Michael C. Thomsett

Candlestick Charting

Micael C. Thomsett

Candlestick Charting

Profiting from Effective Stock Chart Analysis

DE G
PRESS

ISBN 978-1-5015-1580-4
e-ISBN (PDF) 978-1-5015-0739-7
e-ISBN (EPUB) 978-1-5015-0729-8

Library of Congress Cataloging-in-Publication Data
A CIP catalog record for this book has been applied for at the Library of Congress.

Bibliographic information published by the Deutsche Nationalbibliothek
The Deutsche Nationalbibliothek lists this publication in the Deutsche Nationalbibliografie; detailed bibliographic data are available on the Internet at http://dnb.dnb.de.

Published by Walter de Gruyter Inc., Boston/Berlin
Printing and binding: CPI book GmbH, Leck
♾ Printed on acid-free paper
Printed in Germany

www.degruyter.com

MIX
Papier aus verantwortungsvollen Quellen
FSC® C083411
FSC www.fsc.org

Contents

Introduction

The chaotic short-term movements in stock trading create a lot of confusion and add to uncertainty among traders. A novice can observe this reality with trepidation, but even experienced professionals who have been trading for years suffer from the same affliction.

This is where chart analysis becomes valuable. No one can claim a perfect record of timing buy and sell decisions, and no one realistically expects to beat the market with every trade. It is enough to beat the averages and to out-perform the typical profit or loss experience ratio. For many, today's profits are eroded by tomorrow's losses, and so many individual traders find themselves seeking trades just to get back up to dead even. The candlestick chart is a valuable tool that helps you to anticipate trends in a stock's price, and to improve the timing of buy and sell orders. Ironically, even experienced traders who refer regularly to candlestick charts often are not well versed in recognition of patterns or their significance.

Why this Book?

This book describes candlestick charts in detail and then shows how they are constructed. The advantage with this visual aid is that you can find all of the price information in one daily symbol. This includes a day's opening and closing price, the trading range, and direction (upward or downward) of movement. The candlestick also shows each day's *breadth* of trading, from high to low. When you view an array of charts over a number of trading periods, you can determine in an instant whether a stock is high- or low-volatility, trending upward or downward, and most of all, *when* to make a trade. Collectively, this is a valuable set of statistics. Most traders who have analyzed price movement using candlesticks understand these basic attributes of candlesticks; but if this is the extent of a trader's understanding, they need more.

Beyond the basics, this book explains how to recognize different kinds of signs, moves and patterns (bull, bear, reversal, and market) and how to employ double and triple stick formations to better understand why prices behave in a particular manner. Many of these moves and patterns are subtle and their meaning is easily lost in the more recognizable patterns most traders seek.

Candlesticks are also valuable when analyzed in combination with other indicators. For example, two factors often overlooked in price-focused technical analysis are the critical attributes of price movement and risk: Volume and

DOI 10.1515/9781501507397-201

volatility. This book explains how candlestick chart analysis employing these important features will help you to improve your mastery of stock trading. Advanced technical analysis can be greatly enhanced by combining candlestick indicators with the better-known price patterns and trends.

The chapter on buy and sell set-up indicators examines and analyzes the use of swing trading techniques to improve the timing of trades. A set-up is a sign found in candlestick movement and breadth, pointing to the best timing of either a buy or sell; and also serving as a confirmation tool. Adding to this trend, indicators found within moving averages improve insights that are indispensable in your daily trading strategy. Moving averages show you not only where prices are today, but how these are significant in terms of what is likely to happen next. Unfortunately, the popular convergence signals often come too late to take action and maximize the timing advantage. This is where candlestick patterns can help you to anticipate trends well before other indicators solidify the information.

The dozens of technical indicators involve timing of decisions. Candlestick charts are timing tools not only for trends in upward or downward directions, but also for determining the strength or weakness of the current price movement. Some patterns are easily identified, while others reflect a lot of uncertainty among traders. The endless struggle between buyers and sellers usually involves one side or the other dominating the price movement; but at times buyers and sellers are deadlocked. This condition is just as important as a strong bull or bear pattern, because it also helps time your decision to buy, to sell, or to take no action.

After introducing the patterns of single and combined candlesticks, exploring set-up signals and moving averages, the book concludes with an analysis of candlesticks used in combination with technical indicators that most chart analysts employ. Analysis of price movement requires at least a rudimentary appreciation of a few very important price patterns, and these are most readily recognized using candlestick patterns. Whether you are an active day trader, a swing trader, or a technician, this book provides the essential visual and interpretative information you need to expand your technical knowledge. Even the conservative value investor who dabbles in speculation from time to time will find great value in the study of candlestick charts and the associated price patterns they reveal.

The book combines several important features to help you. These include special “boxes” with key points and definitions, checklists, examples and charts of actual companies demonstrating candlestick chart movement and their interpretation. A word about the charts of actual companies: No matter which company’s charts are used or when they are picked, any chart is likely to reflect a range of prices that is out of date by the time this book is published. Most of the charts in this book are from familiar publicly traded companies, because these names are well known to most people; and that familiarity makes the analysis more accessible and practical. However, even an out of date chart is revealing. It's not the price level or current condition of a stock that matters, but the pattern and strength or weakness of price movement. The observations based on these charts apply to all stocks and at all price levels.

The charts are also consistent in their time frame. They are mostly three-month summaries of price movement with each candlestick representing a single trading day. This format was selected because a majority of traders think in terms of the opening and closing price, breadth of trading, and direction on a *daily* basis. Stocks open and close within the easily defined trading day. But it is also important to understand that chartists use a variety of different trading periods—hourly, 15-minute or five-minute charts, for example. The amazing thing about charting is that no matter what length of time you use in your chart analysis, the same rules and observations apply. A pattern is going to be found in a daily or weekly chart and likewise in a one-minute chart. The significance of movement is identical even though the timing of trade decisions is different. So a trader, generally making decisions from day to day, is going to act in the context of "daily" change. A day trader, in comparison, is likely to use the shorter-term charts and make decisions in terms of hours or even minutes. Both are using the same trading information, moving averages, and patterns; that is a fact worth remembering.

Finally, the question must arise: Where do you find free charts? Many websites offer free charts for virtually any listed stock, and you can use these sites to get what you need for stocks you want to track and trade. These sites also offer subscriptions which include more advanced features beyond the basic quote chart. For many traders, the free information provided by brokerage firms, financial companies, and others is enough. For other traders, the cost of a subscription makes the added information worth the price. In this book, the free charts are generously provided courtesy of the website, www.StockChart.com.

This book is intended for the experienced trader and technician who wants to find out how charting can improve technical analysis, or who needs to add to a body of knowledge about interpreting technical patterns and time buy, sell and hold decisions. Candlesticks are one of the best tools for aiding analysis of stock prices, and for confirming indicated reversals and continuations or, equally important, to spot signals that are likely to fail. The point of adding to technical knowledge through confirmation signals is to improve timing and to employ more traditional technical indicators in an effective timing strategy.

The experienced trader or investor is likely to be familiar with candlestick charts, as these have become the standard used by most market participants.

Ironically, though, many do not fully understand or appreciate the true value of candlestick signals and how to use them. This book is intended as a source for expanding the trader's knowledge base and improving the instances of well-timed trade decisions.

Chapter 1
The Basic Candlestick

The candlestick chart is a wealth of information. It combines all of the needed features of daily stock movement: opening and closing, breadth of the day's trading, upward or downward price movement, and high/low prices reached during the day. This is achieved through a combination of shape and color, but the result is a simple, easily recognized visual of the day.

Candlestick chart: A visual summary of all the trading action in a single period, showing the opening and closing prices, breadth of trading, and upward or downward movement in price.

At the same time, candlesticks are simple in design, but complex in what they reveal. If you had to construct your own candlestick chart for a single day, it would not take very long, although building a thirty-day chart would be quite an undertaking. Fortunately, modern technology includes numerous free Internet sites that provide candlestick charts instantly for any period you want to review and with any combination of indicators (price only, volume, moving averages, or momentum oscillators, for example). Candlesticks address a widespread desire among traders to identify reliable means for timing of trades. To the extent that this can be addressed through price patterns, candlesticks deserve the popularity they have gained:

> The stock market is a fascinating phenomenon and [its] movements [have] for a long time caught the interest of . . . banks, individual investors and scientists. Different strategies have been developed over time and [are] being used . . . to predict future price movements in order to give maximum return on an investment. Investors and traders are constantly trying to find profitable patterns, because of this it's an area where very few have managed to create a stable prediction over time. This is usually recognized as a core principle of a free and open market.[i]

In the following chapters, a series of charts are presented to make the point that candlestick signals often accurately predict and anticipate the next price move. This is a form of backtesting that by definition picks and chooses examples to show specific signals at work. Even with inclusion of several failed signals, however, past performance cannot be used to judge likely future price behavior. The value in candlestick signals is in the likelihood that your skills in timing of trades will be improved based on improved averages. No system can ensure 100% positive outcomes:

DOI 10.1515/9781501507397-001

> It is well known that a backtest is just a simulation over the past and does not predict future behavior of a trading system. The ability to accurately simulate a parameter dependent trading system on some chart data can rapidly lead to an overestimation of the parameters by optimizing these parameters to reach the best performance on the historical data.[ii]

The range of information is explained in greater detail in the coming chapters. For now, a review of the basics of candlesticks helps maximize their value.

The Origin and Meaning of the Candlestick

Why is it called a "candlestick"? The answer is its shape: a vertical rectangle box with a smaller "wick" on the top and on the bottom. All of these shapes have great significance in recognizing price behavior and forecasting what is likely to come next. The use of this valuable visual tool is traced to Japan in the seventeenth century. The Dojima Rice Exchange in Osaka traded mainly in rice during that period, and the use of futures contracts became necessary. As the world's first futures exchange, traders on the Dojima developed the candlestick as a way to track futures contract trends.

Key Point: A candlestick is a highly visual representation of price history, showing each period's opening and closing price, the trading range, and price direction.

Trend: The direction of price movement over time, which continues in the same movement until it weakens and moves sideways or reverses.

The introduction of candlesticks as a means for estimating coming price behavior revolutionized the art of charting, enabling traders to apply sensible price patterns to predict how price reaction will likely occur:

> Recognizing behavioral patterns of financial markets is essential for traders. Japanese candlestick chart is a common tool to visualize and analyze such patterns in an economic time series. Since the world was introduced to Japanese candlestick charting, traders saw how combining this tool with intelligent technical approaches creates a powerful formula for the savvy investor.[iii]

This pattern recognition applies equally to stock, index, and futures trading. The candlestick was developed as part of futures trading in Japan. The futures contract—whether for rice or any other commodity—is a market necessity. When farmers plant their crop, they need to know in advance that there will be a market for their product, even though it won't exist for several months. Without knowing whether there is a market, the farmers cannot know how much to plant. The futures contract is a commitment from end users (retail merchants and others who need the rice product in later months). It guarantees a price based on market conditions at that moment. As those conditions change, the value of the futures contract changes as well. With growth in demand, the futures contract rises; if demand falls, so does the futures price. For farmers, buying a futures contract locks in a price. When the product goes to market, they can sell for the market price (if higher) or, if the market has fallen, they can sell their futures contract and get the price they need.

Just as stock prices rise or fall for any number of reasons, commodity prices are also affected by factors no one can anticipate. This explains why it is so important for growers to be able to lock in a minimum price. A large-scale crop failure means less rice and much higher prices, for example. With this in mind, the end user is also interested in locking in the price he or she has to pay so both seller (farmer) and buyer can take advantage of futures contracts to add certainty to the market.

This is where candlesticks enter the picture.

In Japan, by the eighteenth century, the rice market was extensive, involving not only trade between local growers and consumers, but international commerce as well. Analysts in Japan noticed that several factors affected futures prices. These factors included weather patterns as well as the tendencies among traders to act in a particular way based on market conditions. Today, stock market wisdom is based on the same trends and observations. When prices rise, traders tend to become greedy and overbuy, and when prices fall, they tend to panic and sell. So, buying high and selling low is more common in practice than the sage advice to buy low and sell high. The two factors at work—greed and panic—lead many traders to take the wrong actions based on market conditions. The candlestick is used by traders to improve their timing for both buying and selling positions, based not on gut reaction or emotion, but on recognizable trend patterns. The candlestick is a valuable tool because it makes it so easy to recognize those patterns.

As a charting tool, the candlestick reveals much more than the traditional line chart or bar chart, also called the OHLC (open, high, low, close). A line chart tracks daily prices (usually the closing price), but does not reveal breadth of trading during the day. The OHLC is easy to construct, but with online free charting services, the more complex and revealing candlestick chart makes much more sense.

OHLC chart: Abbreviation of "open, high, low, close." A type of stock chart showing a vertical stick for the day's trading range and two vertical, shorter protrusions showing opening and closing prices.

Trading range: The price spread between highest and lowest points on a daily bar or over a period of time; the breadth of trading between those two points.

If you had to build your own charts every day, the OHLC chart would be easier to work with than the candlestick. But with the free Internet services available, you can use candlesticks to get much better visual summaries for the same effort. A side-by-side view of the three types of charts makes this point. Figure 1.1 compares line, OHLC, and candlestick charts for the same price movement of a stock.

Notice how much more information you see—instantly—with the candlestick chart. Some days move downward and show up as a black rectangular session. Others move upward and are white. The extensions above and below the boxes show the trading range from highest price (above) to lowest price (below) for each session. Opening and closing prices are found on the top and bottom of the box. When the trend is downward, the top of the box is the opening price and the bottom is the closing price; vice versa for an uptrend day.

Each of the attributes of the candlestick has a name. Figure 1.2 summarizes the names of each segment of the candlestick.

Comparison, types of charts

line chart

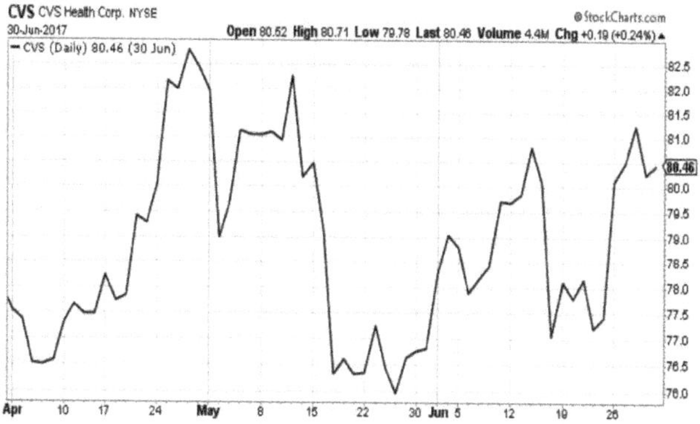

OHLC chart

candlestick chart

charts courtesy of StockCharts.com

Figure 1.1: Comparison, types of charts

The candlestick and its features

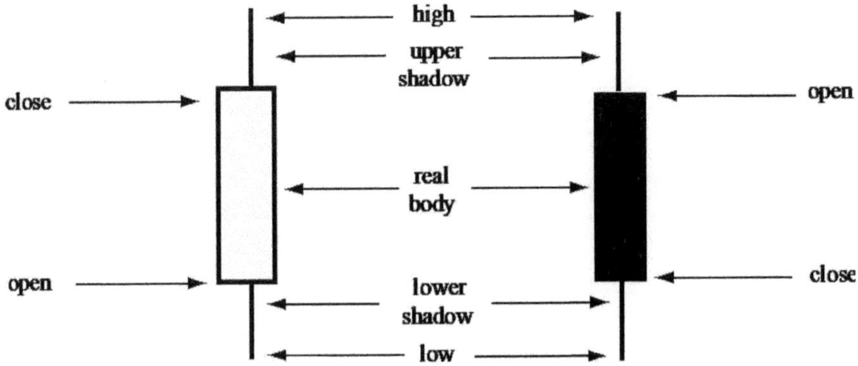

Figure 1.2: The candlestick and its features

Key Point: The white candlestick occurs when prices move up, and a black candlestick occurs when prices move down. This makes it easy to see, at a glance, the direction and duration of every trend.

The open and close are opposite on upward and downward trending days, as the figure shows. The rectangular box (the real body) is the range from the day's opening to closing price. The full breadth of trading, including extensions above and below the range of open to close, is represented by the upper and lower shadows (also called "wicks"). When you compare the candlestick to the same day's OHLC, the candlestick's advantages are clear. It is more visually revealing, especially when you view a series of days next to one another.

Real body: The rectangle in a candlestick, representing the area between the day's opening and closing price but excluding the total range above and below those levels (upper and lower shadows).

Shadow: The portion of the candlestick above and below the real body. The upper shadow shows the distance between the trading range (open to close) and the highest price of the day, and the lower shadow shows the distance between the trading range and the lowest price of the day.

Strengths and Weaknesses of Candlesticks

The most apparent benefit of candlesticks is their immediate revelation of trends. As with most types of analysis, no single day's results are as important as the multiday trend, and this is where candlesticks present a definite advantage.

With the OHLC chart, for example, it is much more difficult to recognize a trend than it is with the highly visual appearance of candlestick charts. In the next few chapters, discussions focus on bull and bear trends and identification of reversal and market patterns. The greatest advantage is in what is revealed in double stick and triple stick patterns. These are two-day and three-day formations that foreshadow likely coming price movements and provide indications of the strength (or weakness) in the current trend.

Even so, candlestick charting and, to a greater extent, technical analysis invite continued controversy. Not everyone is convinced that candlestick charting and other signals are reliable for improved timing of trades. This set of beliefs, based on theory and academic opinion more than on actual trading experience, ignores the reality that skillful use of candlestick signals and confirmation does improve the ratio of profits to losses based on improved trade timing. The controversy, although outdated and contradicted by fact, persists. Evidence reveals, in fact, that technical analysis provides great value to traders:

> A significant body of literature exists on fundamental and technical analysis in various financial domains. Results obtained in the 1960s and 1970s supported the "Efficient Market Hypothesis," which states that the efficient nature of financial markets should mean that market data does not contain any discernable and exploitable patterns. . .. However, some recent results since the 1980s have appeared to indicate otherwise. Well-known anomalies involve abnormal returns associated with: unexpected earnings announcements, firm size, the month of January, the day of the week, and so on . . . numerous financial researches have progressively employed a positive and careful attitude to probe into technical analysis. A fairly comprehensive literature related to technical analysis in various financial domains has addressed numerous effective evidences that trading success can be achieved with technical analysis.[iv]

The predictability of candlesticks as a leading technical indicator is the primary advantage to candlesticks. Because all of the price information is represented in a visual format involving side and color, the importance of the trend as it evolves is more readily seen. This improves your timing for entering and exiting positions. The simple formation of the candlestick gives you a lot of information in a split second.

Traders like to know as quickly as possible whether the short-term trend is bullish (white) or bearish (black). With the OHLC chart, the implications of day-to-day change are not as obvious, so the trend is also more difficult to spot not only in terms of direction, but also in terms of strength or weakness. As a trend evolves, the strength or weakness is likely to change as well, and the candlestick is the most effective tool for recognizing this change.

A drawback to candlesticks is that trends can be misinterpreted if the chart itself is not studied carefully. False and failing signals are common in all forms of charting so everyone relying on the timing provided in charts has to proceed with caution. A series of uptrend days, for example, might indicate a bullish condition in the stock. But if the trading range or the range between high and low is narrowing, the field of white charts could easily obscure a more revealing internal development in the price trend. A continuing uptrend may be weakening, in fact, so the attributes of the candlestick have to be reviewed in full context and not just by the color of the real body.

Traders may proceed cautiously with any technical system, aware of a tradeoff between price sensitivity and consistency of signal reliability. A reliable signal is expected to provide reliable signals as early as possible while also reducing the incidence of false signals. However, if signals lag behind price reaction, resulting price action is less reliable and more likely to simply not yield the expected results.[v]

Candlesticks, like all pricing systems, contain limits. For one thing, they are restricted to price trends. This means that technical data beyond the daily trading range and price direction may be ignored or overlooked in the analysis. To develop a complete view of the current trend, you also need other technical data to make the review as complete as possible. The judgment you bring to the timing of trades requires consideration of many attributes, not just the short-term price trend. Although traders tend to make decisions based on short-term price changes, the intermediate and long-term trend is equally important. This is where it becomes valuable to combine candlestick analysis with moving averages and a few other revealing technical indicators. Fortunately, many free charting sites provide this additional information as part of the complete chart.

Key Point: No single indicator is valuable unless viewed in a larger context. Candlestick charts show the greatest insight when the sticks are augmented with moving averages and other technical data.

Candlesticks are valuable, but by themselves they do not give you the entire story. As you move through the book, additional indicators and their confirmation value are introduced and explained. Bringing a full range of technical signals into your charting activities enriches your overall analytical capabilities. Based on the candlestick as a primary initial indicator, you will also know how to employ volume, moving averages, and a few other important technical gauges. In addition, a tendency among technical analysts is to give weight to past price patterns as part of the candlestick-based analysis of what is likely to occur next:

> For technical analysts the patterns recognized in the past are a valuable clue to predict probable scenarios of market moves in the future. These scenarios are built on psychological analysis of traders and on statistical analysis of past data. . .. The analysis of Japanese candles is more geometrical and visual, closer to modeling human perception and intuition rather than strict functional dependency. Most technical indicators are delayed in time as based on moving averages. The analysis of candle formations is focused on current market behavior—mostly on the previous candle right after it finishes forming its shape. The emphasis is put not only on closing or average values for each timeframe, but also on the structure of the market movement during each period.[vi]

This natural tendency among traders based on behavior may be aggravated by individual confirmation bias—you see what you expect to see and reject contradiction—but this does not reduce the overall value of how information is weighted or how trades are timed based on observed signals and confirmation. The whole purpose is to improve timing of trades based on observed price behavior, and that lends itself naturally to at least some bias.

With any form of charting—whether line chart, OHLC, or candlesticks—improving the instances of well-timed decisions is in itself a worthwhile outcome. Experienced traders know that not every trade will be profitable or well timed and that each poorly timed trade is a learning experience. This is why diversification is so crucial for successful trading. Candlesticks are valuable tools for developing a body of informed knowledge, but no analytical tool can ensure 100% profitability.

With candlestick analysis, as with most forms of technical study, mastery of a large number of patterns helps in understanding their significance, leads to skillful application of these patterns in actual situations, and, finally, knowing how to evaluate outcomes. These steps help you not only to develop working knowledge of candlestick chart analysis, but also to find out what can go wrong. This knowledge—the negative or loss experience—is at least as valuable as having a series of trades that are all profitable. Losing is also an experience, but one that is more painful than what you learn through winning.

Some candlestick books promote the belief that a particular candlestick pattern may be *either* reversal or continuation. This is questionable. A reversal pattern—one indicating a likely change in direction of the trend—is valuable if also confirmed by other signals. However, when a reversal appears in the wrong proximity, it could be nothing more than a coincidence. So, a bullish reversal is expected to show up after a downtrend. If it shows up during an uptrend, does that imply continuation? Or is it just a coincidental series of daily patterns? To avoid confusion, a suggestion is offered here: Identify reversal and continuation patterns and apply them consistently as one or the other.

A mistaken belief or assumption is that a candlestick may serve either as reversal or as a continuation. A candlestick occurring in the wrong place (bullish reversal during an uptrend, for example) does not reveal that a reversal can also be a continuation. Some signals fail and others are simply coincidences of price patterns. The assumption that every candlestick means something ignores the role of chance in patterns:

> A number of candles do not work as expected. This is the big surprise for candle lovers. A candle that functions as a reversal of an upward trend should cause price to drop. Thus, a close above the top of the preceding candle would be a failure because price climbed instead of fell, whereas a close below the previous low would have been a success.[vii]

This points out two aspects of candlestick behavior. First are the inevitable failures that occur some of the time (especially when confirmation is not present). Second is the fact that price reaction is not always immediate. The actual reversal anticipated after a signal might happen only after many days of sideways movement. The candlestick itself does not cause price movement; it only predicts what the pattern is likely to mean.

A second idea also departing from popular belief is what "reversal" can mean on a price chart. Most analysts believe that a reversal can be applied only near the end of an uptrend or a downtrend and that the reversal signal is a warning that price is about to turn in the opposite direction. If this assumption is accepted, it also means that reversal cannot be applied during a period of consolidation, a time of sideways movement in the stock. Consolidation takes up a good deal of a stock's history and often represents more trading activity than bullish or bearish trends. Challenging this assumption requires an expansion of reversal itself.

A "reversal" may be defined as a *change* from the current trend. Under this definition, a period of price consolidation may be signaled to end as a *reversal* signal appears. In this case, the reversal applies to the trend and not just to price direction. The standard definition tells you that consolidation is a non-trend, so no signals can reveal reversal; you can only wait for a breakout to identify a dynamic (bullish or bearish) trend. Under this revised definition, consolidation itself is a trend and an important one. So bullish, bearish, and sideways movements are all in the realm of possibilities, and all may be reversed in six different ways: bullish to bearish, bullish to consolidation, bearish to bullish, bearish to consolidation, consolidation to bullish, or consolidation to bearish.

Considerable confusion is created in the market of technical analysis by intermixing of the terms "consolidation" and "continuation." A consolidation is a trend in its own right, consisting of sideways movement rather than dynamic (bullish or bearish) patterns. A continuation is a signal indicating continuation of the current bullish or bearish trend. Continuation patterns are either bullish or bearish and contain specific characteristics not interchangeable with reversals. However, many sources of information about technical analysis confuse this distinction. For example, in discussing triangles (which are continuation signals), perhaps the best-known book on the topic of technical analysis, written by Edwards and Magee, refers to triangles as reversal signals and, at the same time, defines consolidation as a trend "terminating an up or down movement only temporarily and setting the stage for another strong move *in the same direction* later on."[viii]

The inclusion of italics by the authors emphasizes a claim that after consolidation, the previous trend will continue. An analysis of chart patterns reveals that consolidation, as a trend distinct from bullish or bearish moves, is no more temporary than these types and may conclude with movement in the same direction *or* in the opposite direction. Consequently, the confusion created is twofold. First, the statement identifies continuation patterns as either reversals or as patterns that may be either. Second, it confuses continuation with consolidation.

A breakout from consolidation may occur with a reversal signal. This new definition allows reversal to apply not just to price behavior, but also to change in the trend itself. With this new definition of reversal, the candlestick reversal signal is powerful not only to spot changes between bullish and bearish price movement, but also to spot changes associated with the sideways movement of a consolidation trend. Many traders see consolidation as a time to wait for new dynamic trends to emerge. Consequently, by the time this occurs, timing opportunities have been lost.

So, there are two new "rules" offered here. First, a signal is either reversal or consolidation and cannot be interchanged. Second, "reversal" can be applied to trend direction and not just to price changes.

When a signal is identified as 50% reliable, it is of no immediate value by itself; many signals fall into this category. However, as a basic premise for effective charting, no signal should be acted on without independent confirmation. This is found in other candlesticks, volume, moving averages, or momentum.

This leads to a final flaw in charting overall. What action should you take when you find no signals or when two signals contradict one another? This occurs frequently. As a level of trading discipline, patience is invariably rewarded. The lack of signals or appearance of divergence between signals indicates a confusing situation. At such times, a "wait and see" attitude makes the most sense. Acting without signals or when signals are contradictory is a problem and a mistake.

Traders easily fall into the trap—especially when strong signals are not present—of confirmation bias. This is a behavior based on assumptions as a starting point, followed by a search for confirming information. So if you believe a stock's price is going to rise, you may look for confirmation of that starting assumption. Bias often leads to finding "proof" that the assumption is correct. However, because this exploration reveals only part of the truth (such as weak signals or signals without confirmation), it often leads to poorly timed trades or even to trades that should not be made at all.

Even so, given the discipline of methodical analysis for signals and confirmation, it is likely that chart readers will be able to improve the timing of trade entry and exit, prediction of price movement, and overall understanding of price behavior. Analysis may be applied to overcome reliance on emotion or instinct, which improves the rate of well-timed trades. By tracking price movement and recognizing how supply and demand interact with price patterns, the rational and objective results define candlestick analysis as one of the most reliable technical strategies for traders.[ix]

The skillful application of candlestick science demands not only a clear identification of signals and patterns, but also a requirement for confirmation. Without fail, reversal and continuation signals found in candlesticks must be confirmed before you act. Signals should be compelling and indisputable. There are no guarantees, but locating strong signals and equally strong confirmation is going to improve overall timing for both entry into trades and exit from trades. Candlestick signals are a strong starting point, but experienced traders know that any technical system involves many pitfalls.

Paper Trading as a Testing Ground

Considering the complexity of candlestick signals and their interpretation, developing interpretive skills as a first step makes sense. But this can also be expensive, so charting skills are best developed by employing a paper trading program. This is a trial run in which you start out with a fictitious portfolio, enter buy and sell orders, and see the resulting profits and losses.

Because you are improving your observations while going through these paper trades, you do not actually lose money, but you can discover how trades are likely to come out and how analysis of candlesticks improves what you already know how to do. So, reliance on a chart pattern that is not as reliable as you had thought is very instructive. Paper trading helps you to better appreciate the subtle meaning of patterns and how information can be misread. For any system, paper trading is a smart way to learn without risk of loss. Even experienced traders can benefit by trying out expansions on a technical program in a paper trading forum before putting real money on the line.

Paper trading: A method for becoming familiar with strategies, in which a fictitious portfolio is traded using "virtual money." This enables you to see the outcomes of different timing strategies, but without losing real money.

Many sites offer free paper trading software, many promoted as contests or games (with prizes awarded for the best performing paper portfolio), and others are simply free initially, leading to promotions for membership in more advanced services. Many brokerage firms offer variations of this idea. The following sites also offer free paper trading programs:

Investopedia: www.investopedia.com
Trading Simulation: www.tradingsimulation.com
Market Watch: vse.marketwatch.com
How the Market Works: www.howthemarketworks.com
Wall Street Survivor: www.wallstreetsurvivor.com

Of course, all websites offering free features also promote sponsored subscription services or try to sell upgrades to you. These sites are useful for starting out in a paper trading program, though, and they provide opportunities for you to apply what you learn about candlestick charts as you move through the learning process.

Key Point: Paper trading is a method for making simulated trades without risking capital. This aids in improving your analytical and timing skills.

The most valuable insight you can expect from a paper trading program as an ongoing technical management process is to seek a correlation between your interpretations of candlestick patterns with actual price behavior. This involves two aspects. First, economic factors are involved, which are complex and far reaching but can be summed up and described as the forces of "supply and demand." Most traders know how this works: Increased demand for stock drives up the price, and weakening demand drives down the price. This involves far more than market forces in their pure form; however, outside economic news, earnings, competition, consumer confidence, cyclical changes, and many other factors provide change to prices in both directions.

It's the second factor that is more interesting and subtle: the trading behavior of "the market" as a collection of investors. Much of the daily price movement of stocks is chaotic and represents overreaction to news and information. Swing traders know this and trade on the emotions of the market. Whether you are swing trading or using candlesticks as confirmation tools, being aware of how short-term price movement works greatly improves your timing. By resisting the urge to jump onto the emotional rollercoaster of the market, you are able to look for patterns as they emerge and improve your short-term entry and exit strategies.

This behavioral factor limits the value of paper trading. Although an excellent forum for learning the mechanics of the market, paper trading is not the real market and cannot duplicate the behavior experienced with real money at risk:

> One question that new investors ask me a lot is, "Why do I do better at paper trading than I do when I trade with real money?" The answer is easy: Fear, doubt, complacency, greed, anxiety, excitement, and false pride can all interfere with rational and intellectual thoughts. When dealing with real money, you are faced with the realization that you and your money can actually be separated.[x]

This is the flaw in paper trading. It is beneficial but limited. Detailed tracking of candlestick charts for a particular stock reveals how prices change based on current news and financial reports. It is interesting to see how different stocks react to the same news; for example, if one company's quarterly earnings report is below expectations, that company's competitors might see a temporary upward movement in the stock price. If a national statistic is promising, stocks in affected sectors will react positively (or when the statistic is negative, the same stock prices might fall).

None of the short-term cause and effect in stock price movement is meaningful in the long term. Value investing calls for holding onto shares for months or years. However, that short-term price movement is where you find trading opportunities. By tracking stock price changes through candlestick charts (along with other technical indicators), you discover patterns that signal the time to make a move. These are most often based not on long-term fundamental value, but more on what is taking place today and tomorrow.

There are two major areas to focus on in the use of candlesticks within your technical program. First is the tendency for the stock to react to market news; some stocks react with volatile price changes to even the slightest change, while other stocks tend to ignore news. The second area to focus on is the development of chart patterns and trends. This is where most chart watchers focus, but studying both the stock's reaction to market news *and* the development of chart patterns and then acting on logic (rather than emotion) leads to success as a contrarian investor. Candlesticks are exceptional vehicles for building the analytical skills needed to spot opportunities and to zero in on the timing of trades. Avoiding emotional gut reactions and making decisions based on *observation* invariably improves charting skills and increases the percentage of profitable trades over losses.

The Skills Every Trader Needs

Anyone embarking on a new strategy has to accept the learning curve that goes with it. Even experienced traders who analyze stocks based on candlestick formations for the first time have to proceed cautiously. Every trader needs to review his or her strategies and portfolio continuously even after years of experience to make sure he or she is not violating his or her own trading rules (specifically, goals set based on risk tolerance and market conditions).

Risk tolerance: The degree of risk you are willing and able to take in your portfolio based on many factors, including knowledge about the market, experience, capital, budget, portfolio size, and personal financial situation. The defined risk tolerance level identifies the kinds of investments anyone can afford to make.

Traders and investors may be defined in terms of how they view risk. Risk avoidance is fairly well understood among investors and traders, who are likely to acknowledge that highly volatile price behavior inhibits the ability to predict or anticipate coming price movement. For this risk-avoiding trader, a less volatile alternative is preferred. In contrast, a risk seeker will prefer taking chances over guaranteed (but lower) net returns.[xi]

Key Point: Knowing how much risk to take is critical for every investor; equally important is mastering analytical tools like candlesticks to ensure that you can use them most effectively.

Risk levels are further complicated when an individual exposed to knowledge becomes overconfident. This leads to bias and a false belief in a trader's own superior ability to skillfully time trades. A danger in this is a related belief that the caution suggested in the use of candlesticks and the critical need for confirmation is secondary to that overconfident opinion of knowledge, capability, and likelihood of superior trade selection.[xii]

To avoid this trap, traders may develop skills and knowledge while also recognizing that nothing is certain in chart analysis. There are five important skills every trader needs based on experience as well as personal risk tolerance. These five important skills are:

1. *A complete appreciation of the risk element in all trading.* Everyone knows that risk, as a general concept, is the chance of losing money instead of making money. But in fact, risk has numerous other aspects that everyone needs to know about. These include the double exposure to taxes and inflation, for example. You need to know your breakeven rate, the rate you need to earn *net* of taxes, to match inflation and break even.[xiii]

   Many of these risks (like the tax and inflation risk) are invisible. For example, you might be exposed to an invisible risk if you have diversified your portfolio into many different stocks and sectors, all of which are exposed to the same economic or cyclical effects. To determine whether or not you are adequately situated based on your own risk tolerance level, you need to evaluate a range of different risk-related questions.
2. *The ability to* ***effectively*** *diversify without going too far.* The concept of diversification is more complicated than some traders realize. It is not enough to own several different stocks if they are in the same market sector or are subject to similar or identical market forces. Diversification can take many forms, including division between direct stock and mutual fund shares; equity and debt; nonstock trading in futures, options, or ETF shares;[xiv] and using hedging strategies to reduce risks (for example, offsetting stocks with gold or currency positions).

   At the same time, there is another danger: overdiversification. If you spread capital around too much, you can gain only the average rate of the entire portfolio. This could mean your potential profits are reduced because strong positions are absorbed by weaker ones. This is one of the major arguments against sector-based ETFs, in which the basket of stocks is going to include a range of both strong and weak sector stocks. You can also overdiversify by holding shares of too many diverse stocks; depending on market conditions and risk tolerance, it is often more effective to own a small number of carefully selected stocks and focus attention on the trading patterns and trends of those few instead of trying to play a larger segment of the market.
3. *Mastery over the advantage (and trap) of leverage.* The concept of leverage is widely known. It is using a sum of money to borrow additional money to invest. It is far riskier than just investing on a cash basis, but leverage also has

its place. Most people who buy a house use leverage when they borrow money through their mortgage, for example. For investors, it is practically automatic to be granted a margin line of credit by your broker. You can borrow up to half of the money you need to buy shares of stock. This gives you a great advantage as long as the stock's value increases.

On the other side of the issue is the cost and risk. When you borrow through your margin account, your broker charges you interest. And if the value of your holdings declines, you still have to pay back what you borrowed. If the value of your portfolio falls below the initial margin, the difference has to be made up—that means you need to invest more cash. This is common knowledge among traders, but it helps to insert this reminder in the context of trading *risk* and reward. When you get a margin call, a question should always be asked: Is it worthwhile to keep the position open, or should my losses be cut here and now? If you want to cut your losses, you have to close the position as soon as possible. If you want to keep it open, you need to deposit funds immediately. If you do not close the position or deposit the additional sum to meet margin requirements, your broker will sell some of your holdings.[xv]

4. *Control over and planning for liquidity.* One of the least understood concepts in the market is liquidity. The word has several meanings, but for traders it simply means having enough cash on hand to make trades when you want to. If your capital is fully committed, you cannot take advantage of new opportunities when they arise. One of the greatest mistakes traders make is taking profits when they are available, but keeping loss position securities in their accounts. This attrition results in a portfolio fully invested in stocks that have declined in value. The illiquidity of this situation ties you up and prevents you from making any further investments even when great opportunities come along.

   A solution is to manage liquidity with a few common sense rules. First, always keep some cash on hand (opinions vary, but between 5% and 10% of your portfolio kept in cash is a reasonable level). Second, if you take profits, offset a portion of the gain by also selling loss position stocks.
5. *Acceptance of the constant need to acquire more knowledge.* Even the most experienced trader faces an ever-changing body of knowledge about the markets and needs to keep informed of what is going on. This is true in the overall markets and communications technology, which enables efficient access to market information; it is also true of individual companies and their technical and fundamental information. The status of every company (in terms of price strength or weakness, emerging trends, and changes in

comparison to competing from companies) is also changing every day. So knowledge has to be maintained on several levels, the basic skills every trader needs, the company-specific attributes affecting prices and current or future trends.

Your ability to renew and maintain your knowledge base defines how much control you have over your trading experience. The more you monitor an individual company's trends and volatility levels, the better your timing becomes. With candlestick charts, you have powerful visual tools for recognizing subtle but important changes in the current trend and the beginnings of reversals and continuation patterns.

Key Point: By knowing the popular myths of the market, you are better able to avoid the mistakes associated with them. Wise investing is often simply a matter of knowing the difference between fact and myth.

Beyond the logical skill set you need to master technical analysis and charting, you also need to be aware of the popular myths and pitfalls that permeate the market and the trading psychology of a highly superstitious trading culture. Technicians can easily fall into one or more of these pitfalls, including:

- *The tendency to think there is a secret formula out there somewhere.* Realistically, you know there is no such thing, or else getting rich within a few trading sessions would be easy. The uncertainty of trading is what makes it so challenging and interesting. You cannot know the future any more than you can change the past—that's the reality.
- *An unconscious belief that an entry price is the start of every trend and that prices will always move in the desired direction from that point onward.* So many traders, even those who have been in the business for years, mistakenly fall into the trap of thinking that once they enter a position, prices will begin to move as they desire. This is based on the use of entry signals or simply on monitoring price and picking the "right moment" to jump in. But an entry price is not the zero point in a trend; it is part of a continuing change in price affected by numerous interactions within the market. While everyone knows this logically, they do not always know it emotionally, and that's where the pitfall lies.
- *The assumption that price movement is somehow a "conscious" element of the market.* It is easy to treat price and its trend as a conscious element, and many traders fall into this belief. It is a form of magical thinking, the belief (or desire) that something can be made to occur by the power of the mind of through outside forces (like wearing a "lucky shirt" when you enter trades).

Many will not admit it, but some form of magical thinking is used widely. (For example, a trader named Dell might belief that Dell Computer stock value will rise because he shares the same name.)

Candlesticks: General Observations Concerning Their Use

Using candlestick charts as a primary tracking and timing tool requires that you also have a mastery of a few basic technical theories. A short list of technical indicators is useful in determining the significance of a trend or a sudden change in price (level and direction). By itself, the chart—candlestick or other type—has limited value. Besides recognizing a specific shape to a short-term movement based on the visual development of a day's trade as seen in the candlestick, you also need to be aware of the overall pattern in the price trend. Concepts like support, resistance, and patterns like breakouts, gaps, head and shoulders, double or triple bottoms (or tops), and moving averages reveal meaningful changes or confirmations in the current trend. Besides tracking the pattern of single candlesticks or a series of candlestick developments, you also need to follow the larger technical picture. The candlestick chart is the easel, and the broader indicators are the paint.

Combining candlestick pattern recognition with other technical indicators adds to the body of knowledge traders need to increase skills. However, financial literacy (contrasted with academic study) tends to increase risk tolerance, which may in turn lead to increased exposure to higher risks than intended.[xvi]

The last chapter in this book analyzes the most popular and important technical indicators. These are the essential tools for measuring the strength of trends and even the safety in the current price level of stock. So, the candlestick chart provides a single source for starting the analytical task and much more, including:

- The significance of single candle signs within the context of the current trend.
- Developing double moves and triple patterns of candlesticks and understanding what they mean within the larger trend.
- Coordination of the candlestick formation and short-term trend with the longer-term trend revealed by the technical pattern, trading range, and moving averages.
- Important signals involving a combination of the candlestick patterns, volume of trading, and technical indicators, used collectively to develop a *singular* opinion about the timing of entry or exit decisions.

The simple signs and moves revealed by candlestick charts are only the starting point. Even the more complex candlestick patterns that grow from this initial trend have to be used as part of a more encompassing technical program. It is essential to learn the meanings of candlestick movements, but the two-stick and three-stick indicators that evolve signal changes of great importance.

Sign: A single candlestick that provides initial indications about a reversal or continuation in the overall trend.

Move: A double-stick formation that foreshadows either a reversal or continuation in the current price trend.

Pattern: A candlestick formation of three or more trading periods that strongly indicates a reversal or continuation of the current trend.

Key Point: The concept of *confirmation* is a cornerstone of every technical system. No one piece of information should be relied upon for timing entry and exit. Every indicator is at its highest value when it is confirmed by a separate but equally important one.

Why is it so critical to confirm even a strong and compelling indicator, especially given price patterns making a conniving argument for what happens next? Confirmation is essential due to the frailty of human nature and its tendency to act in a manner not always rational or justified. Traders, like all people, may be susceptible to acting not based on an understanding of probability, but more in response to instinct and gut feelings:

> Any discussion of the modern history of research on everyday judgment must take note of the large shadow cast by the classical model of rational choice. . .. According to this model, the "rational actor" (i.e., the typical person) chooses what options to pursue by assessing the probability of each possible outcome, discerning the utility to be derived from each, and combining these two assessments. The option pursued is the one that offers the optimal combination of probability and utility. . . . But is the average person as attuned to the axioms of formal rationality as this stance demands? . . . Evidence is collected indicating that people's assessments of likelihood and risk do not conform to the laws of probability.[xvii]

The dominance of instinct over analysis is a chronic and very human problem. It points out the essential attributes of technical analysis in general and candlesticks specifically. In spite of how convincing intuition may be, confirmation bias tends to cloud judgment and lead to ill-timed decisions rather than to decisions based on analysis of price patterns and the probability those patterns reveal.

This is why using candlesticks as an initial indicator of what is about to occur is a wise idea. Daily price action is the starting point for the more developed technical signal. Candlesticks are early indicators of changes not only in direction, but also in emerging strength or weakness in the current trend. So if you think of the candlestick pattern in this way, then the more traditional technical signals *confirm* the indicators first seen in the daily candlestick. The concept of confirmation is a basic idea used by technical analysts to strengthen their opinions about how to interpret price patterns. It is analytical and based on observation, rather than intuitive or based on emotion and confirmation bias.

Confirmation: The use of an indicator to verify the meaning of a separate indicator occurring at the same time or earlier, consisting of movement in an index or individual stock price, changes in price trend direction, or initiation of an entry or exit signal.

No approach to price analysis should take place in isolation. This means that you cannot make reliable entry and exit decisions based *only* on short-term price movement seen on the candlestick chart. You also need a range of indicators stretching over the longer term, an understanding of each stock's volatility level, and the strength or weakness of the current trend. This is why you need to combine candlestick charts with other technical indicators. The more indicators you add together, the better your information pool.

A word of caution: Using too many indicators clouds the results. You need to be able to make an informed decision and confirm that decision through secondary indicators. There comes a point at which you have enough data to make an informed decision, and going beyond this will not add to your information. The time element, plus the simple excess of information, then turns and confuses the picture rather than clarifying it.

Expanding the Information Pool Effectively

Beyond the technical side, it also makes sense to pay attention to a company's fundamentals, those financial values defining a company's capital strength and profitability. Even though short-term traders tend to shun the backward-oriented financial indicators, they can be used to narrow down the range of stocks you want to trade based on price volatility and financial strength. Considering there are thousands of stocks to choose from, which ones do you want to use for short-term swing trading and timing of entry and exit? You need some criteria for narrowing down the range of stocks you want to use. This is where the fundamentals can be valuable.

Combining the fundamental and technical sides certainly enriches the pool of input to the decision-making process. However, a distinction has to be made between the attributes of each side and what actually drives the market. Confusion about the distinction exists partly because

> textbook definitions of fundamental and technical analysis differ slightly from what the strategists mean when they state that a market is either fundamentally or technically driven. For example, a stock with high price momentum is probably an attractive investment in terms of textbook technical analysis, but what's driving that momentum could in fact be related to fundamental factors.[xviii]

Understanding the distinction between definitions of what each side contains and what drives price behavior is a starting point in enhancing analytical skills. In terms of the fundamentals, it makes sense to limit your trades to companies with a few important financial attributes. These could be any of dozens of indicators, but some very important ones include:

1. *Basic profitability*. Even the most speculative trades can be limited to those companies that have reported growing revenues *and* profits. For some traders, the question is: Why buy shares in a company that has never shown a profit? As a rudimentary selection question, this eliminates those troubled companies that have fallen from previous years of competitive strength as well as those that have not yet proven that they can carve out a competitive place for themselves.
2. *Strong working capital*. The ability of a company to finance its operations and pay for expansion is an essential test, perhaps even more important than profitability. A favorite ratio is the comparison between current assets (those

convertible to cash within twelve months) and current liabilities (debts payable within twelve months). This is an important test, but an equally valuable one is the debt capitalization ratio. This is the percentage of total capitalization represented by debt. Total capitalization is the sum of long-term debt and shareholder's equity. If debt is growing each year, it erodes the company's ability to fund future growth. Dividends have to fall as interest obligations rise. For example, by 2008, before General Motors filed bankruptcy, its debt capitalization ratio was *over* 200%. This meant that the shareholders' equity was worth less than zero, which is not a good sign. A company's chances of ever recovering from such an extreme situation are very poor.

Total capitalization: The sum of capital that funds a company's operations, consisting of equity (shareholders' capital) and debt (long-term loans and bonds).

---

3. *Higher than average dividend yield.* Another important fundamental test is dividend yield. A company that is able to pay better than average dividends is the exception, and this itself is a sign of financial success. A company must have cash from profits in order to pay dividends. An expanded qualification is to limit the selection to "dividend achievers," those companies whose dividend per share has grown every year for the past ten years or more.
4. *Acceptable price/earnings ratio range.* The comparison of price per share to earnings per share, or the P/E ratio, is one of the most important indicators of whether the price is a bargain or not. The P/E multiple (price divided by earnings and reported as a single number) is significant; it is the number of years' annual earnings represented in the price per share. So, a P/E of 10 is the equivalent of a price worth ten years' net earnings for the company. The higher the P/E range, the more expensive the stock becomes. As a general rule, most traders and investors like to see the P/E between 10 and 25. But as it gets higher, the risk level increases as well.

Fundamental indicators, just like technical indicators, are rules of thumb for a company's value and strength. Because of this, no indicators should be viewed alone. They only gain significance when analyzed comparatively on two levels. First, they have to be compared between companies in the same market sector (thus, a drug company with a dividend yield of 6% and P/E of 12 is stronger than a competitor with a 2% dividend yield and a P/E of 45). Second, they have to be viewed as part of a fundamental trend (for example, a company with a debt capitalization ratio that is falling by 5% per year and is now at 35% is more promising than one whose debt capitalization ratio keeps going up and is greater than 50% of total capitalization).

Key Point: Everyone needs to place a limit on the number of indicators they will watch. The most sensible approach is to combine a limited number of technical *and* fundamental trends.

It's all relative, in other words.

That is the key to every form of analysis, and the same applies to candlestick charts. If you look at the charts of two competing companies, you gain insight into price strength and the current trend of each. If you review the chart along with moving averages over the past year in addition to over the past month, you advance your knowledge about that company's longer-term direction. The more expanded the field of vision, the better your information.

The next chapter introduces the basic signs you find in single candlesticks and explains what they mean. The central lesson to remember is that, even with some exotic names of patterns and lines, candlesticks are easy to read. You can tell at a glance whether the current price movement of the stock is upward or downward and whether it is strong or weak. Chapter 2 shows how this works.

[i] Martinsson, F., & Liljeqvist, I. (2017). Short-Term Stock Market Prediction Based on Candlestick Pattern Analysis. *Examensaybete Inom Teknik, Grundnivå*, 5.

[ii] Maier-Pappe, S., & Platen, A. (2014). Backtest of Trading Systems on Candle Charts. *Institut für Mathematik.*

[iii] Mahmoodzadeh, S., Shahrabi, J., Torkamani, M. A., & Sabaghzadeh, J. G. (2007). Estimating Correlation Dimension on Japanese Candlestick, Application to FOREX Time Series. *World Academy of Science, Engineering and Technology*, 30.

[iv] Wang, J., & Chan, S. (2007). Stock Market Trading Rule Discovery Using Pattern Recognition and Technical Analysis. *Science Digest*, 304–315.

[v] Teeples, A. W. (2010). An Evolutionary Approach to Optimization of Compound Stock Trading Indicators Used to Confirm Buy Signals. Graduate Thesis, Paper 820, Utah State University.

[vi] Ciskowski, P., & Zaton, M. (2010). Neural Pattern Recognition with Self-Organizing Maps for Efficient Processing of Forex Market Data Streams. *Artificial Intelligence and Soft Computing*, 307–314.

[vii] Bulkowski, T. N. (2008). *Encyclopedia of Candlestick Charts*. New York: John Wiley & Sons, 8.

[viii] Edwards, R. D., & Magee, J. (1957). *Technical Analysis of Stock Trends*, 4th ed. Mansfield Center, CT: Martino Publishing, 87.

[ix] Caginalp, G., & H. Laurent. (1998). The Predictive Power of Price Patterns. *Applied Mathematical Finance*, 5, 181–205.

[x] Person, J. L. (2004). *A Complete Guide to Technical Trading Tactics: How to Profit Using Pivot Points, Candlesticks & Other Indicators*. New York: John Wiley & Sons, 7.

[xi] Weber, E. U., & Milliman, R. A. (1997). Perceived Risk Attitudes: Relating Risk Perception to Risky Choice. *Management Science*, 43, No. 2, 123–144.
[xii] Barber, B. M., & Odean, T. (February 2001). Boys Will Be Boys: Gender, Overconfidence, and Common Stock Investment. *The Quarterly Journal of Economics*, 261–292.
[xiii] To compute your after-tax and after-inflation breakeven, divide the current rate of inflation by your after-tax income or the difference between 100% and your effective tax rate (be sure to include both federal and state taxes in this calculation). The formula is:
(rate of inflation ÷ (100 – effective tax rate)).
For example, if you pay a combined federal and state tax rate of 42% and the current rate of inflation is 3%, your breakeven requirement is:
(3% ÷ (100 – 42)) = 5.2%.
This is the rate you must earn just to cover your risks based on taxes and inflation.
[xiv] ETFs are exchange traded funds, mutual funds that have a pre-identified "basket" of stocks and trade on exchanges like stocks, rather than directly with the fund's management. Because the portfolio is identified in advance and does not change, management fees are lower because no management is required other than maintenance of the existing portfolio. However, the ETF is going to perform only at the average of all of the stocks in its portfolio, including those performing well above and well below the average. For many traders, ETFs are a form of overdiversification. For others, it is an effective way to spread risk and reduce single-stock risks.
[xv] The rules governing initial margin fall under the Federal Reserve Board's Regulation T. This provides that you can borrow up to 50% of the value of securities in your account.
[xvi] Gustafsson, C., & Omark, L. (Spring 2015). Financial Literacy's Effect on Financial Risk Tolerance. *Umeå School of Business and Economics*, 17–18.
[xvii] Gilovich, T., Griffin, D., & Kahneman, D. (2002). *Heuristics and Biases: The Psychology of Intuitive Judgment.* Cambridge, UK: Cambridge University Press, 2.
[xviii] Biwer, T., Jacobsen, B., & Kurkiewicz, A. (May–June 2012). Market Drivers: Fundamental vs. Technical. *CFA Magazine*, 10–13.

Chapter 2
Single Stick Signs

The most practical way to master candlestick charting is to start with the single stick sign and evaluate it, then move to double stick moves, and finally move to the more complex multi-stick patterns. Each of the formations you find in charts is important in what it reveals about the current trend: strength or weakness, direction, or pending reversal.

Key Point: Single stick attributes are extremely valuable but are made much more significant when studied within a current trend *and* as part of a longer formation.

Every analyst faces the challenge of interpretation. Even with excellent understanding of how formations develop, the immediate pattern can represent a false start, which supports the idea of requiring confirmation before acting on a signal. Every trend will exhibit a series of these misleading indicators, apparent reversals that are in fact short-term retracements, and even outright false signals. The apparent direction or change in status misleads you if you do not fully understand how to combine many different candlestick and technical indicators. Can you see patterns emerging or use candlestick analysis to anticipate the next step in a trend? That is the big question.

Understanding trend movement and price behavior all too often relies on the use of limited data. In technical analysis, for example, reemphasis has always been placed on a day's closing price. In fact, the price activity during a session is equally important in understanding price activity and in predicting future price movement. This is where candlesticks add a wealth of information in the analysis of price:

> The advantage of candlestick theory to investors is that the candlestick chart is visual; a market reversal or continuation candlestick pattern can be easily identified by an experienced investor. There is rich information existing in a financial time series database, but most of the traditional approaches only scratch the surface of the wealth of knowledge buried in the data. For example, many financial time series prediction approaches only use a single type of value, such as daily closing price, as raw data to construct the forecasting model.[i]

This skillful use of candlesticks is the essential attribute that adds the greatest value to chart analysis. However, candlestick charting is a relatively new concept in the Western world. It was first introduced in 1991 when Steve Nison be-

DOI 10.1515/9781501507397-002

gan publishing his observations of the centuries-old Japanese art of candlestick analysis:

> Since the western world was introduced to Japanese candlestick charting, traders saw how candlesticks could give them an edge by combining them with western technical analysis methods. Recognizing patterns in the stock market is a critical resource for today's trader. Combining candlestick charting techniques with traditional technical approaches creates a powerful formula for the savvy investor.[ii]

The combined use of candlesticks with other, better-known technical indicators does not guarantee success in each and every trade, but it does improve the percentage of successes over failures in timing. While it is true that chart analysis improves with practice, there is no reason that even investors with little experience cannot rapidly come to understand the significance and predictive power of price patterns. So much of this is obvious, and with the visual advantage of candlesticks the learning curve is not necessarily extensive. So much relies on the ability to understand the true meaning of signals and on the discipline of requiring confirmation. Finally, avoiding errors by being aware of confirmation bias enables every trader to master the basic skills of candlestick charting. Even so, a great deal of this overall skill relies on the interpretation and combination of fundamental and technical analysis. This means that "the understanding and identification of candlestick rules are determined by the personal experiences of individual investor. Investors can obtain different information from the same candlestick chart."[iii]

Uptrends and Downtrends

In all forms of chart analysis, you rely on chart patterns to determine whether the current trend is bullish (upward) or bearish (downward). This trend is not identical to the longer-term primary trend in the market as a whole. For swing traders, the "trend" is the price direction that is set for three days or more.

Key Point: A technical trend is established when three or more periods move in the same direction, both on the top and bottom of the price range.

The trading day is used as a typical trading period because most people analyze stock prices from each day's opening and closing levels. Traders come in many varieties, however, so the trading period you end up using could be shorter. The sixty-minute, fifteen-minute, and five-minute charts are used by people wanting fast action and a lot of in and out of positions. These day traders also tend to be risk takers, so the use of short-term charts is not appropriate for everyone. References to trading periods used in this book are normally references to single-day movement.

Risk takers, when applied to investing and trading, tend to apply certain expectations of outcomes, and this further defines whether the individual is a speculator or a cautious trader:

> Risk is commonly defined as being the chance or possibility that a real investment return will be different from what was expected; it is also referred to as being the uncertainty involved in an investment in a security or portfolio. In economics, risk measures the expected loss for an investment in monetary units. Risk is defined by the factors influencing any securities' performance.[iv]

Managing risk is a constant challenge for all traders. This is where effective charting—especially the use of candlesticks—becomes a valued aid. Even so, chart users come in many types. Some speculate moderately and risk only a small amount of cash. Others use a lot of cash and leverage and rely on small changes applied to big dollar amounts. In either case, chart watching relies on well-defined uptrends and downtrends.

An *uptrend* is made up of three or more periods of rising prices, but with a distinct pattern. Each day's candlestick consists of a series of higher highs offset by higher lows. So the candlestick of the second day has to exceed the previous day's high *and* low to qualify as an entry in a true uptrend. For example, consider the following comparison of prices:

Day	Uptrend Pattern	Non-Uptrend Pattern
1	high 45 / low 43	high 45 / low 43
2	high 47 / low 44	high 47 / low 42
3	high 48 / low 46	high 46 / low 44

In this short example, the uptrend pattern shows growth in an upward direction in both the daily high and low prices. A true uptrend consists of higher high prices and higher low prices, and a downtrend consists of a series of lower highs and lower lows. In the non-uptrend, even though there was upward movement, the high and low requirements were not met. The subsequent high of the third day was lower than that of the second day, and the second day's low was lower than the first day's.

Uptrend: A short-term pattern of three or more periods characterized by each period's higher high price levels and higher low price levels.

A *downtrend* is also carefully qualified. It consists of a series of changes lasting three periods or more combining lower lows and lower highs. A trend is set only if it consistently produces the defined results for three periods or more, although the trend can also last many more periods; three is the generally acknowledged minimum. For example:

Day	Downtrend Pattern	Non-Downtrend Pattern
1	high 45 / low 43	high 45 / low 43
2	high 43 / low 42	high 43 / low 40
3	high 42 / low 41	high 44 / low 41

Downtrend: A short-term pattern of three or more periods characterized by each period's lower low price levels and lower high price levels.

In the true downtrend, the second and third days report lower highs *and* lower lows. In the non-downtrend variety, the overall trend is downward, but it lacks the defined qualities. The third day's high is higher than the second, and the second day's low is higher, not lower, than the first. The trend ends at the point where a subsequent signal occurs, often a narrow range day (explained later in this chapter) or other signs found in candlestick formations.

Under some definitions, a trend cannot be analyzed as part of a *current* price pattern without also referencing past price behavior. The concept of prediction in charting may be assumed to exploit past price patterns, assuming that history will be repeated in current and near-term future price patterns.[v]

This is not necessarily the premise for trend analysis, nor does it limit the application of candlestick signals. The purpose in candlestick chart analysis is to identify proximity between signal and trading range, to quantify the strength or weakness of signals, and, as a result, to intelligently estimate the likely next price move. Whether showing a sideways movement, an uptrend, or a downtrend, the candlestick is probably the most powerful tool for making such a prediction.

On all charts, uptrends and downtrends are easily recognized. It is far more difficult to determine when a current trend will end and flatten out or reverse.

This is where candlestick signals and confirmation have the greatest value, serving as advance warnings of changes about to occur.

The Significance of a Candlestick's Shape

As a first step in working with candlestick charts, an initial determination should be what a particular candlestick formation reveals. Terms applied to visual patterns are crucial to working with candlestick. These terms—real body, upper shadow, and lower shadow—are of interest because the size of each of these components makes up the signs, moves, and patterns themselves, as well as the strength or weakness of the overall signal. When you need to distinguish between bull and bear patterns or between reversal patterns and continuation patterns, the individual candlestick attributes take on great importance.

Key Point: There is a tendency to look at the entire candlestick as a single factor in the trend, using either the real body only or the price range only. Both are important in setting trends and in anticipating reversals about to occur.

In addition, it is important to make a distinction between the real body (the white or black rectangle) and the larger trading range. The range extends from the tip of the upper shadow (the high of the day) to the tip of the lower shadow (the low of the day). There is a tendency among technicians to pay more attention to the range from high to low than from open to close. In fact, the OHLC chart more readily shows this range-based pattern, even though the totality of range and open-close differences is collectively important. The meaning of these outcomes together is significant, and neither range or open-close works by itself. Candlestick terminology is somewhat different than the corresponding OHLC terminology. For example, an OHLC chart shows a "long range" from highest to lowest price, and the candlestick, with more emphasis on open-close, is described as a tall (long) or short candle (the difference in size of the real body, which is the open-close range).

The long candle (also called a tall candle) can be defined as a "significant" move for the day in relative terms. Simply being longer than the previous day's candle is not significant by itself. But if today's candle is twice the extension of the typical candle range, it takes on much greater meaning. Big price movement is invariably worth paying attention to. So for example, if a stock's daily price movement is typically in the one-half to one-point price range, an unexpected two-point candle is very significant.

A long candle means different things if the rectangle is white (uptrend) or black (downtrend). The longer the candle real body is, the stronger the move appears in the indicated direction. This trend is not necessarily revealed in the total range (as emphasized with OHLC charting) because many intraday factors might affect the range, including high volatility in the first hour of trading that is not typical of the entire day, reaction to economic news that takes place and later reverses, or higher volatile change due to rumors that are later proved to be false. So relying on range instead of open-close can be deceptive and misleading.

The relationship between the open-close range and the shadows is also significant; another reason that candlesticks are valuable analytical tools. When a bullish long candle forms (a larger than average white rectangle), that is an uptrend in the day's price. However, an additional sign adds to the indication that the movement is a *strong* upward movement. This sign is found when the day's price opens near the low price for the full day and closes near the high. This is quickly recognizable because there will be little or no upper or lower shadow. This is an important change when the formation appears after an extended downtrend in the stock's price. It can indicate the end of the downtrend. The opposite can be interpreted when the long white candle shows up after a long uptrend. The longer than average price movement could signal exhaustion in buyer interest and foreshadow a leveling out and a decline in price to follow in coming sessions.

The opposite observations apply to bear long candles (black real bodies). A long black candle opening near the high and closing near the low is quickly recognized by the small or missing shadows. When this appears at the end of an uptrend, it may signal the end of the trend and a coming reversal. When this long candle shows up after a period of downtrend, it could be a sign that sellers are exhausted, which is followed by a reversal and movement in the other direction.

Longer real bodies tend to show shorter than average shadows. This is typical. However, what does it mean when a day's outcome combines a long body with a long upper or lower shadow? As a general rule, extended shadows reveal which side (buyers or sellers) is in control. When the upper shadow is extended along with a long real body, it implies that buyers are in a stronger position; when the lower shadow is longer, sellers are calling the shots. Of course, these are generalizations and do not apply universally, but the signs and shapes are revealing when taken as part of a larger trend.

Variations on the Bullish Long Candlestick

Although the white candlestick denotes an upward movement, not all bullish days are the same. You can learn a lot from the subtle differences in bullish candlesticks to improve your timing. In some cases, a single candlestick provides you with the most important indication about the current trend or its coming exhaustion and reversal. As a general rule, you rely on a series of patterns to time buy and sell decisions; some exceptions apply when you use candlesticks.

Key Point: Although candlesticks tell the most when they are part of a trend, some single sticks tell a lot as well. The long white candlestick is a bullish formation.

***Marubozu*:** A long candlestick with varying lengths of upper and lower shadows. The word in Japanese means "with little hair."

The long white candlestick is clearly bullish. The combined long body and small upper and lower shadows tell you the bulls were in control through the session. A few subtle variations of the bullish long candlestick are found in the *marubozu*. This is a long candlestick with varying amounts of shadow (also called the "wick" or "tail") above, below, or on both sides. In Japanese, the word *marubozu* means "bald" or "with little hair." There are four variations.

1. *Marubozu* with small upper *and* lower shadows. When a long white candle appears with some upper and lower shadow and the price does not rise above the upper shadow of that long candle, two assumptions can be applied. First, the long white candle is clearly bullish and probably signals a coming uptrend in price. Second, as long as the price in subsequent days remains above the lowest point of the lower shadow, it represents a *support* level. Support is the lowest price the stock is expected to trade (in comparison, *resistance* is the highest price likely to be traded, and the space between support and resistance is the current trading range).
2. *Marubozu* with no upper or lower shadows. When there is no shadow on either end of this candle, it is the most bullish of all. This tells you the day's price opened exactly at the bottom and closed exactly at the top, with no additional range in between. When you see this, it indicates that a strong uptrend has started. Candlestick analysts are likely to use this strong indicator (along with the trend pattern and other technical indicators) as confirmation of the entry signal.

3. *Marubozu* with upper shadow only. Also called an opening bullish *marubozu*, this one has an upper shadow. Referring back to the first type with shadows on both sides, you can use the upper shadow to check subsequent trading; when prices of the next few days remain at or below the shadow's highest point, it is one of the two bullish signs. The second is the bottom of the candle, which has no shadow but still serves as the support level. As long as price does not fall below this level for the next few days, all signs point to an uptrend.
4. *Marubozu* with lower shadow only. The last type is called a closing bullish *marubozu*. The same rules for resistance and support apply, although in this instance (because the price did fall below the opening price) the potential support level is lowered for the following sessions.

The distinction between "opening" and "closing" *marubozu* candlesticks is reversed for bearish long candles. In both cases, the value of the long candle itself is not always clear and is best acknowledged as a significant signal only when it fits well into the proximity of a current trend, notably at a point of reversal.

A summary of the variations of long candlesticks is provided in Figure 2.1.

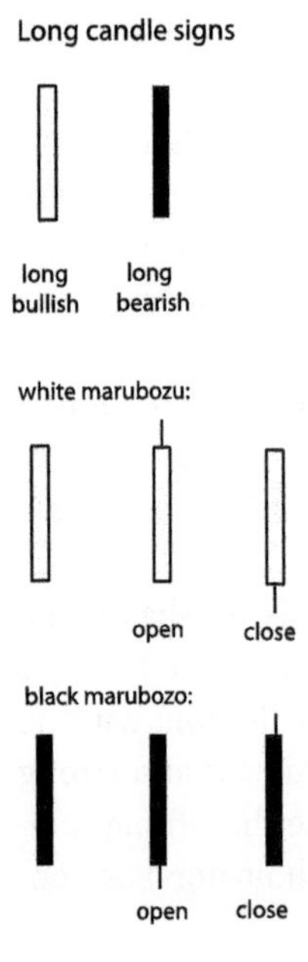

Figure 2.1: Long candle signs

The Mistake Pattern

A second candlestick formation is called the *doji*, which is the opposite of a long day. The word in Japanese means "mistake." It is a candlestick for days that open and close at the same price level so that there is no body, just a horizontal line. A *doji* often appears at the point where the trend is about to turn in the opposite direction. It is also the extreme version of a "narrow range day" (NRD), used in swing trading as a strong signal that price is about to turn and move in the reverse direction.

***Doji*:** A candlestick sign developed when the day's opening and closing prices are identical or very close; the real body is a horizontal line rather than a box.

Key Point: The *doji* is the most extreme narrow range day because opening and closing prices are identical or close to identical. When a lower shadow is prominent (making it a dragonfly *dojo*), it is an exceptionally strong bullish signal.

One of the most important bullish candlesticks is the dragonfly *doji*. This is a pattern in which opening and closing price are identical, but a lower shadow also forms. In other words, price fell below the open but closed *at* the same price as the open in spite of the day's decline below that level. In this formation, the bears dominate through the early part of the day, but before the close the bulls take over and return price to its initial level. So the longer the lower shadow of the dragonfly *doji*, the stronger the bullish indicator.

Dragonfly *doji*: A type of *doji* with a lower shadow; the longer the shadow, the greater the bullish indication.

The lower extension of the shadow forms a short-term support level that can be used to check coming trading sessions and to identify and time your entry. But this assumed support level can also act as a cautionary signal that the dragonfly *doji* represents a false bullish indicator. If the following trading levels trend *below* the extension of the *doji*'s lower shadow, it means the support is not holding and that prices are likely to fall lower.

You will not always find the dragonfly *doji* in a perfectly flat narrow range day. It is more likely you will find one that is close, with a small trading range and even a very small upper shadow. The dragonfly can just as easily fail, establishing a false indicator.

The opposite of a dragonfly is the gravestone *doji*. Just as the dragonfly is a bull signal, when the real body appears at the bottom of the stick, the gravestone is a bear signal. The ideal gravestone shows up at the very top of a bull trend; it strongly indicates coming reversal, with a long upper shadow showing that bulls were not able to move price higher by the close.

Gravestone *doji*: A type of *doji* with an upper shadow; the longer the shadow, the greater the bearish indication.

There are more kinds of *doji* signs, each worth analysis as part of your candlestick charting program. The opening and closing prices are identical or very close in order for the *doji* to form; they do not have to be exactly identical, so a *doji* is any candlestick with even a thin line, representing little or no gap between opening and closing prices.

Long-legged *doji*: A *doji* sign with exceptionally large upper and lower shadows, indicating a coming reversal in the current trend.

The long-legged *doji* has unusually long upper and lower shadows. This often appears at the end of a current trend and signals the beginning of a reversal. The long-legged *doji* is interesting because, although the period's opening and closing prices are the same (or very close), the trading range moved far above and below that level during the session. In the dragonfly, the bears took prices down but the bulls prevailed. In the long-legged variety, both bulls and bears had their turn. The bears took the price down and the bulls brought it back up; or the bulls ran the price higher and the bears brought it back down. This action can occur in either sequence and even go back and forth many times during a single trading day.

The long-legged *doji* is also a symptom of an exceptionally volatile day, with a lot of back and forth in the price and, during the session, without any clear domination by either side. This is a bullish pattern when previous trading has been on a downtrend. The day's struggle between bulls and bears could be a sign that an uptrend is going to ensue. This applies especially when the pattern has established a downtrend of three sessions or more. (Of course, the opposite applies equally after three uptrend sessions and may signal the start of a downtrend.)

The signal is qualified, of course, as all signals are. Any signal is only as good as the degree to which it confirms other signs. This is as true of the long-legged *doji* as for any other formation. The long-legged *doji* signals a change in trend when subsequent price action remains above support (after the existing downtrend) or below resistance (after the existing uptrend). However, when a long-legged *doji* is followed by price falling below support (or above resistance), it was probably a false reversal signal. A false signal is followed by a continuation of the existing trend.

Key Point: Confirmation that the *doji* exists when following prices remain at above resistance or below support, depending on the direction. When this does not occur, the *doji* has to be viewed as a false signal.

A *doji* entry signal can also work as an exit signal. If you are watching a stock looking for the entry point, the long-legged *doji* (given the qualifications about false signals) can serve as a confirming entry point. By the same argument, if you are already in a position, the long-legged *doji* can work as a warning to close out the position. If you are long in stock and enjoying a strong uptrend, the long-legged *doji* could be the red flag telling you to sell. If you are short and profiting from a downtrend, the same pattern could signal that it is time to cover the position and get out. In either case, the long-legged *doji* should not be ignored.

When a session is close to a *doji* but has a very small real body, it is called a near *doji*. This is a common formation and should be accepted as having similar value to a pure *doji* when it is part of a more complex candlestick signal.

Near *doji*: A candlestick with an exceptionally thin space between opening and closing prices; while these are not identical, the range is so small that the candle is granted the same significance as a perfect *doji*.

As a general rule for the *doji*, when the horizontal line appears on the upper half of the shadow extension, it is a bullish sign (the opening price held and closed even though the bears took the price lower during the day). And if the vertical line is found in the lower half, it is usually bearish for the same reasons; even though the bulls took price above the opening and closing line, the bears were able to bring it back down. A range of *doji* formations is shown in Figure 2.2.

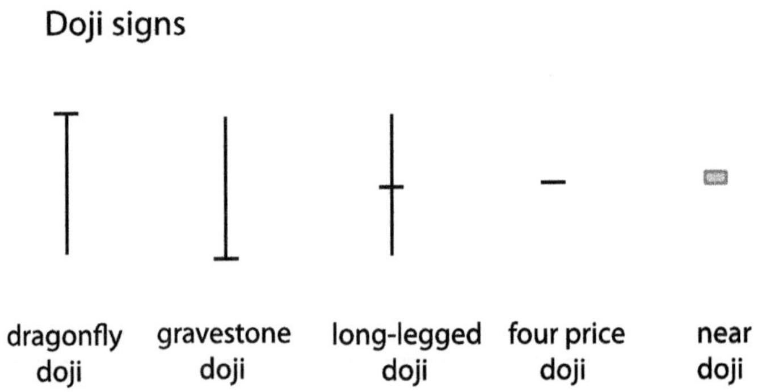

Figure 2.2: Doji signs

Expanding on the appearance of a *doji* are general price patterns concluding with a *doji* session. A *doji* gapping up is a bullish continuation signal. A typical formation is shown in Figure 2.3.

Figure 2.3: Doji gapping up

This chart contains two examples of the continuation signal. Note that the session preceding the *doji* may be of either color and that the dominant attribute of this signal is the trend direction itself. To work as a continuation, a gap should appear before the *doji* moving in the prevailing direction. In the example, the preceding sessions were white, but even in a bullish trend, a single black candle preceding a gap up and a *doji* is valid for confirmation.

The opposite is a *doji* gapping down, which is a bearish confirmation signal. The preceding candle may be of either color, but a downward gap is essential immediately before the *doji* in order to set up a continuation pattern. An example of this is found in Figure 2.4.

Doji gapping down

Chart courtesy of StockCharts.com

Figure 2.4: Doji gapping down

As in the previous example, the preceding days were the same color as the direction of the trend—bearish trend and black sessions. When the colors of the preceding candles conform with the direction, it implies a stronger confirmation, but that is not always true. The existence of two signals of the same directional indication is a cross-confirming indication. This means that the two signals confirm one another. Confirmation of the continuation signal is confirmed by another of the same shape and pattern.

Some direction *doji* signals may also provide reversal signals. One example is the Northern *doji*, which is a bearish reversal. The name refers to the direction of movement, but no gap will be found between preceding days and the *doji* day. Figure 2.5 highlights a Northern *doji* occurring at the top of a very brief uptrend and leading to immediate bearish reversal.

Northern *doji*: Any *doji* appearing above a previous uptrend is considered a strong bear signal.

Doji, Northern

Figure 2.5: Doji, Northern

The opposite is a bullish reversal, consisting of a downtrend leading to the *doji* and expected to immediately reverse and move in a bullish direction. An example is seen in Figure 2.6.

Doji, Southern

Figure 2.6: Doji, Southern

Southern *doji*: Any *doji* appearing below a previous downtrend is considered a strong bull signal.

In both of these directional *doji* formations, the lack of a gap of any substance makes a distinction between the gapping continuation and directional reversal attributes of these signals. However, all *doji* signals occur often and easily give off false signals, so confirmation is definitely required before acting on a *doji*, whether appearing by itself or as part of a more complex pattern.

Key Point: The *doji* shows up frequently, especially during volatile trading patterns. While the *doji* is important, it is not always an indication of a signal that the trend is about to change.

The Spinning Top, Hanging Man, and Hammer

Three more revealing single stick candles are the spinning top, hanging man, and hammer. A spinning top is represented by a fairly small real body (a narrow trading range) along with both upper and lower shadows. To be a true spinning top, two attributes should be present. First, the real body should be found approximately midway in the full range and the shadows should be at least as long as the real body, preferably longer.

Figure 2.7 shows how the spinning top acts as a reversal signal. The small real body defines the difference between the very similar long-legged *doji* (with no real body) and the minimal near *doji* formation seen here. These are the most effective forms of narrow range days because they represent a trading range in which both buyers and sellers had the chance to move price without success.

Spinning top

Chart courtesy of StockCharts.com

Figure 2.7: Spinning top

Spinning top: A candlestick with a relatively small real body and upper and lower shadows. The real body is approximately midway in the day's range, and both shadows are at least the same size as the real body.

The confusing attribute of the spinning top is that its color (white or black) is not the most important attribute. Instead it is where it appears in the current trend. Swing traders look for narrow range days or what candlestick analysts call either *dojis* or spinning tops. If the current trend is an uptrend, a black spinning top is somewhat stronger as an indicator that the trend is about to turn. If it is a downtrend, a white spinning top indicates a reversal. But either a white or black spinning top can be used as an indicator of the same kind of reversal when it shows up at the *end* of the current trend. The difficulty is knowing when you are at the end of the trend, again pointing to the importance of confirmation.

Key Point: The spinning top may signal reversal, but caution is needed here: This candle also forms mid-range and can give out a false read.

A failing spinning top can show up in the middle of a trend. When the color of the real body is the same as the existing trend direction, it does not always indicate that the trend is about to change direction. These signs can be misleading, so keeping a close eye on price action in the days following is necessary. As an observation of market psychology, you can experience a series of spinning tops midway through a strong trend with none representing true reversal indicators.

The *hanging man* and the *hammer* look identical. A small real body of either color is found at the top of the pattern, with a longer than normal lower shadow. The hanging man is a bearish signal, seen at the top of an uptrend, and a hammer is bullish, appearing at the bottom of a downtrend. To be sure that either of these is a true reversal signal, you need confirmation by trading on the following days.

Hanging man: A pattern with a small real body, no upper shadow, and a longer than usual lower shadow. It appears at the top of an uptrend and is a bearish day indicating an impending reversal, or it appears as confirmation during a downtrend.

An example of the hanging man is found in Figure 2.8.

Hanging man

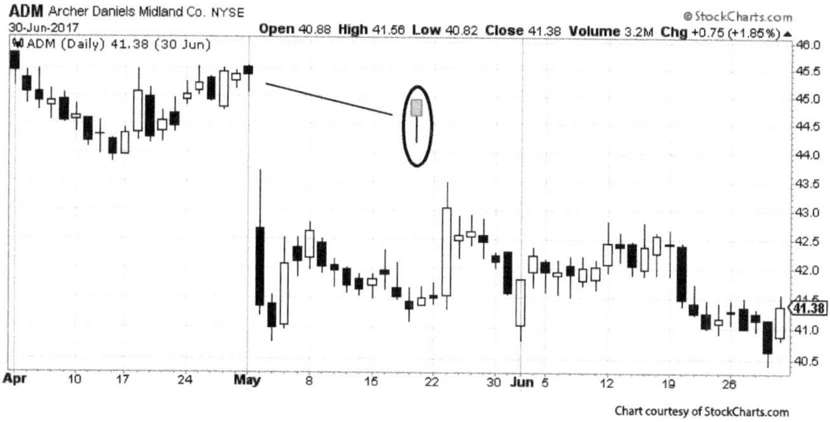

Figure 2.8: Hanging man

This appeared at the very top of an uptrend and was followed by a strong downward gap and further movement down. The opposite of this pattern is the *hammer*, which looks the same but appears at the bottom of a downtrend, indicating bullish reversal. Figure 2.9 contains a highlighted example of the hammer.

Hammer

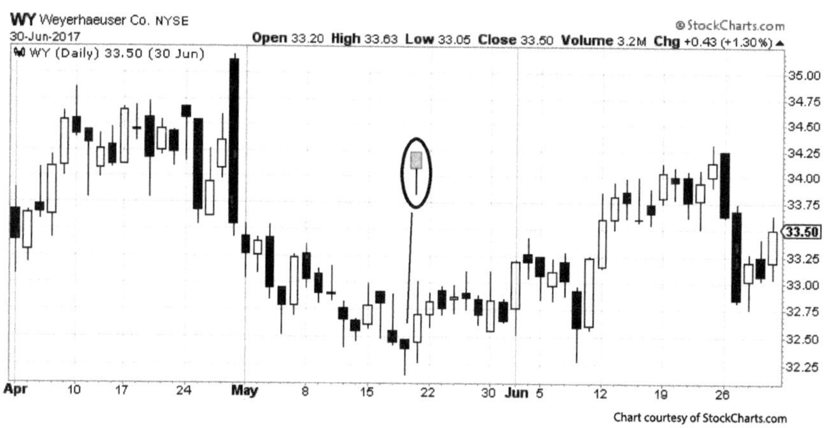

Figure 2.9: Hammer

Hammer: A pattern with a small ready body, no upper shadow, and a longer than usual lower shadow. It appears at the bottom of a downtrend and is a bullish day indicating an impending reversal, or it appears as confirmation during an uptrend.

In this example, the downtrend preceding the hammer and the uptrend following were relatively weak, but one month later, the bullish trend took off, at least briefly.

Like the spinning top, both hanging man and hammer can provide false signals; you need confirmation before relying on either as a reliable signal. As with most chart signs, the preliminary indication should get your attention, but you need to confirm what it appears to show before you act.

Key Point: Confirmation for the hanging man and hammer occurs with price movement in the days after the candle appears. If price does not move in the direction predicted (upward for the hammer or downward for the hanging man), then the signal is not confirmed; it is a false indicator.

Line Signals

The *takuri line* and *umbrella days* signals are reversals consisting of single sessions with relatively small bodies and long shadows. First among these is the *takuri* formation, shown in Figure 2.10.

Takuri line

Figure 2.10: Takuri line

This appears near the end of the chart, but the following three sessions moved upward strongly before reversing once again. Like the hanging man and hammer, the real body can be either color. In this case, the real body was white and it signaled the end of the brief downtrend. It also confirmed the two long lower shadows preceding the *takuri* session by two and three days. Collectively, these lower shadows confirm weakness on the sell side of the trade.

The *umbrella line* is also a reversal and it may contain either a white or black real body with a lower shadow much greater than that of the hanging man or hammer. Whether white or black, the long lower shadow indicates the signal is a bullish reversal. The inability of sellers to successfully push price lower is a bullish pattern. The opposite or *inverted umbrella* is bearish for the same reason. The long upper shadow demonstrates buyer weakness. Both forms of umbrella days are summarized in Figure 2.11.

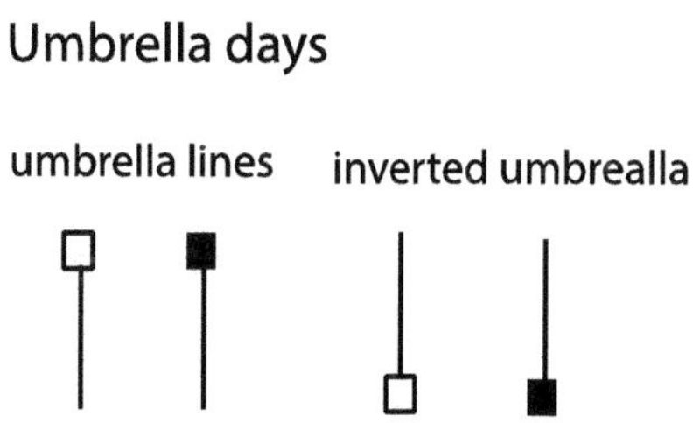

Figure 2.11: Umbrella days

The Significance of Tails

The upper shadow and lower shadow shows the trading range extending beyond opening and closing prices and provides intelligence about the strength or weakness of price movement. When studied as indicators, exceptionally long shadows are also called tails.

Tails: An alternate term for especially long upper and lower shadows: used as indicators of the degree of strength in bullish or bearish trends.

The longer the shadow, the more analysts tend to pay attention to it. As a general rule, a very long upper shadow is bearish because it implies that price is driven upward by buying interest that is not sustained; the ending price retreats. This indication is confirmed when two or more long upper shadow tails appear in subsequent trading sessions. A long lower shadow is the opposite. It is a bullish signal, but only if confirmed by the appearance of two or more tails over a period of trading sessions.

The lack of demand found in a bearish tail (an "overbought" condition), meaning that the high side is exhausted and there are no more buyers entering positions, may be a sign of buyers taking profits, notably the case when price retreats following the sale of many shares. Bullish lower tails indicate that demand is growing and that the low level of prices (beneath the real body) is not going to hold, subject to confirmation.

Key Point: A tail, an exceptionally long shadow, indicated the inability of buyers to sustain a growing price level (upper tail) or for sellers to hold price down (lower tail). If confirmed, the tail serves as a reliable indicator of a reversal.

Either formation—bullish or bearish tails—can also be false. Tails appear during strong trends in either direction as part of the higher than average volatility in a strong trend. For this reason, the tail itself should never be used as the only timing mechanism for either entry or exit. It serves as one of many useful patterns that needs to be considered as part of a larger picture.

Tails may also indicate something different from the signal for entry and exit. They may show you where resistance or support levels are starting to be newly established. In many of the multiple-candle moves and patterns, the confirming factor of an indicator is often found in whether subsequent days' prices remain lower than resistance or higher than support. Do you treat the tail extensions as these levels or only the range between opening and closing price?

Analysts normally look at the full range of trading to define the trading range, including extensions above and below the real body. Traders tend to time purchase entry at or close to support level and exit at or close to resistance. In other words, assuming the trading range holds, this approach assumes that price is going to continue moving back and forth between these levels, as it so often does. (The opposite moves apply to short selling, with resistance serving as the entry point and support the exit, or closing purchase transaction.) The extension of the tail on either the top (at resistance) or bottom (at support) not only indicates whether this approach is wise, but also helps you gauge the strength of either side of the trading range.

Tail size tends to increase at these levels (larger upper tails near resistance and large lower tails at support). A tail is simply a larger than average shadow on the candlestick. By itself, the size of the tail is not enough of an indicator to require an entry or exit, so limiting the timing of trades to those levels is improved when the specific candlestick sign is combined with the proximity of price to resistance or support.

Another time that tails appear is when, even within the middle of the trading range, the stock is overbought or oversold. This does not always occur at resistance or support; it is normally a condition following too rapid a trend in one direction. So when prices move upward strongly, the stock is overbought, and when prices move strongly downward, the stock is oversold. At such times, tails may appear even if the price is not right at resistance or support levels. The condition (overbought or oversold) is a stronger indicator of an impending reversal and is more reliable than proximity of resistance or support for three reasons.

1. *Trading range is dynamic.* It is easy to assume that the current trading range is fixed and permanent, but it is not. The range tends to move upward or downward over time. In fact, a reliable test of volatility is the size of the range rather than actual price levels. For example, if a stock tends to trade within a four-point range, it is less volatile than a stock trading in an eight-point range. Either of these stocks can retain the same range breadth even when their prices move upward or downward. So if you rely only on price proximity, you miss many opportunities. Tails that begin appearing after strong trends are more reliable for timing of entry and exit.
2. *Prices may move considerably within the range without approaching the edges.* The chartist who waits for price to approach resistance or support is likely to be frustrated when prices move a lot over time without ever reaching those top and bottom edges. The range may be narrowing, for example, so that an outdated trading range is being used and the changed conditions are difficult to spot. This is where the emergence of tails is very useful. The range is not reliable over time, but the appearance of tails at the top or the bottom foreshadows reversal and serves as a better, more finely tuned signal.
3. *The appearance of tails is more of a signal than price level by itself.* The price level of a stock is chaotic in the short term, as every trader realizes. The timing of entry and exit can be guesswork more than science, and the constant search for reliable signals is made more difficult by that short-term unreliability. There are times when price action is so erratic that no obvious trend emerges and you cannot know whether the stock is going through an uptrend or a downtrend. However, if you see the appearance of tails, you have a strong initial indicator of price movement and you can also spot the implied direction. Getting confirmation in the next two to three sessions is crucial, valuable information. In comparison to reliance on trading ap-

proaching resistance or support, the recognition of tails is a far better system. Confirmation is essential because even with the best single stick indicator, no isolated day's pattern tells the whole story.

Single stick patterns reveal a lot about the continuation or reversal of a trend as well as its strength or weakness. However, confirmation is always a requirement. The next chapter expands on this theory by showing how double stick moves work as indicators or their own, as well as in confirming what the single patterns reveal. Single sticks are very interesting but only in the context of how they serve as signals requiring additional confirmation. With the double stick formation, two candlesticks provide a more definitive signal that—while also requiring confirmation—a specific price direction reversal is about to occur or that the current trend is likely to continue.

---

[i] Lee, C. L., & Liu, A. (2006). A Financial Decision Supporting System Based on Fuzzy Candlestick Patterns. *Joint Conference on Information Sciences (JCIS).*

[ii] Mahmoodzadeh, S., Shahrabi, J., Torkamani, M. A., & Ghomi, J. S. (2007). Estimating Correlation Dimension on Japanese Candlestick, Application to FOREX Time Series. *World Academy of Science, Engineering and Technology*, 30.

[iii] Qiujun Lana, Q., Zhang, D., & Xiong, L. (2011). Reversal Pattern Discovery in Financial Time Series Based on Fuzzy Candlestick Lines. *Systems Engineering Procedia*, 2, 182–190.

[iv] Linares Vásquez, M., Losada, H, Fernando, D., & González Osorio, F. (2008). Exploiting Stock Data: A Survey of State of the Art Computational Techniques Aimed at Producing Beliefs regarding Investment Portfolios. *Ingeniería e Investigación*, 28, No. 1, 105–116.

[v] Deboeck G. J., Ed. (1994). *Trading on the Edge. Neural, Genetic, and Fuzzy Systems for Chaotic Financial Markets*, Hoboken, NJ: John Wiley & Sons, Inc.

Chapter 3
Double Stick Moves

One of the critical lessons of candlesticks is that you need a broad view of stock price activity before you take action, requiring some form of confirmation. Single stick signs hold great importance, but they most often serve as part of a larger trend. Confirmation is the key, and single sticks often prove to be false signals of reversal, which points out a weakness in relying too heavily on one-session signals. The only ways to consistently analyze candlesticks is to observe multiple formations of at least two candlestick moves, confirm what appears to be occurring, and improve future timing by anticipating change based on solid data from more than one source.

Reversal formations: Candlestick developments signaling the end of the current trend and anticipating the likelihood that price will next move in the opposite direction.

In the trading moment when price is changing rapidly, information might seem solid enough only to be disproven on the next trading session. This is why following the trend is essential. A single stick sign is only an entry; a trend starts with the second stick in a series. In this chapter, the strategic importance of double stick moves is explored to show how to interpret information as it evolves.

This addresses the potential for false signals and expands on the reliability of strong candlestick signals. This contains several elements: strong initial signal, equally strong confirmation, and occurrence of reversal signals at or near the trading range borders (resistance or support). Augmenting these elements, a two-day signal is stronger than a one-day signal in general because the second day confirms the first day as a starting point. The top and bottom points of trends are the proximity point for the strongest reversals:

> Successful trading operations should occur near the reversal points of price trends. Traditional technical analysis, which usually appears as various trading rules, does aim to look for peaks and bottoms of trends and is widely used in stock market.[i]

As effective as traditional technical signals are in this effort, combining them with candlesticks adds great power to the value of signals for predicting the next move.

DOI 10.1515/9781501507397-003

Key Point: To accurately analyze price movement, no single day's sign can be interpreted as definitive. You need the double stick move to identify and confirm reversal.

A double stick move is defined by a set-up session followed by a signal session. These can work as part of a continuation or a reversal of the current trend. Even with the use of two candles instead of one, the importance of confirming the indicated significance of the move remains. Even a double stick that appears to be confirmed can end up being a false signal, so you need to rely on patience and keen analysis.

Set-up: The first trading period in a multi-stick formation, followed by the signal trading period.

Signal: The last trading period in a multi-stick formation, which occurs after the set-up.

Two Reversal Moves: Engulfing and *Harami*

A revealing sign of either bullish or bearish movement is called the engulfing pattern. In this pattern, the second day's extension of opening and closing prices exceeds the previous day's full trading range on both sides, engulfing it. A bullish engulfing consists of a downward moving set-up and then an upward-moving signal day.

Key Point: When price range in the signal days exceeds the range on upside *and* downside (engulfs), this serves as a significant reversal indicator.

Engulfing pattern: A double stick move in which the range of the set-up period's stick is surpassed by the range of the signal period and in which the setup stick's shadows are longer than those of the signal period.

A bearish engulfing move exhibits the opposite set-up and signal. The set-up is an uptrend day and the signal day reverses and creates a downtrend while completely engulfing the trading range of the previous day.

Figure 3.1 provides a single chart containing two examples of a bullish engulfing move. Both appear in the appropriate proximity, which is at the end of a downtrend, and both correctly anticipate an uptrend to follow.

Engulfing, bullish

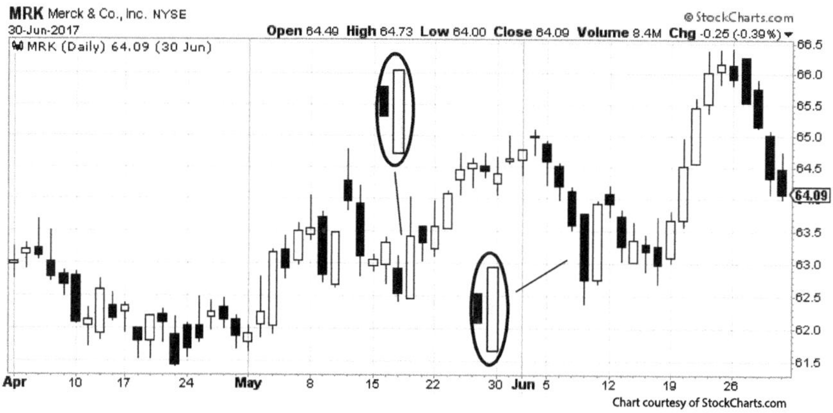

Figure 3.1: Engulfing, bullish

A failing engulfing move, whether bullish or bearish, occurs when price does not trend in the direction indicated or expected. The importance of confirmation applies to engulfing moves as it does to all others. In the previous example, both engulfing moves properly anticipated the strong uptrend that followed shortly after. Failure in engulfing moves tends to occur very soon after the pattern appears, so confirmation can be found in a single subsequent trading session. Use support in bullish engulfing to confirm and use resistance in a bearish pattern. If the next day's trading range violates the established support (bullish level) or resistance (bearish level), it indicates that the engulfing move is failing.

The behavior of the engulfing pattern has been described in psychological terms as well as in simple price behavior. In discussing the bullish engulfing, the observation is that the pattern

> acts as a reversal almost two-thirds of the time (62% to 63%), but its performance suffers. . . Downward breakouts show respectable performance, but upward breakouts yank and rank back like a bungee cord on the rebound. The candlestick appears most often at minor lows but less often at major turning points.[ii]

A similar qualification is applied by the same author to bearish engulfing patterns. However, the roles of confirmation and proximity have to be considered in evaluating the strength or weakness of this signal. If the bearish engulfing appears at the top of a bullish trend and close to resistance, or in the bullish version it shows up at the bottom of a downtrend and close to support, its placement makes the signal very powerful. This assumes that confirmation is located at the same time, making the strength of this (or any) signal a feature that goes beyond the structure of the sessions and is based more realistically on a larger context: placement, proximity, and confirmation.

The bullish signal should appear at the proper place in the downtrend and, by the same argument, a bearish engulfing should be found near a price top. An example of the bearish engulfing has the same pattern as the bullish, but with opposite colors, as shown in Figure 3.2.

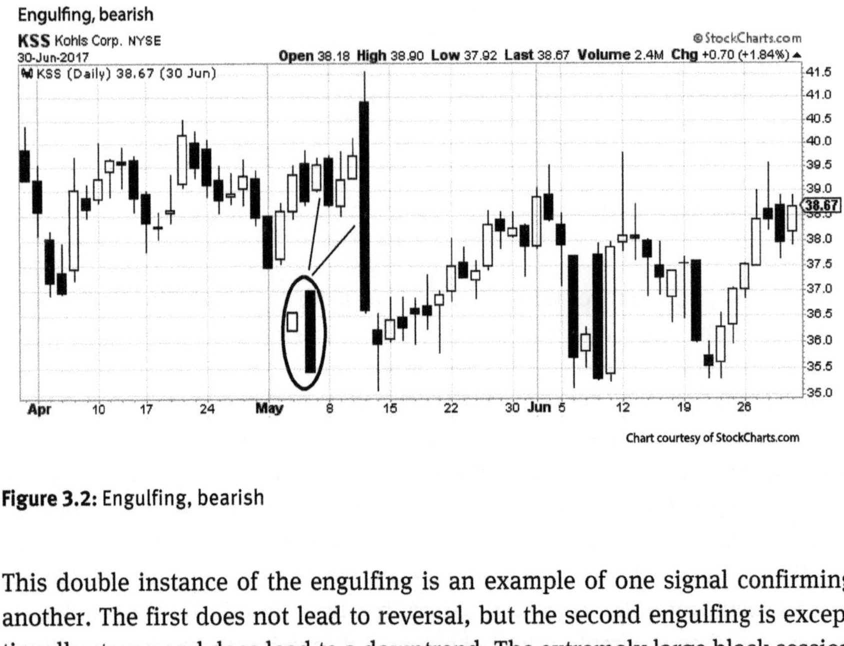

Figure 3.2: Engulfing, bearish

This double instance of the engulfing is an example of one signal confirming another. The first does not lead to reversal, but the second engulfing is exceptionally strong and does lead to a downtrend. The extremely large black session is unusual but makes the signal especially strong.

A move opposite that of the engulfing is called *harami*. This word means "pregnant" in Japanese, so named for the protrusion in the signal day. In the *harami*, the rules are opposite those of the engulfing move. A bull *harami* is characterized by a downward movement in the set-up and an upward movement in the signal session. The set-up's shadows are longer than those of the signal, and the signal is smaller on both upper and lower sides of the range.

***Harami*:** Meaning "pregnant," a double stick move in which the set-up day's range is longer than the signal's days, extending above the high and below the low, and when the set-up's shadows are longer than those of the stick in the signal period.

Key Point: The *harami* is the opposite of the engulfing move; the signal day has a smaller trading range than the set-up day. Even so, it also provides a strong indicator of a reversal in the current trend.

An example of a bullish *harami* is found in Figure 3.3.

Figure 3.3: Harami, bullish

Although this appeared at the bottom of a downtrend, the reaction was not strong. Even so, the pattern met the specifications of the bullish *harami*. The *harami* is not a particularly strong signal by itself; in fact, it is among the weakest of reversals. However, when it is found with strong confirmation or when the *harami* itself confirms another reversal signal, it is a valuable indicator. This value as part of a signal and confirmation matrix is true of many candlestick patterns.

The opposite, a bearish *harami*, has the same pattern but opposite colors. An example is shown in Figure 3.4.

Figure 3.4: Harami, bearish

This is another example of an exceptionally strong signal based on the length of the white session. As expected, the immediate price reaction was a downtrend; however, it did not last long, so ultimately the signal failed. Even though the signal was made exceptionally strong by the long candle, the basic attribute of the *harami* has to be kept in mind. Without confirmation, it is not a reliable or strong reversal signal.

The same rules of confirmation and potential failure apply for *harami* as for engulfing moves. If support holds (for bull *harami*) or if resistance holds (for bear *harami*), that is a sign that the signal is real. If and when you see a subsequent violation of the established support or resistance level, it indicates a failing *harami*. To believe in the meaning of engulfing or *harami* moves, the direction you expect to see should be established immediately.

***Harami* cross:** A type of *harami* in which the signal day forms a *doji* and is subject to the same range requirements of other *harami* moves.

A variation of this is the *harami* cross. This is a *harami* in which the signal day forms a *doji*, that is, a day in which opening and closing prices are identical or very close, resulting in a horizontal line for the real body of the stick. A bull *harami* cross consists of a downward moving day with the same attributes as other *harami* formations and a signal day of a *doji* within the trading range of the set-up. A bear *harami* cross consists of an upward moving day followed by the *doji* formed within the set-up's borders.

Figure 3.5 is a chart showing a bull *harami* cross move.

Harami cross, bullish

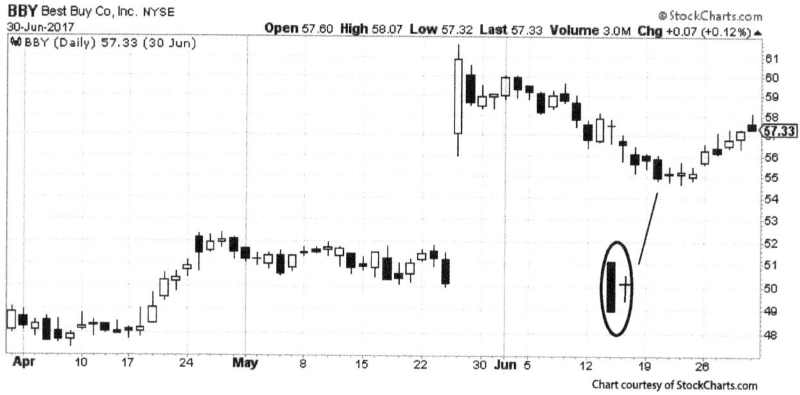

Figure 3.5: Harami cross, bullish

Key Point: A *harami* cross is simply a *harami* in which the signal day forms a *doji*, which is a very strong reversal indicator.

When support is not adhered to (in a bull move), the *harami* cross may fail, and when resistance is violated (in a bear move), the same guidelines should be observed. In Figure 3-5, the bullish *harami* cross acted as expected. The opposite, a bearish *harami* cross, is expected to appear at the top of an uptrend and forecast reversal to the downside. An example is shown in Figure 3.6.

Harami cross, bearish

Figure 3.6: Harami cross, bearish

This signal was perfectly placed at the height of the preceding uptrend, and the following price movement reversed and moved downward.

More Reversals: The Inverted Hammer and *Doji* Star

The engulfing and *harami* variations are found often in charts. However, they need to also be confirmed by other signals to take confidence levels high. Similar patterns have the same requirements. For example, the inverted hammer does not occur often, but it is a very significant move when it is found, serving as a very strong indicator in the direction away from the established trend. A bull inverted hammer occurs at the end of a downtrend and consists of two parts: the set-up is a downtrend long candle and the signal (hammer with inverted shadow on the top rather than the bottom) follows after a downward gap between the two periods. The hammer can be either white or black. These formations are seen in times of higher than average volatility.

Inverted hammer: A double stick move made up of a downward trending long candle, a low-side gap, and a hammer (a bull formation), or an upward moving long candle, a high-side gap, and a hammer (a bear formation).

An example of a bull inverted hammer is seen in Figure 3.7. Price had been volatile, but this signal followed a very brief downtrend. Even so, the reversal reaction was strong.

Inverted hammer, bullish

Chart courtesy of StockCharts.com

Figure 3.7: Inverted hammer, bullish

The bearish inverted hammer is expected to occur at or near the top of an uptrend and should forecast a reversal. Figure 3.8 provides an example. The long black candle that followed confirmed the inverted hammer. Subsequent strong downward price movement took back all of the gains in the previous bullish price move. The turning point was the topping off of the bullish trend and the inverted hammer.

Inverted hammer, bearish

Figure 3.8: Inverted hammer, bearish

Key Point: The inverted hammer is one of the strongest reversal signals. The signal day follows a gap and then confirms the reversal by the hammer in which the dominant side in the current trend was not able to sustain price changes.

This is an example of a "delayed reaction" signal. Once the uptrend peaked, it moved sideways for a full month before the reversal signal appeared. However, the inverted hammer succeeded in anticipating a strong downtrend.

A similar pattern is the *doji* star. This consists of a black session (bullish), a downward gap, and a *doji*, or a white session (bearish), an upward gap, and a *doji*. An example of the bullish variety is seen in Figure 3.9.

Doji star, bullish

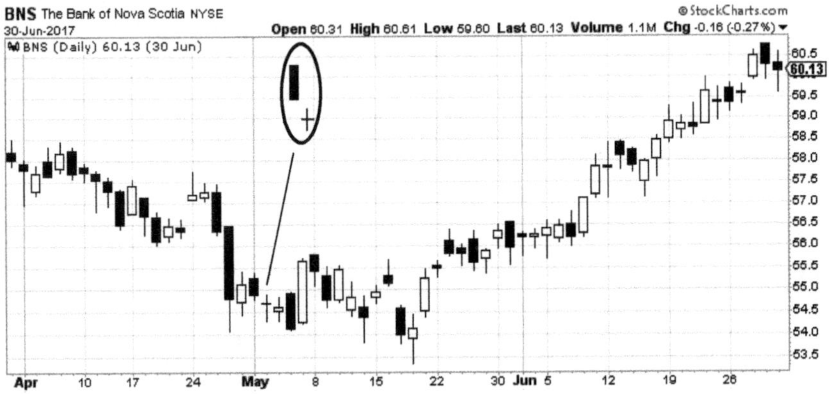

Chart courtesy of StockCharts.com

Figure 3.9: Doji star, bullish

Although this is an accurate example of a bullish *doji* star, the reversal was delayed by three weeks. This is not unexpected, as reaction is one of the unpredictable features of candlesticks. An analyst would not assume it failed, however, as price remained sideways moving but did not fall any further. The preceding black candles were strong, even though the downtrend was ending. In spite of the following delayed reaction, the *doji* star accurately predicted the next move.

A bearish *doji* star is the opposite, and an example is found in Figure 3.10.

Doji star, bearish

Chart courtesy of StockCharts.com

Figure 3.10: Doji star, bearish

***Doji* star:** A variation of the inverted hammer in which the signal day forms as a *doji* instead of a hammer candle.

Key Point: The *doji* star replaces the hammer with a *doji*. The combined gap and price action in the signal day make this a very powerful reversal formation.

The problem with this example is that it appears at the top of a minimal uptrend, consisting of only three sessions. However, it did lead to a small downtrend, so the criteria were met, but only minimally.

A final version of the *doji* star is the "collapsing reversal." In this version, the *doji* session follows a gap, and a subsequent gap takes price further in the same direction. When a white sessions gaps down to a *doji* and then gaps further to a black session, it is a collapsing bearish reversal. An example is shown in Figure 3.11.

Doji star, collapsing

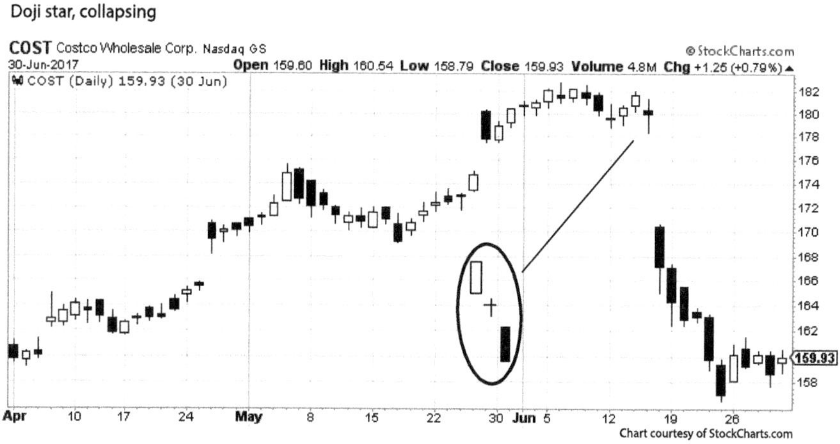

Chart courtesy of StockCharts.com

Figure 3.11: Doji star, collapsing

This reversal is an extreme case because the second gap (after the *doji*) was exceptionally wide, dropping the price more than ten points in a single session. It strongly established a bearish move, which did continue after this pattern appeared. Even though the preceding uptrend was brief, the *doji* star did collapse into a bearish reversal.

Gaps and Lines

Two-session candlesticks take many varieties, some subtle and others more obvious. Inverted hammers and stars require gaps in between sessions. Another form of two-session signals involves both sides occurring without gaps.

First is the two black gapping candles. This is a bearish continuation signal. A downtrend sees a downward gap followed by two black candles. An example is shown in Figure 3.12.

Two black gapping candles

Chart courtesy of StockCharts.com

Figure 3.12: Two black gapping candles

The preceding candle color is not important. The key feature here is the gap followed by two black sessions. The downtrend did continue even after a false rise, which initially had the appearance of a bullish move. The continuation signal (meaning the current trend is expected to keep moving in the same direction) is opposite of a reversal, which indicates a turn in the trend.

A bullish continuation was found in the two white gapping candles signal. Figure 3.13 shows an example. The existing uptrend continued after the gap, as expected.

Two white gapping candles

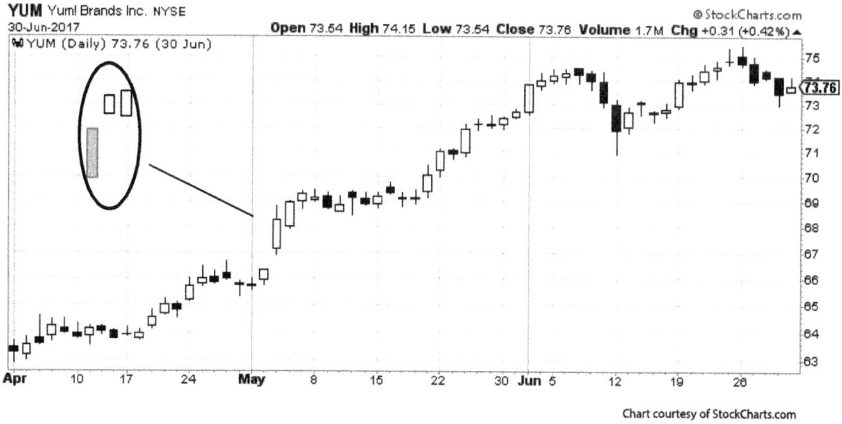

Figure 3.13: Two white gapping candles

A reversal signal was found in the meeting lines. A bullish meeting line was set up with a black session followed by a white. The closing price of both was at the same price (meeting). When a black session is followed by a white set-up with these criteria, it is a bullish meeting line, as shown in Figure 3.14.

Meeting lines, bullish

Figure 3.14: Meeting lines, bullish

The meeting between the black and white closing prices provides a strong bullish reversal, and, as predicted, price does turn to the upside immediately after the appearance of this signal. The bearish meeting line consists of the same proximity between two consecutive sessions. However, the first is white, and the second opens higher but moves down to close at the same price, signaling a bearish reversal. In Figure 3.15, this is spotted at the very top of the preceding uptrend, and a bearish reversal followed.

Meeting lines, bearish

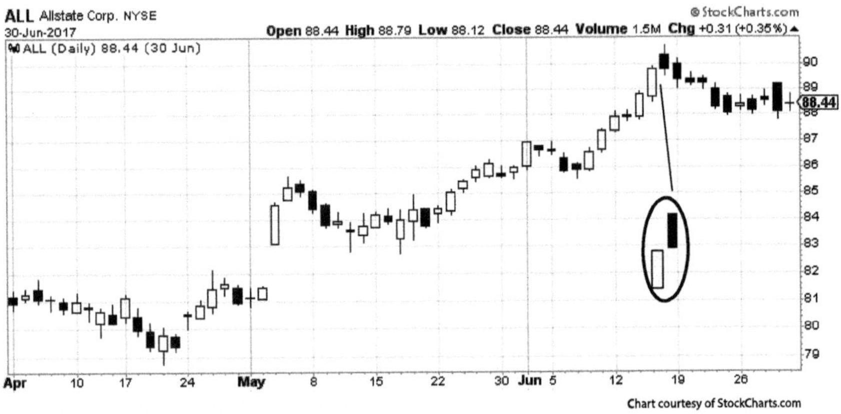

Figure 3.15: Meeting lines, bearish

Meeting lines: A double stick move with the bottom of the set-up day's real body meeting the top of the real body in the signal day. In a bull move, the set-up day is downward moving and the signal day is upward, creating a downward gap between the closing price of the set-up and the opening price of the signal. A bear meeting lines move exhibits the opposite direction in both sessions and an upside gap in between.

Key Point: A lot of chart analysis focuses on the trend while overlooking the relationship of the real body between days. The meeting lines move can be very significant in foreshadowing reversal because it contains an invisible gap.

Yet another version of a two-session reversal is found in the development of patterns called raindrops and stars. Raindrops are single sessions followed by downward gaps and small day real bodies. They are usually bearish reversals. Stars contain single sessions followed by upward gaps and small day real bodies. They normally predict bullish reversal. Both raindrops and stars may contain either color in both of the sessions. All of the possible combinations are summarized in Figure 3.16.

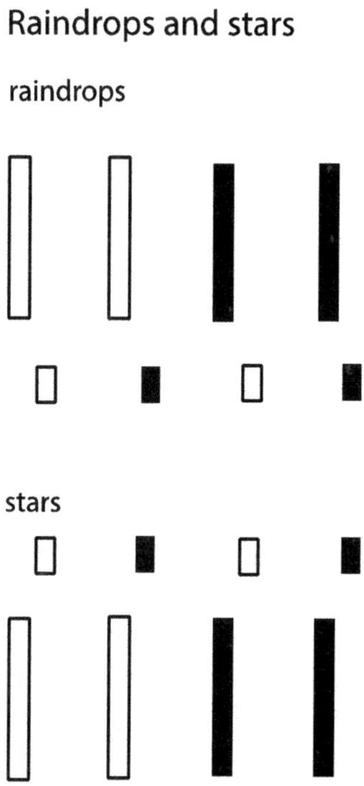

Figure 3.16: Raindrops and stars

Another two-session reversal is found in the frequently occurring piercing lines. A bullish version consists of a black session followed by a white session that opens below the previous close, and then closes within the range of the previous real body. Figure 3.17 contains three examples of the bullish piercing lines.

Figure 3.17: Piercing lines, bullish

Although the pattern on this chart was volatile, the bullish piercing lines appeared consistently at the bottom of short-term downtrends. The bearish piercing lines (also called dark cloud cover) appear at the top of an uptrend and consist of a white session followed by a high-opening black session that declines and closes within the range of the first session's real body. An example is found in Figure 3.18 and the result was a very strong downtrend.

Figure 3.18: Piercing lines, bearish (Dark cloud cover)

Key Point: A confirming move can relate to a very short-term trend or, when multiple versions of the same move appear, may provide strong confirming signs of continuation in the longer-term trend.

Piercing lines: A double stick move with two long candles. A bull formation has a downward movement in the set-up and a lower, upward movement in the signal, with trading ranges overlapping to form an invisible gap.

Dark cloud cover: Alternate name for the bear piercing lines move.

Double sessions like this may also represent continuation patterns, appearing mid-trend and forecasting that the same direction will prevail and not reverse. The thrusting line is one of these continuation patterns. The bullish thrusting line begins with a white session followed by a high-opening black session closing within the first day's real body range. An example is shown in Figure 3.19.

Thrusting lines, bullish

Chart courtesy of StockCharts.com

Figure 3.19: Thrusting lines, bullish

Thrusting lines: A double stick confirming move consisting of two long candles. In a bull formation, set-up is upward and a higher signal day is downward. In a bear formation, set-up is downward and a lower signal day is upward moving.

This continuation pattern is reassuring because it follows strong gapping days. This often precedes reversal, but the appearance of a bullish continuation pattern predicts that the uptrend is not over. Even though the movement was minimal, it did continue advancing as the continuation signal indicated.

A bearish thrusting lines move is the opposite. The first session is black, followed by a lower-opening white session that advances to close within the first session's real body range. Figure 3.20 provides a very unusual and exceptionally strong bearish reversal found in the appearance of three bearish continuations in close proximity. The downtrend continued after this pattern.

Figure 3.20: Thrusting lines, bearish

In examining the timing of entry and exit decisions, rate your ability to correctly call both reversal and confirming indicators. The failing indicators are just as important as those that succeed; the failure of even a strong double stick move reminds you that these are only indicators and not certainties, that all of the elements need to be present for the pattern to apply reliably, and that the goal is not to achieve completely perfect timing but to improve your overall success. A *confirming* indicator is different from a confirmation sign within a reversal pattern. When working with reversal, you seek confirmation of what the candlestick move seems to be revealing; when seeking a confirming move, you are looking for signs that the current trend is still in effect.

Key Point: The confirming move tells you the current trend will continue. Compared to the more popular reversal move, confirming moves can be more difficult to spot.

Confirming moves tell you that the current trend is going to continue, at least until it weakens and reverses. The duration of a trend is impossible to forecast without relying on developing patterns within the trend itself. Among these, the thrusting line is one of the most important.

Another two-session continuation signal is found in the separating lines. The bullish version begins with a black session in the first day and a white session opening at the same price but moving upward. Figure 3.21 contains an example of a bullish continuation pattern in the form of separating lines. The stock price had been rising steadily, but continuation was not clear until this small but important signal appeared on May 6 and 9 (Friday and Monday).

Separating lines, bullish

Chart courtesy of StockCharts.com

Figure 3.21: Separating lines, bullish

Separating lines: A confirming double stick move creating a gap equal to the real body of the set-up day. A bull formation is formed with a downward set-up and a higher upward signal. A bear move is formed with an upward set-up and a lower downward signal.

In the bearish version, a white first session is followed by a black session opening at the same opening price of the previous day, but then moving lower. An example is seen in the chart in Figure 3.22. In both cases of the separating lines indicator, the gap between the first session's opening price and the second session's closing price is the most important feature.

Figure 3.22: Separating lines, bearish

Key Point: The separating lines move, like many other double sticks, includes an invisible gap. This should not be ignored; gaps are significant and revealing, even in confirming moves.

Neck Lines, Crows, and Rabbits

Another series of two-session indicators consists of a series of very specific patterns, developing to indicate continuation (neck lines) or reversals (crows and rabbits).

Neck line: A double stick confirming move with long candlesticks. The set-up is upward and a higher signal is downward (bull pattern) or the set-up is downward and the signal is upward (bear pattern). In both cases, a gap is closed in the set-up day, confirming the current trend.

The on neck is a continuation pattern that appears during a trend and forecasts that the same direction will prevail for the immediate future. A bullish on neck begins with a white session followed by a higher open in a black session, which closes at the same price (on the neck) as the previous day. An example is found in Figure 3.23.

On neck: A variation of the neck line move in which the two days' real bodies intersect at approximately the same price level.

On neck, bullish

Figure 3.23: On neck, bullish

Although the preceding trend was relatively weak, the continuation of a bullish move did occur. In a bearish on neck pattern, the opposite configuration occurs. This is a black session followed by a lower-opening white session that advances to close at the same closing price of the previous day. Figure 3.24 provides an example.

On neck, bearish

Figure 3.24: On neck, bearish

Key Point: Whenever you find two consecutive long candles with opposite price directions, it is invariably important and requires further study.

A similar continuation is represented by the in neck pattern. The distinction here is that rather than closing at the same price, the second day of the in neck closed with the range of the first session's real body. In the bullish case, a white session is followed by a high-opening black session that closes with the range of the first day's real body. An example is seen in Figure 3.25.

In neck - bullish

Chart courtesy of StockCharts.com

Figure 3.25: In neck, bullish

In neck: A variation of the neck line move in which the two days' real bodies overlap somewhat in price levels.

The signal is subtle but appears during the uptrend and does predict further upward movement. In a bearish in neck, a first day's black session is followed by a lower-opening white session that advances to close within the real body's range of the first day. An example is found in Figure 3.26.

In neck - bearish

Figure 3.26: In neck, bearish

Key Point: Whenever you find two long candles with opposite price directions, it is invariably important and requires further study.

A trader witnessing the unusually high open of the session that followed could easily interpret this as a bullish upside gap. However, a combination of that day's downward move and the previous appearance of the bearish continuation pattern revealed what was taking place.

Compared to continuation, two-session reversals present a special challenge in chart analysis. A recurring problem with reversal double sticks is that they often turn out to be false signals. When prices move opposite of the direction the reversal pattern indicates, timing can be made worse instead of better. This is why you need to rely on confirmation signals and to ensure that *all* of the attributes are in place. Most reversal double sticks show up at the end of the trend. You expect to see a bullish reversal move at the end of the downtrend and the bearish reversal at the end of the uptrend. False signals can occur anywhere, but they are more likely to show up in the wrong place. This means that a bull reversal move that you find within a bull trend is questionable, and the same is true of a bear reversal move within a bear trend. In order to serve as a true reversal formation, there must be a trend to reverse. If you forget this important rule, you might end up buying near the top of an uptrend or selling near the bottom of a downtrend; these actions are exactly what you hope to avoid by using candlesticks, so be aware not only of the shape of the move, but also where you find it.

Reversals come in many forms. For example, the two crows is a bearish reversal set-up as a gap to the upside followed by two black sessions. An example is found in Figure 3.27.

Figure 3.27: Two crows

The resulting downtrend was brief, but it did follow after the reversal predicting a change in direction. A requirement for this indicator is that the second black session has to fill the gap created before the first session. In the upside gap two crows, the same configuration is found, but the gap is not filled. Figure 3.28 shows this.

Figure 3.28: Upside gap two crows

Even though the pattern was identical to the two crows, the initial gap did not fill until several sessions later.

On the opposite side of this gapping reversal is the downside gap two rabbits. An example is found in Figure 3.29. Following a strong downtrend, the two rabbits predicted an end of the trend and a bullish reversal. Even though the first of the two "rabbit" sessions was a *doji*, the pattern remained accurate.

Figure 3.29: Downside gap two rabbits

Another reversal pattern is the stomach. The bullish version is called stomach above and is made up of a black session followed by a white opening within the real body of the first day but advancing to close higher. The difference between the first day's close and the second day's open is a gap, which is the strength to the stomach. This is shown in Figure 3.30.

Figure 3.30: Stomach above

The proximity is exactly what would be expected. It is located at the bottom of a downtrend and followed by a strong uptrend. The stomach below is a bearish version of this pattern. It begins with a white session followed by a gap to a black session opening within the real body but then declining to close lower. An example is found in Figure 3.31.

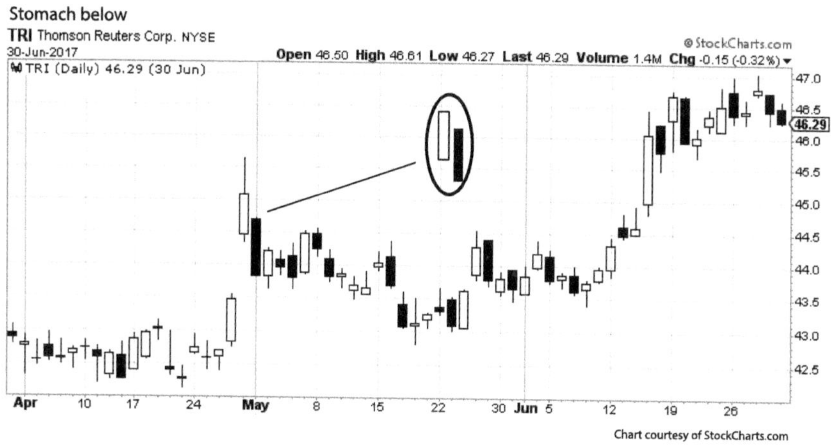

Figure 3.31: Stomach below

The uptrend in this case consisted of a single upward gap. Although very brief, the gap itself presented a problem. Gaps are normally expected to fill, so the appearance of the bearish stomach was of interest to the chartist seeking the likely point of reversal.

The "window" is a pattern appearing within a trend and indicating confirmation. For example, a window rising is bullish confirmation. Two window rising signals are shown in Figure 3.32.

Figure 3.32: Window rising

In each case, the prevailing uptrend indicates continuation due to the appearance of the window signal. These are characterized by gaps in between the two sessions. In the bearish version, known as the window falling, black sessions decline and forecast continuation of the downtrend. The two sessions are separated by a gap, as shown in Figure 3.33.

Window falling

Figure 3.33: Window falling

The continuation in this instance was subtle because the sessions consisted of gaps, but also were close to *doji* in formation. However, continuation did occur, and the window falling was a successful forecast.

A bearish reversal occurs in the form of a descending hawk. This two-session pattern consists of two white days, with the second residing entirely within the real body range of the first. An example is seen on the chart in Figure 3.34.

Descending hawk

Figure 3.34: Descending hawk

This is a subtle indicator, but it was confirmed immediately by the bearish *harami* that followed. After this, the price turned and moved downward as the descending hawk forecast. An opposite pattern is the bullish reversal called the homing pigeon. This is made up of two black sessions, with the second session engulfed entirely within the range of the first. An example appears in Figure 3.35.

Homing pigeon

Figure 3.35: Homing pigeon

Proximity was correct here, with the two-day session appearing at the end of a downtrend and then followed by an uptrend. Although this (like the descending hawk) is a short and simple indicator, it is also a strong reversal signal.

Reversal and Confirming Moves—Relative Values

Most chartists are comfortable with reversal moves because they represent action points. These are entry and exit signals calling for immediate action (upon confirmation). Consequently, a reversal move contains several important attributes:

1. It provides a sign that the trend is turning.
2. The action—entry or exit—is indicated in the candlestick shape.
3. Confirmation is often straightforward, represented by the next day's price action, changes in trading volume or momentum, or changing shadows *and* real bodies of the candles involved.

Reversal is considered the most important point in the trend because it signals the end of the current trend and the beginning of the next trend. If this seems obvious, it is not. The indicator can be a false sign as well as a true one, which is why timing is only made better with the appearance of the all-important confirming indicator and with the lack of any contradictory signs (for example, reversal moves immediately after the confirming moves).

Key Point: Reversal moves are popular because as timing signals, they tell you when and where to make a decision, either entry or exit.

A confirming move tells you the right action is to *hold*, whereas reversal moves signal the time to buy or sell. The hold action is just as important as a buy or sell decision and is an equally important attribute of timing based on chart analysis. The confirming move is the sole indicator telling you the trend has not yet ended. Even though most traders are accustomed to looking for reversal moves, confirming moves should be part of the analysis as well. Using both reversal and confirming moves can double overall analytical effectiveness. Knowing when to act is a key to success, but knowing when not to act is just as important.

Key Point: Confirming moves are just as important as reversals in the sense that they tell you when *not* to act. Instead of a buy or sell indicator, the confirming moves tell you to hold on.

To this point, focus has been on single candlestick signs and double candlestick moves. The next chapter delves into the complex pattern involving three or more candlesticks. These are more difficult to find than double stick moves, but can also act as initial *or* confirming indicators.

---

[i] Lin, X., Yang, Z., & Song, Y. (2011). Intelligent Stock Trading System based on Improved Technical Analysis and Echo State Network. *Expert Systems with Applications*, 38.

[ii] Bulkowski, T. (2008). *Encyclopedia of Candlestick Charts*. Hoboken, NJ: John Wiley & Sons, 317.

Chapter 4
Complex Stick Patterns

Any pattern of three or more candlesticks appearing in consecutive sessions is a *complex* pattern. Three stick patterns are stronger indicators than two stick moves if only because it takes more pattern to create a specific set of attributes. A complex pattern is not limited to only three consecutive sticks, however. A pattern can easily become a trend when it moves beyond three sticks. Complex patterns can be divided into two broad categories. Reversal patterns appear at or near the end of the current trend and anticipate a change in the opposite direction. Directional patterns are indicators pointing to a new trend as it develops or as continuation of an existing trend.

Complex patterns: Candlestick formations consisting of three or more consecutive trading sessions and creating one of several specific reversal or directional indicators.

Key Point: A complex pattern is any pattern with three or more candles.
These are frequently extensions from established two stick moves. These patterns can indicate continuation of an existing trend or reversal and establishment of a new trend.

The third entry into the pattern either confirms what the two stick move indicated or contradicts it. The three stick pattern is worth waiting for when a two stick move has appeared to confirm that the timing hinted at in the two stick move is strong enough to confirm the initial signal and to take action.

While complex patterns involve a series of requirements including direction of each stick, gaps, and the relationship between each session, the following observations apply:

1. *The observations are guidelines, not absolute requirements.* You might discover some complex patterns with *most* but not all of the requirements. For example, a third stick in a three stick move might open slightly above the trading range of the second stick. Does this negate the indication? No, it only modifies the strength of what the formation reveals, but ideal and perfect formation is rare. The candlestick analysis is intended not to adhere to a strict set of inflexible rules but to provide meaningful guidance about improving the timing of entry and exit.
2. *No formation is a guarantee, only an indicator.* Not every formation will be followed by price movement in the direction indicated. The purpose of

DOI 10.1515/9781501507397-004

chart analysis is to improve your timing, but there are no assurances. Formations also fail. However, when analysis is performed consistently, complex patterns are likely to improve your overall experience and timing. Judging the confidence level helps improve the odds of positive outcomes regarding the timing of trades. This also helps avoid the potential for making ill-timed decisions due to confirmation bias.

3. *Complex patterns are excellent forms of confirmation of two stick moves.* The majority of complex patterns are extensions of the two stick moves introduced in the previous chapter. The complex pattern is not always distinct; it is often the case that the third entry into the formation strengthens what the first two sticks indicate and serves as excellent confirmation of the initial pattern.
4. *The prediction may not occur in a strict sequence of three or more sessions.* Some chart watchers are "purists" about candlesticks, and they recognize a pattern only when there are three or more sticks that adhere in strict sequence to the required pattern. But as you study the charts presented in this chapter, you will observe that in some cases, a strong complex pattern is going to be found over a four-day period with the second or third day a passing or nonconforming phase. Thus, the complex pattern often evolves in a nonconsecutive sequence. The danger of stretching patterns over a period that includes nonconforming days is that you can easily twist the pattern to suit what you want to see or what you think should be taking place or to fall victim to confirmation bias. But when an interim stick does not violate any trading range borders for the sticks on both sides and the adjusted pattern is exceptionally strong, you can consider it a valid complex pattern. It is a matter of judgment. Check what price action follows an "interrupted pattern" of this type to decide whether allowing exceptions within the pattern is productive or distracting.

Key Point: Flexibility in interpreting complex patterns aids in improving trade timing. Specific patterns are most valuable when they adhere to their requirements, but the complex pattern can also include interim sessions not part of the formation.

Reversal Trend Change Patterns

The first set-up complex pattern deals with reversals in an existing trend. This means that you would expect to see these formations at or near the end of an existing trend. A reminder, however: Formations do not always appear when you expect them, and they are never completely reliable. They only indicate the likelihood of changes to come.

The existing trend is likely to exhibit clear signals of decline in momentum, plateauing, and, ultimately, reversal. During the trend, these signals can anticipate a coming reversal, which may be confirmed by candlestick and traditional Western reversal indicators as well as signals found in momentum, volume, and moving averages. Trend analysis of price is purely technical in nature and does not take into consideration the underlying fundamental strength or weakness of the company. This means that

> technical analysis evaluates solely on the market prices themselves rather than on any fundamental factor else outside the market. Traders who are solely equipped with technical analysis suppose that a careful analysis of daily price movement as well as a long term trend is all that is required to predict a price trend for their trading.[i]

As a potentially limiting factor of technical analysis, this isolated trend analysis may easily overlook emerging fundamental information such as mergers, earnings, changes in management, or industry news. So, a holistic trading system is best when it combines observation of price patterns and signals with tracking of financial and other news. This two-part effort recognizes the contribution to price movement of both fundamental and technical factors, and aiding in this is the search for complex candlestick patterns. These, more or less complicated one- and two-session indicators, tend to incorporate the fundamental developments underlying price behavior.

Key Point: You are likely to spot complex patterns over a three-session period. But they can extend for a much greater number of sessions as well. The number three is only the minimum.

The first among these is three (or more) candles moving consecutively and in the same direction. An upward formation may take any number of pattern forms, and what occurs immediately after the pattern is also important. The ladder top is one example. It consists of a series of three or more upward-moving sessions and then a downward gap followed by a black session. Because of the gap and black session, this makes the ladder top a bearish reversal. Many signals involving subsequently higher white sessions are considered bullish; however, when it appears at the top of an uptrend, a reversal and bearish change makes sense. An example is shown in Figure 4.1.

Ladder top

Figure 4.1: Ladder top

In this example, the bearish reversal was strong due to the large gap occurring as price direction reversed. The opposite, a ladder bottom, should appear at the bottom of a downtrend and consists of three or more consecutive black sessions, an upside gap, and a white session. These attributes define the ladder bottom as a bullish reversal. An example is shown in Figure 4.2.

Ladder bottom

Figure 4.2: Ladder bottom

The ladder pattern is easily recognized. The end of a current trend followed by a gap in the opposite direction is among the strongest of reversal patterns.

Compared to the ladder reversals, consecutive sessions of the same color and appearing in the expected proximity to the prevailing trend also provide a different type of reversal. The three white soldiers consist of three white sessions appearing consecutively. Each has higher high closing prices and higher low openings. An example is seen in Figure 4.3.

Figure 4.3: Three white soldiers

Three white soldiers: A complex candlestick formation consisting of three or more consecutive upward candles. Each has a higher opening and a higher closing than the previous candle.

The required attributes were all present: a downtrend preceded the signal, the three consecutive sessions displayed higher opening and closing prices, and, most important of all, an uptrend followed. This pattern is typical of a strong trend that begins with reversal and continues with momentum. A widespread belief is that a trend—especially a strong one—is likely to continue in the same direction until an opposite signal appears. Thus a trend starting out with a convincing signal forecasts a strong trend to follow. As a technical signal, any strong reversal contains similar attributes, even if based only on price patterns and lacking an underlying fundamental reason. The strength of a three-part reversal often defines the strength of the trend to follow.

A downward formation is called three black crows and consists of three sessions with lower low openings and lower high closings. Figure 4.4 contains an example. This is not a perfect three black crows because the downtrend began three sessions before the set of black crows showed up. Even so, as a reversal, the signal did lead to a strong movement over five days. This was followed by a consolidation movement of more than one month before the trend began moving once again.

Three black crows

Chart courtesy of StockCharts.com

Figure 4.4: Three black crows

Three black crows: A complex candlestick formation consisting of three or more consecutive downward candles. Each has a lower opening and a lower closing than the previous candle.

One of the rarest of reversal signals is called a squeeze alert. It is unusual because each session trades within the range of the previous session and the color of the leading session is opposite what most signals would contain: the squeeze alert begins with a black long candle for a bullish reversal and a white long candle for a bearish reversal. The bullish version is shown in Figure 4.5.

Figure 4.5: Squeeze alert, bullish

Bull squeeze alert: A three-session candle with the first one downward, the second with a narrower opening and closing range, and the third with yet narrower ranges. Although second- and third-session candles may be upward or downward, the strongest version of the squeeze alert contains three black candles.

The pattern is subtle because it is not immediately visible. Because it is not seen often, the tendency among chartists is to not look for the squeeze. A "perfect" bullish squeeze alert would contain longer black sessions and all three would be black. This is a rare pattern. An acceptable variety requires only that the first session is black and that the next two are each smaller, but may be of either color. Ultimately, the pattern is successful if the price reverses and begins moving upward.

The opposite or bearish squeeze alert begins with a long white candle and two additional sessions of either color, each opening and closing within the range of the previous session. An ideal bearish squeeze alert would have large white candles with all three sessions white; this is as rare as a bullish all-black set.

Bear squeeze alert: A three-session candle with the first one upward, the second with a narrower opening and closing range, and the third with yet narrower ranges. Although second- and third-session candles may be upward or downward, the strongest version of the squeeze alert contains three white candles.

An example of the bear squeeze alert is shown in Figure 4.6. This is a reasonably strong example because it contains two out of three white sessions, appears at the top of an uptrend, and immediately leads to reversal and a downtrend.

Figure 4.6: Squeeze alert, bearish

Inside and Outside Formations

Another range of complex patterns forecasting reversal is the inside and outside pattern. The first of these, the inside pattern, consists of a *harami* followed by a strong move in one direction or the other. The *harami* is a two stick move with two attributes: the two sessions have opposite colored real bodies and the second day is smaller in both opening and closing price. The inside up (bull) move contains a black first day followed by two white days, a *harami*, and another white session closing higher.

Inside up: A three-stick formation with a bull *harami* in the first two sessions (a black first day and a smaller white second day in a narrower range) and then a third upward day.

An example of the inside up is found in Figure 4.7.

Inside up

Chart courtesy of StockCharts.com

Figure 4.7: Inside up

This is a bullish reversal. The expected *harami* formed in the first two sessions. Even though only a minimal downtrend had preceded the inside up, a strong uptrend followed and advanced five points over two weeks.

Inside down: A three-stick formation with a bear *harami* in the first two sessions (a white first day and a smaller black second day in a narrower range) and then a third downward day.

A much stronger reversal is seen in the inside down appearing in Figure 4.8. In this case, an uptrend gapped to a new high, a bearish *harami* appeared, and price reversed to move downward.

A set of opposite patterns appear in the outside up and down signals. Each begins with an engulfing pattern, followed by a third session confirming the indicated reversal direction.

Key Point: The complex pattern is commonly a two stick move with confirmation in the third stick. The inside down formation is a good example, strengthening what is implied in the initial *harami* of the first two sessions.

Outside up: A complex pattern consisting of a bull engulfing (two sticks made up of a black day and then a larger white day with higher high and higher low) and a third day moving higher.

Inside down

Figure 4.8: Inside down

An outside up formation was found on the chart in Figure 4.9. The gap between the second and third sessions is not a requirement, but clearly it makes the signal much stronger. This chart is typical of a mild downtrend, a reversal, and a mild uptrend. A tendency for strength or weakness in the preceding trend to be mirrored in the reversal is seen often.

Outside up

Figure 4.9: Outside up

In the outside down, a bearish engulfing appears at the top of an uptrend, indicating likely reversal. This is confirmed by the third session, which is black and moves downward. In this regard, the inside and outside signals are stronger than the initial two-session signals due to the all-important third session and the direction it confirms. In Figure 4.10, an unusually strong bearish reversal was created by the long black candle in the second session. This was preceded by a mild uptrend, but followed by a strong downtrend.

Figure 4.10: Outside down

Outside down: A complex pattern consisting of a bear engulfing (two sticks made up of a white day and then a larger black day with higher high and higher low) and a third day moving lower.

Reversal Stars and Abandoned Babies

Some reversal three stick patterns are less visible than others, and like other patterns, these less visible ones combine previously explained two stick moves with a third component. This third consecutive day's movements strengthen the indicated change in direction.

Key Point: Some of the most valuable reversal indicators involving complex patterns are not obvious. The less visible pattern provides valuable confirmation and is worth looking for. Most chart watchers will spot the obvious patterns easily, but it takes greater powers of observation to find less visible ones.

The first of these is the morning star, a bullish indicator showing up at the end of a downtrend. It consists of a bull hammer (a downward day, downward gap, and small real body day with a lower shadow [hammer] or upper shadow [inverted hammer]). The hammer session is followed by a gap and another, higher upward day.

Morning star: A bull three-stick pattern combining a bullish hammer with a subsequent third day moving upward, with spaces between the sessions.

The morning star, like the hammer, does not always succeed. It is simply an indicator and not a promise of the coming price direction. Even so, when it is found at the bottom of a downtrend and confirmed by other signals, the morning star may be a strong candlestick signal of high confidence. An example of the signal is found in Figure 4.11.

Morning star

Chart courtesy of StockCharts.com

Figure 4.11: Morning star

The length of the black session, the first of the three in the morning star, created an exceptionally strong hammer and an equally strong morning star with the additional of the third day. A two-week period of uncertainty followed before the expected bullish reversal took hold.

Evening star: A bear three stick pattern combining a bear hammer with a subsequent third day moving downward, with spaces between the sessions.

The evening star consists of a white session, upward gap, black session, then a lower gap and another black session. Figure 4.12 appeared at the right place, but did not lead to a strong reversal.

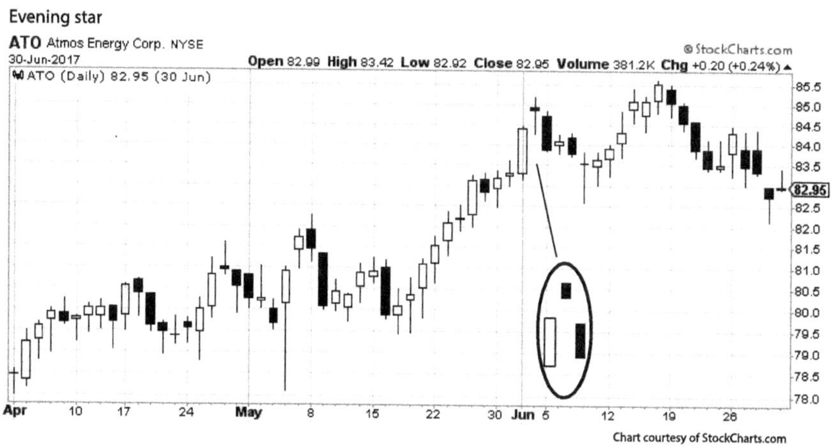

Figure 4.12: Evening star

Morning star and evening star formations are strong and reliable much of the time, but they can also appear as failed signals. Strong confirmation is required before acting on either of these apparent reversal predictions.

A similar pattern is the abandoned baby, which is an expansion of the two stick *doji* star. In the bull abandoned baby, the bull *doji* star (a downward day, downward gap, and *doji*) is followed by an upward gap and then an upward day. The *doji*, residing all by itself between two gaps, is the "abandoned" segment of this formation.

Bull abandoned baby: A complex pattern consisting of a bull *doji* star (a downward day, downward gap, and *doji*) followed by an upward gap and then an upward day.

An example of the bull abandoned baby is seen in Figure 4.13. Although the preceding trend was minimal, this formation did accurately forecast a new uptrend that continued throughout the duration of the chart.

Abandoned baby, bullish

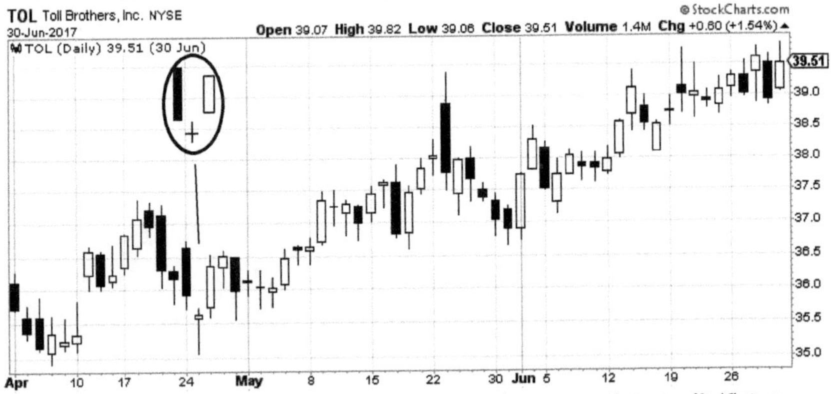

Chart courtesy of StockCharts.com

Figure 4.13: Abandoned baby, bullish

Key Point: The abandoned baby pattern is a strong indicator because of the reversal after the *doji* day. This tells you the direction supported by the pattern has a lot of strength.

Bear abandoned baby: A complex formation consisting of a bear *doji* star (an upward day, upward gap, and *doji*) followed by a downward gap and then a downward day.

A bear abandoned baby is the opposite. It is the combination of a bear *doji* star, a gap, and a downward day. Figure 4.14 provides an example. This chart is fairly volatile, but even in the condition of volatility, a series of candlestick reversals showed up. These included repetitive bearish *harami* signals at all of the price peaks after the abandoned baby.

Figure 4.14: Abandoned baby, bearish

Line and Gap Continuation Signals

Besides easily recognized reversal patterns, some complex patterns confirm a trend. These trend patterns should be expected to appear during an existing trend and can be used to determine that no reversal is likely to occur in the immediate future. The patterns forecast a direction, often immediately after a brief delay in price movement.

The first of these are the side-by-side lines. These can be confusing because there are four distinct formations, two each for bullish and bearish continuation. First is the bullish white side-by-side lines.

Side-by-side white lines bull: A pattern of three white sessions. The first is followed by an upside gap and then two additional upward-moving sessions.

Figure 4.15 contains two examples of the bullish white lines continuation signal. Price did not conform precisely as expected, as it moved to a plateau and consolidated for the rest of the charted period. Even so, the appearance of two continuation signals during a strong move was a good example of how this signal is used.

Side by side white lines, bullish

Figure 4.15: Side by side white lines, bullish

The side-by-side black lines bear is similar to the preceding one but provides all black sessions and indicates downward continuation.

Side-by-side black lines bear: A formation of three black sessions. The first is followed by a downside gap and then two additional downward-moving sessions.

An example is seen in Figure 4.16. A period of uncertainty preceded this, but once it appeared, a downtrend was established and the move did occur.

Side by side black lines, bearish

Figure 4.16: Side by side black lines, bearish

A second set of side-by-side line signals combined white and black sessions but also work as continuation signals. First is the side-by-side black lines bull, constructed with a white session, upward gap, and two black sessions. Reference to this as a "black" signal refers to the second and third sessions.

Side-by-side black lines bull: A formation of one white session, an upside gap, and two black sessions. Price support prevents the bears from moving price down to fill the gap and forms new support, making this a bullish indicator.

A bullish side-by-side black lines pattern is most likely to be found during an uptrend. The pattern reveals that although trading during the second and third sessions moved in a bearish direction, the price trend did not fill the gap, creating new support at the lower extension of the first day's range and making the pattern bullish. An example is seen in Figure 4.17.

Figure 4.17: Side by side black lines, bullish

This was a strong signal due to the appearance of two of the same continuation signals. These are not going to appear frequently, so a double continuation is noteworthy.

The bearish version is the side-by-side white lines formation, which contains the opposite attributes and creates a new level of resistance at the top of the first day's trading range. The downward gap is followed by further downward price movement as bulls prove to be unable to fill the gap.

Side-by-side white lines bear: A pattern of one black session, an upside gap, and two white sessions. Price resistance prevents the bulls from moving price up to fill the gap, making this a bearish indicator.

For example, Figure 4.18 shows an exceptionally large gap between sessions one and two, adding strength and confidence to the interpretation of the downtrend continuation. Even with the strength of the signal, prices moved sideways for the following months before the downtrend began with momentum.

Side by side white lines, bearish

Chart courtesy of StockCharts.com

Figure 4.18: Side by side white lines, bearish

Key Point: Side-by-side patterns are strong because they reveal a gap followed by the *lack* of reversal or fill. This is a very strong sign of support for the direction forecast.

Continuation consisting of gaps tends to be strong. Beyond the "lines" formations, more gapping patterns also indicate likely continuation. A *tasuki* is a Japanese sash used to hold up a shirt sleeve, similar to a garter. The *tasuki* gap pattern is so called due to the shape of the three sticks. The first session is followed by a gap and then "held up" by the second and third session's price movement. An upside (bull) *tasuki* gap contains an upward day followed by an upside gap and then a second upside day followed by a somewhat lower range. It opens within the range of the second day and finishes below it. Usually found either within an uptrend or after a period of sideways trading, the important element is that even with the third day moving to the downside, the gap holds up; this is why the pattern is bullish. Although this portends an uptrend, the result might be delayed by several trading sessions.

Upside *tasuki* gap: A complex pattern creating a bull trend with an upward candle, an upside gap, a second upward candle, and then a downside candle that does not fill the gap. It is a bull formation because the gap holds up.

For example, in Figure 4.19, after a large downward gap, the stock price began rising. In this volatile situation, traders are going to be nervous. The appearance of the *tasuki* gap was reassuring in its promise of a continuation in the brief uptrend. Prices rose seven points as this signal appeared. These are difficult to spot and do not occur often, but when uncertainty in the trend is present, a rare but strong continuation signal is a promising development.

Figure 4.19: Tasuki gap, upside

A downside *tasuki* gap consists of a downward candle, a downside gap, a second downward candle, and then an upside candle. The third candle opens within the trading range of the second session but does not move high enough to fill the gap. This inability to take prices back to previous trading levels defines the continuation of the bear trend.

Downside *tasuki* gap: A complex pattern creating a bear trend with a downward candle, a downside gap, a second downward candle, and then an upside candle that does not fill the gap. It is a bear formation because the gap holds up.

Key Point: A *tasuki* gap is exceptionally strong because the price direction is maintained without a fill of the gap or price reversal.

The chart in Figure 4.20 revealed an example of the downside *tasuki* gap. Unlike the previous example of volatility, this price pattern was uncertain during the preceding month. As a result, the certainty of a downtrend was weak. The continuation pattern led to a downtrend briefly, and the continuation pattern was the convincing element that this was likely to occur. Even so, this overall formation was not strong. When the entire period was reviewed, short-term trends were found but a longer-term directional trend was lacking.

Figure 4.20: Tasuki gap, downside

The *tasuki* often serves as a strong indicator because the gap does not get filled by subsequent price movement. If a gap is a common gap (one occurring frequently in the course of normal trading), you expect it to fill within a short time. So, a nonfilled gap becomes important in setting up or reinforcing a trend.

A distinction is found in a different continuation, the filled gap. In this pattern, the gap is filled but the low of the first session (in a bull pattern) is not violated. In the bull-filled gap pattern, the opening price of the first session sets a support level, and this is confirmed by the third session. So an upside gap filled consists of an upward session, an upside gap, a second upward session, and then a downward session that fills the gap but does not fall below support.

Upside gap filled: A bull complex pattern with an upward session, an upside gap, a second upside session, and then a third session moving to the downside. However, although the third session fills the gap, it does not fall below the support level set by the first day's opening price.

An example is seen on the chart in Figure 4.21. Uncertainty was present in the previous trend. The uptrend was interrupted by a strong downward gap before the trend continued. However, this introduced great uncertainty. The upward gap introduced a bullish gap filled that, although small, set a new support level at $102. This held for the following two weeks before the uptrend resumed, and strongly. Price moved from $102 to $118 in two weeks.

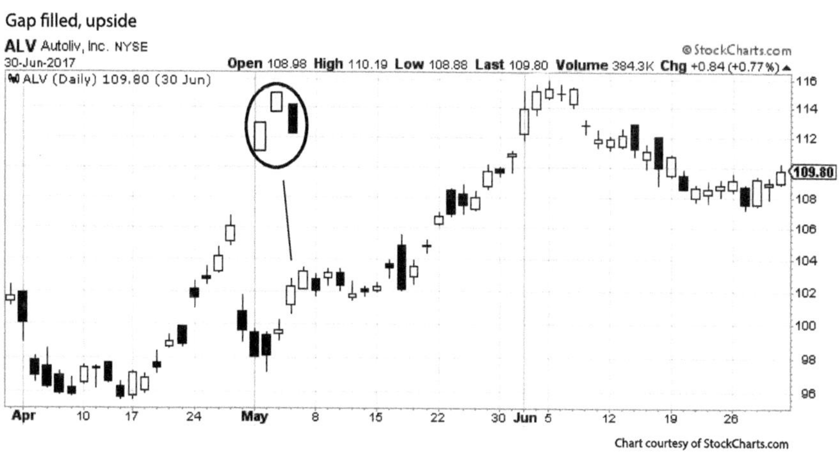

Figure 4.21: Gap filled, upside

Key Point: The established support (bull) or resistance (bear) levels define the value of a gap-filled pattern. Price often moves strongly in the direction opposite to the gap, so when this does not take place, it deserves more attention.

A downside gap filled is the opposite. It consists of a downward session, a downside gap, a second downward session, and then an upside movement that

(a) fills the gap and (b) does not violate the newly set resistance level of the first session's opening price.

Downside gap filled: A bear complex pattern with a downward session, a downside gap, a second downside session, and then a third session moving to the upside. However, although the third session fills the gap, it does not move above the resistance level set by the first day's opening price.

An example of a downside gap filled is seen on the chart in Figure 4.22. A downtrend was stopped at the price of $19.10 set during the development of the downside gap filled. However, this was also an example of a failed continuation pattern. Price rose immediately after, finally retreating back to the same level. For the remainder of the period shown, price traded in a consolidation range between $18.60 and $19.30 with interim volatility. The downside gap filled might have been viewed as a success if the price behavior a month later had continued downward; however, it did not, and the prediction of continuation did not materialize.

Gap filled, downside

Figure 4.22: Gap filled, downside

Whether patterns reverse the established trend, confirm existing movement, or set a new trend, it pays to observe them as they emerge. Any unusual developments, including exceptionally long days (or short days represented in the *doji* day), big increases in volume, or price gaps, indicate that something significant is about to take place. For most traders, the focus of interest in such developments concerns reversal. Whether used for entry or exit, a reversal signal is the key top timing of your decision. As the preceding example revealed, the appearance of a signal does not promise the expected result. It only adds to the *likely* next step.

The fact that reversals increase the likelihood of well-timed entry or exit is the main point in candlestick analysis. Some have referred to an "intellectual vacuum at the core of technical analysis" based on a belief in the efficient market theory.[ii] However, this assumption of flaws in technical analysis is questionable given the flaws in efficiency itself. The assumed vacuum of technical analysis has been offset by tendencies among traders described as "noise traders," those who pay attention to past price behavior and recognize patterns in price (in other words, technicians and chartists).[iii]

Even so, candlestick charting is by no means free of flaws, false leads, and unreliable signal appearances. A flaw in charting analysis is a tendency to quickly spot common signals but to not see the less frequent ones. This applies both to continuation and reversal. For example, rising three and falling three methods involve patterns of five days or more. With focus on brief signals of one, two, or three days, it is easy to miss these exceptionally complex patterns.

The rising three method (also called the bullish mat hold) occurs during an uptrend, and its middle part looks exactly like a bearish reversal, either a three black crows or three identical crows; the middle session in these three downward days can be either color. The key difference defining the rising three method as a bullish signal is what occurs before and after this middle section. Before acting on the assumption of a bearish reversal, a chartist needs to be aware of the potential for development of a bullish continuation pattern.

Rising three method (bullish mat hold): A complex bullish continuation pattern combining upward movement, a gap, three downward-moving days, and a resumption of the uptrend.

An example of the rising three method was found on the chart in Figure 4.23. The middle three sessions looked like a three black crows. However, lacking confirmation, a trader acting on this apparent reversal would make an ill-timed trade and miss the continuation that followed. The lesson for chartists is clear: When a reversal appears, do not consider it a legitimate reversal until you also find confirmation or until it develops into a continuation pattern.

Rising three method (mat hold, bullish)

Figure 4.23: Rising three method (mat hold, bullish)

The falling three method (also called a bearish mat hold) provides a similar indication in a downtrend. Because it is a continuation pattern, a trader seeing what appears to be a bullish reversal should demand confirmation before acting and be aware that rather than a bullish reversal, it could be a bearish continuation.

Falling three method (bearish mat hold): A complex bearish continuation pattern combining downward movement, a gap, three or more upward-moving days, and a resumption of the downtrend.

Figure 4.24 includes an example of the falling three method pattern. The gap appeared between the initial black and first white sessions, although it was not visible immediately. The white session opened lower than the black session's close. Once the falling three method concluded, the downtrend resumed.

Figure 4.24: Falling three method (mat hold, bearish)

Beyond continuation some complex patterns work as reversals. Recognizing these as a dynamic trend tops or bottoms out improves a trader's ability to understand what is occurring in the trend itself and to anticipate reversal and enter trades with improved timing.

Tower Tops and Bottoms

The tower top is an unusual pattern, a variation on the well-known double top in price pattern. A tower top is a multiple-session topping pattern reversing a bullish trend and predicting a bearish reversal. It consists of an initial white session (the first tower) representing the end of the current uptrend, leading to two topping sessions and a new lower black session, introducing the resulting downtrend.

Tower top: A bearish reversal clearly marking the final white session of the uptrend, two topping days, and introduction of a downtrend with a lower black session.

An example of the power top is seen on the chart in Figure 4.25. Although the initially indicated white session could be replaced with the larger white session two days later, either interpretation identifies the power top. A trader would be likely to recognize the reversal with the greatest certainty with the appearance of the lower black session. The advantage is that the ending price will be likely to end up close to the price where the pattern began to develop.

Tower top

Figure 4.25: Tower top

A tower bottom is a bullish reversal appearing at the bottom of a downtrend. Like the tower top, it is initially difficult to recognize because it requires several days to develop, and recognition is likely to occur toward the end of the pattern, not at the beginning or middle. It begins with a final downtrend black session (first tower), continues downward to the bottom, and concludes with a higher white session (second tower). The key is found in the two lowest narrow range sessions, followed by a move in the opposite direction.

Tower bottom: A bullish reversal clearly marking the final black session of the downtrend, two bottoming days, and introduction of an uptrend with a higher white session.

An example is shown in Figure 4.26. The strong upward-moving gap added strength to the tower bottom as a bullish reversal. However, even with the clarity in this signal, subsequent price movement did not go much higher. The price pattern remained in consolidation established on this chart, between $38.50 and $40.50 per share.

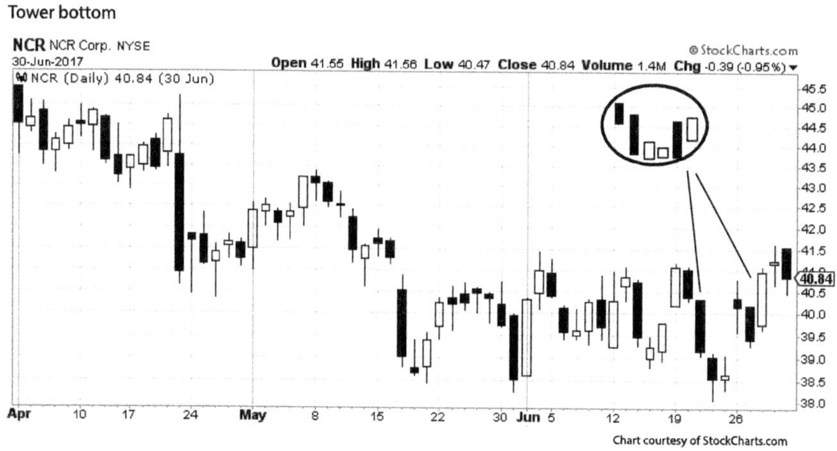

Figure 4.26: Tower bottom

The challenge for every trader in the use of candlesticks is in determining the strength or weakness of reversal and continuation signals. Several of the examples in this chapter led to failures. This occurs in every chartist's analysis, and there are no guarantees. The purpose of candlestick analysis is to improve the timing itself and to create a greater likelihood of improved timing, but not to create a 100% guarantee of success.

Adherents of the efficient market hypothesis, primarily consisting of academics and not of traders, point to the fact that because markets are efficient, technical analysis cannot work. The flaw in this thinking is that EMF does not describe market performance but the efficiency with which information is taken into prices. However, this includes all information with equal value, including true information as well as false information or rumor. The numerous examples of candlesticks confirmed in their prediction, resulting in the predicted price movement, makes the point that "efficiency" does not mean that forecasting does not work. Even so, some who accept EMF rationalize the true nature of the market as exceptions or anomalies:

> It is found in many stock exchanges of the world that these markets are not following the rules of EMH. The functioning of these stock markets deviate from the rules of EMH. These deviations are called anomalies. Anomalies could occur once and disappear, or could occur repeatedly. From the study of anomalies we can conclude that investor can beat the market, and can generate abnormal returns by fundamental, technical analysis, by analyzing the past performance of stocks and by insider trading.[iv]

Using candlestick signals along with trend analysis and confirmation challenges the academic acceptance of efficiency within the markets. Diligent application of the principles underlying candlestick charting demonstrates that traders can effectively improve the timing of their entry and exit decisions. It is no anomaly that these techniques work broadly and consistently.

The next chapter expands on this discussion by examining a range of candlestick patterns enabling the analysis of reversal and continuation. These patterns tend to exist within the trend and as attributes of its behavior rather than as separate signals revealing likely new price direction. Traders recognizing pattern tendencies will be aware that past patterns do not always repeat. The purpose in the analysis is to establish that particular price behavior and certain types of gaps, tops and bottoms, and incidents of resistance or support can all be used to expand appreciation for price predictability. This can be applied in a pattern analysis with equal value as it is applied to recognition of specific one-, two-, and three-day candlesticks.

---

[i] Fong, S., Tai, J., & Si, Y. W. (May 2011). Trend Following Algorithms for Technical Trading in Stock Market. *Journal of Emerging Technologies in Web Intelligence*, 3, No. 2.
[ii] Kee, K. B. (November 2010). Stock Return Synchronicity and Technical Trading Rules. *Global Development Finance Conference*, 24–26.
[iii] Kyle, A. S. (November 1985). Continuous Auctions and Insider Trading. *Econometrica*, 53, No. 6, 1315–1336.
[iv] Latif, M., Arshad, S., Fatima, M., & Farooq, S. (2011). *Research Journal of Finance and Accounting*, 2, No. 9/10.

Chapter 5
Reversal and Continuation Pattern Analysis

So much of charting is involved with reversal recognition. As the entry and exit point for the majority of technical strategies, reversal is more widely acknowledged as a more important signal than continuation patterns. When you see a continuation indicator, the prescribed action is to take no action; technicians are likely to be more interested in identifying the best times to enter and to exit. This is how profits are maximized and losses are avoided. However, continuation should not be overlooked as a valuable contribution to the better understanding of trend and trend behavior.

The refusal within the academic community to recognize the value of technical analysis holds back the advancement of pattern recognition. This would not matter except for the fact that academic publication has great influence in the investment world, in spite of the flawed EMH standard. Practitioners (versus academics) recognize with increasing certainty that information is available to improve timing of decisions. In fact, that

> thousands of individuals in the capital market spend so much time in gaining access to information, in evaluating the information, and in translating the evaluation into investment decisions must suggest that the marginal benefits of acting on information exceed the marginal costs. This reality is inconsistent with the minimal marginal benefits set by the efficient markets hypothesis. Trading volume itself is a reminder that investors constantly fail to find all available information fully reflected in stock prices. Either the hypothesis has an inherent flaw, or Wall Street and its customer base are in truth totally irrational.[i]

The debate has no common ground or areas of agreement. One side, based in theory (academic), insists that it is impossible to beat the market because of its efficiency. The other side, based in practice and experience (traders), believes and even *knows* that technical analysis improves timing and analytical skills. This debate is summarized with the observation that over many decades

> a conspicuous contradiction has existed in the financial economic literature. On one side of the contradiction is the efficient market hypothesis (EMH), one of the most widely accepted theories in economics that is a cornerstone of academic finance. Simply stated, the EMH asserts that security prices fully reflect all available information and that the stock market prices securities at their fair values. As a result, the stock market is always perfectly mediated, with no opportunity for above-normal profits, and expenditures on research and trading are a waste of energy and resources. The other side of the contradiction is the conventional (nonacademic) wisdom that astute analysts can beat the market using tech-

DOI 10.1515/9781501507397-005

> nical or fundamental stock analysis. Thousands of individuals in the investment management industry spend considerable amounts of time daily, gaining access to information, evaluating that information, and making investment decisions based on that information.[ii]

Traders who adhere to EMH eventually transition to the other side. Academic theories are comforting and reassuring, but often are also inapplicable in the real world. Experience demonstrates repeatedly that theories concerning the nature of efficiency in the market simply are not true and that technical analysis improves identification of the two forms of signal: reversal and continuation. Without the ability to use analysis to find these signals, what is the point? Those subscribing to EMH have to conclude that there is no rational reason to trade or invest at all because the inevitable efficiency of the market negates any effort to excel. Practical traders reject this suggestion based on their own experience, repeatedly, that given the rules of candlestick analysis, the science works. It requires strength of signals, equal strength of confirmation, and ideal proximity within a trend (midtrend for continuation and at resistance or support for reversal).

If prices behaved in a manner expected by statisticians, stock chart patterns would be predictable and would be distributed in a manner expected with finite populations. However, the "population" of price outcomes is massive and contains too great a number of variables to conform to ideals of efficiency. As a result, "Statistical studies indicate that price fluctuations are not identically distributed, exhibiting the so-called clustered volatility, meaning that statistical properties of the distribution, such as the variance, change in time."[iii]

This is a problem for the statistician and EMF believer, but a great advantage for traders. It is the very fact that price does not behave efficiently that makes a candlestick forecast so imperative as the forecasting signal for what will occur next. This relies, of course, on the recognition of all required elements for legitimate signal recognition; however, given that these elements are present, candlestick signal recognition may be highly reliable, entirely dispelling the myth of market efficiency.

To reiterate the "rule" concerning reversal and continuation: Much of the literature about candlestick charting makes the point that reversal should occur in proper proximity. Thus a reversal signal for a downtrend should be preceded by an uptrend, and vice versa. However, the belief is widespread that when a reversal signal appears in the wrong place (for example, a downtrend indicator in the middle of a downtrend, or an uptrend reversal indicator during an uptrend), it should be treated as a continuation signal. This belief brings into question the integrity of the entire candlestick system. There are times when an apparent signal is simply a coincidence in pattern, and a distinction should be made between signals as either reversal or continuation. These should not be interchangeable.

Key Point: Every candlestick formation forecasts either a reversal or continuation. These are not interchangeable and cannot be substituted based on the circumstances.

A second fine point in the analysis concerns signals occurring in a consolidation trend. The sideways-moving, range-bound trend is just as legitimate as an uptrend or downtrend and often takes up more time than either dynamic movement. However, a popular belief is that candlesticks are useless at such times because there are no price movements to reverse. This also ignores a "rule" worth applying: *Reversal* does not apply only to price movement, but to trends as well. So a change from consolidation to a dynamic trend may be signaled by a reversal pattern. When this occurs, it should not be ignored. It is among the strongest of signals. The ultimate strength in a trend reversal signal is the combination of a reversal pattern, followed quickly by a continuation pattern indicating the same direction. This observation strengthens timing of trades and provides a means for spotting the end of consolidation.

In earlier chapters, basic reversal and continuation patterns were explained and demonstrated in charts. However, recognition and analysis are not the same process. Analysis includes judgment about whether the signal is true or false, the degree of strength or weakness in the signal, and whether or not it confirms another indicator (or is confirmed in turn). Confirmation can include additional candlestick patterns, moving averages, and traditional technical signs. The relationship between the initial reversal or continuation pattern and other signals matters greatly, and methods of analysis should be most productive to serve a technical trading program.

Key Point: Reversal signals by themselves are useful but never the whole story. When combined with traditional technical analysis, they vastly improve your timing for entry and exit from positions.

Strong Top and Bottom Signals

A bull reversal occurs at the end of a downtrend. If a downtrend is not present, there is nothing to reverse. A mistake made by some chartists is to overlook this crucial fact. In the desire to enter a position, you may find yourself seeing an apparent reversal pattern and then deciding to enter a long position. This is a mistake. The reality is that at times, the signal a trader seeks simply does not materialize.

Key Point: A reversal can only occur if there is a current trend to reverse. If this is not present, then an indication of reversal is not valid.

An essential attribute of the reversal pattern is that it must show up at the trend's conclusion. The identical pattern may appear during an uptrend or in the middle of a sideways price movement. This is not a bull reversal indicator, but merely an aberration in the pattern of current trades.

Placement of a signal helps distinguish between actual indicators and coincidental price design, or aberration. A pitfall in analysis is in assigning value to such coincidental patterns where no value actually exists. To overcome this problem, reliance on strong and well-evolved multiple-session candlesticks provides higher confidence:

> While candlesticks are able to provide valuable insight into a market's situation, single candlesticks are usually regarded as too fragile to allow for a prognosis of required reliability. Hence, instead of relying only on a single candle's shape, forecasts are based upon constellations of successive candlesticks. These so-called Candlestick Patterns usually consist of a series of three candlesticks with certain properties. In addition to the candles' shapes, their positions relative to each other, as well as the prevailing direction of movement, are taken into consideration.[iv]

A potentially low-reliability formation is a sign that, in fact, the signal could be merely a coincidental price pattern. This often is found in the wrong proximity (bearish reversal during a downtrend or bullish reversal during an uptrend, for example). To illustrate how a reversal pattern can appear in the wrong place (meaning it is not a true reversal), a primary point has to be kept in mind: A bull reversal has to appear after a downtrend or it is not legitimate, and a bear reversal should appear at the top of an uptrend.

The purpose in exploring the many reversal and continuation trends found on charts is to demonstrate how these signals appear not only in the combination of white or black sessions, but also as they function as part of broader price behavior. It is this second feature—analysis of each pattern—that is of greatest value to every trader. It enables you to more effectively understand how the candlestick signal functions within the trend itself. A related purpose is to aid traders to resist a tendency toward confirmation bias. This is a destructive force because it distorts observed price patterns. The application of discipline in a candlestick program enables a trader to rely on signal and confirmation rather than on the bias that grows from the possibility of wishful thinking. The bias

> refers to the search for, or the interpretation of evidence in ways that favor existing beliefs or expectations. A related phenomenon has been extensively investigated in the management literature under the heading of "escalation of commitment."[V]

In fact, reliance on the strength of specific signals and confirmation is most effective in overcoming confirmation bias. This fact—reliance on price patterns as they emerge rather than on instinct or outright wishful thinking—is one aspect of interposing science into theory. Seeking strength in signal patterns is one of the key methods for increasing confidence in discovered signals.

For example, finding strong topping and bottoming patterns provides exceptional (but only initial) reversal indication. Confirmation is required before deciding that a reversal is a certainty, but the strength of an initial signal begins the process.

The so-called dumpling top is, at first glance, an understated reversal signal. This is so because it lacks dramatic movement. The strength in this position is derived from several days of sideways movement, setting up a strong resistance point. When this is seen after a strong uptrend, it strongly flags a likely end of the trend and coming reversal.

Dumpling top: A series of narrow days setting up a resistance level after an uptrend, forecasting reversal and a new downtrend to follow.

An example of a dumpling top formation is found in Figure 5.1. The color of the candlesticks at the top does not matter; the strength of this reversal is in the leveling out of top price levels and establishing of stationary resistance.

Dumpling top

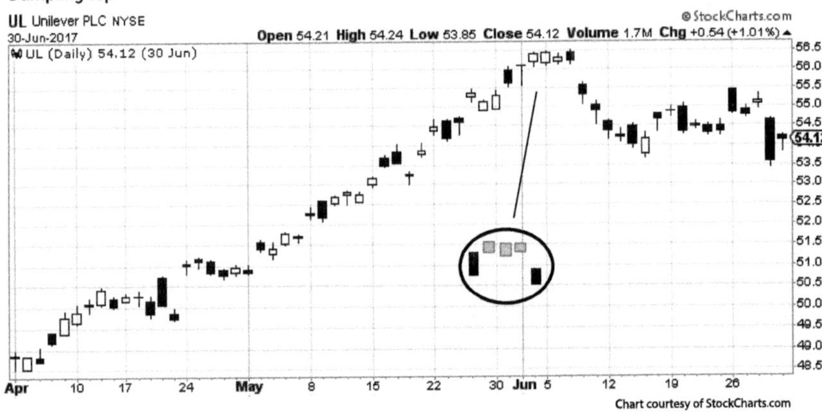

Figure 5.1: Dumpling top

The opposite reversal sets up an uptrend and is called the frypan bottom. Like the dumpling top, this signal consists of several sessions (at least three or four) establishing a new and level support price after a downtrend. It signals the end of the trend and a coming bullish reversal.

Frypan bottom: A bullish reversal signal consisting of several sessions setting up new support after a downtrend and predicting the end of the trend.

An example of the frypan bottom is seen in Figure 5.2, which shows two instances. The first ended the initial downtrend and strongly pointed to reversal with a six-session support level. The resulting uptrend was brief. A second occurrence followed a mild downtrend characterized by starts and stops. For example, the price consolidated briefly in the first half of May before continuing downward. The late May and early June bottom was set up with the frypan bottom before strong reversal going into a new uptrend.

Frypan bottom

Figure 5.2: Frypan bottom

A similar peaking effect is typical of tweezer patterns. A tweezer top is set up by two or more high prices with upper shadows. The color of the top real bodies is not important. When these occur at the top of an uptrend, it is an initial reversal signal.

Tweezer top: A bearish reversal with two or more high price sessions and upper shadows, forecasting reversal and a new downtrend.

Tweezer tops are seen in Figure 5.3. The resulting downtrend was brief in spite of the strength in this signal. A correlation is often seen between the strength or weakness of a trend and the reversal signal. The preceding uptrend was less than ten points, and the reversal only six points. In this case, a brief and mild uptrend was followed by an equally mild downtrend.

Tweezer top

Figure 5.3: Tweezer top

The tweezer bottom is found at the bottom of a downtrend. The consecutive lower shadows are the reversal points for the trend, and like the tweezer top, the candlestick colors do not matter. An example is seen in Figure 5.4.

Tweezer bottom: A bullish reversal with two or more low price sessions and lower shadows, forecasting reversal and a new uptrend.

Tweezer bottom

Figure 5.4: Tweezer bottom

The setting up of new trading range levels is also found in the high waves reversal. This is a multi-session signal appearing at the top of an uptrend and projecting a coming reversal. The color of the high real bodies does not matter.

High waves: A signal of several sessions setting up new resistance and signaling likely bearish reversal.

An example is seen in Figure 5.5. The repetitive upper shadows could be interpreted as a tweezer formation, but in this case three consecutive sessions with the same attributes create the high wave. The downtrend began immediately, and even with the upside move a few sessions later, the final outcome was an exceptionally strong downward move.

High waves

Chart courtesy of StockCharts.com

Figure 5.5: High waves

Stars, Kicks, Swallows, and Sandwiches

A few creatively named reversals enrich the broad range of reversal signals. Among these are the tri-star patterns, consisting of rarely seen consecutive *doji* sessions. The bullish tri-star consists of three consecutive *doji* sessions, with the middle session lower than the first and third.

Tri-star, bullish: A three-session bullish reversal consisting of three *doji* sessions, the middle one lower than the first and third.

This is a rare pattern and not always a strong one. For example, the tri-star shown in Figure 5.6 meets the pattern criteria, but does not follow a downtrend. As a consequence, the appearance is correct but it does not provide a reversal by itself. However, within a few sessions, price gapped higher and evolved into a bullish trend. This is typical of a bullish indicator that would require strong confirmation before entering a trade.

Tri-star, bullish

Figure 5.6: Tri-star, bullish

The bearish tri-star is equally rare and consists of three *doji* sessions with the middle session higher than the first and third. As a rate signal, the tri-star may provide a true bearish sentiment even when the price pattern before it appears is not ideal.

Tri-star, bearish: A three-session bearish reversal consisting of three *doji* sessions, the middle one higher than the first and third.

The bearish tri-star in Figure 5.7 followed a bullish trend, but reversal did not appear immediately. In fact, this was a good example of a failed reversal signal. Subsequent price movement continued upward after the period shown on the chart. This demonstrates that the appearance of a rare reversal pattern does not mean the signal is strong or reliable.

Tri-star, bearish

Chart courtesy of StockCharts.com

Figure 5.7: Tri-star, bearish

The "kicking" pattern identifies a gapping price behavior and reversal. The placement within the chart may be odd and even wrong, but it often is set up with a long candlestick in the second session, implying a likelihood of strong reversal. This does not always occur as expected.

Kicking, bullish: A two-session bullish reversal consisting of a black day, an upward gap, and a white day.

An example is seen in Figure 5.8. The large gap between the two parts of the kicking signal is properly placed as a bullish move. The second session, following the gap, was a long white candle. This is a particularly strong bullish sign. Oddly, however, the uptrend was brief, extending only three periods after the kicking signal.

Kicking, bullish

Figure 5.8: Kicking, bullish

The bearish equivalent is expected to occur after a bullish trend and to lead to a downward reversal. It is especially strong as a signal when the second session is a long black candle. However, the reliability of a kicking signal is not always high, pointing to the importance of strong confirmation.

Kicking, bearish: A two-session bullish reversal consisting of a white day, a downward gap, and a black day.

A bearish kicking signal is seen in Figure 5.9. The uptrend extended for a month, but had consolidated after a quick run-up. The bearish kicking signal had the expected attributes, notably the long black session in the second day. However, price reaction initially moved upward twelve points before declining to net only two points in response to the kicking signal. The price reaction was not strong.

Figure 5.9: Kicking, bearish

Key Point: Spotting reversals is not always easy. A key method is to look for gaps that also fit a reversal indicator. Gaps are exceptions and may foreshadow a change in direction.

Another range of reversals is the belt hold. The bullish version sets up a rounded bottom, a strong bullish reversal pattern. There are several criteria for the belt hold. First, a period of downward-moving black sessions takes place, representing the conclusion of a downtrend. Next, a lower-opening white session appears. In the perfect bullish belt hold, this session contains no lower shadow (a very small lower shadow may occur, however). Finally, the trend reverses and price begins moving upward.

Belt hold, bullish: A reversal signal consisting of multiple sessions: downward-trending black sessions, a lower-opening white session with little or no lower shadow, and finally a series of upward-moving sessions.

An example is seen in Figure 5.10. Although the downtrend was brief, consisting of only five sessions, the appearance of the white session marked this as a belt hold. The subsequent upward trend finalized the opinion, and price did turn around to move higher.

Belt hold, bullish

Chart courtesy of StockCharts.com

Figure 5.10: Belt hold, bullish

The bearish belt hold acts in the same manner with opposite direction and session color. First is a series of upward-moving white sessions, then a black session opening higher and without an upper shadow, and finally a move of price to the downside.

Belt hold, bearish: A reversal signal consisting of multiple sessions: upward-trending white sessions, a higher-opening black session with little or no lower shadow, and finally a series of downward-moving sessions.

Figure 5.11 contains an example of the bearish belt hold. Note the singular flaw in this example: the black session opened slightly higher but also had a small upper shadow. Although price did trend downward after this, the formation is far from perfect. Even so, it appeared after an extended uptrend and led to a complete reversal, as the belt hold predicted.

Figure 5.11: Belt hold, bearish

An unusual reversal pattern is called the concealing baby swallow. It is distinctive, however. As a bullish reversal it consists of four black sessions. The first two are separated by a downward gap and two additional black sessions. After this formation, price is expected to turn to the upside.

Concealing baby swallow: A bullish reversal consisting of four black sessions; the first two are *marubozus*, followed by a downside gap, a third black candle, and then an engulfing black candle. This pattern sets a new support level for the trading range.

The pattern is shown in Figure 5.12. The downtrend was brief, but the pattern met the criteria and led to a bullish reversal. Although the preceding trend was very short, a trend may consist of many sessions or only a few.

Figure 5.12: Concealing baby swallow

The stick sandwich is another form of reversal combining two colors of candlesticks in three sessions; the first and third are the same color, and the middle session is the opposite color.

Stick sandwich, bullish: A reversal pattern of three consecutive sessions. The first and third are black, and the middle session is white. The middle session's real body should reside within the real bodies of the other two sessions.

An example is shown in Figure 5.13. The signal is a subtle one, but its predictive value is strong. In this instance, a delayed reaction of about three weeks occurred before the consolidating pattern finally emerged and was converted into a bullish move.

Figure 5.13: Stick sandwich, bullish

Just as the bullish version appears at or near the bottom of a downtrend, the bearish stick sandwich is seen at or close to the top. It anticipates a bearish reversal. The signal is not obvious at first glance but tends to provide high confidence in the likelihood of a reversal.

Stick sandwich, bearish: A reversal pattern of three consecutive sessions. The first and third are white, and the middle session is black. The middle session's real body should reside within the real bodies of the other two sessions.

Figure 5.14 provides an excellent example of how a bearish stick sandwich forms and how reversal is expected immediately after. In this case, an uptrend extended for a lengthy period, and the bearish stick sandwich predicted the end of the trend.

Stick sandwich, bearish

Chart courtesy of StockCharts.com

Figure 5.14: Stick sandwich, bearish

Matching and Star Reversals

A final range of reversal patterns identifies trading ranges (resistance and support levels) and strong changes in direction associated with sharp contrast in session direction (white versus black). Among these are the relatively simple but powerful matching signals.

The matching low is a clear end to a downtrend in which consecutive black sessions drop to the same closing price. This sets up the expectation for a reversal and uptrend.

Matching low: A bullish reversal consisting of two black sessions with matching closing prices, which sets up a new bullish price move.

Like all reversals, the matching signal may set up after an extended downtrend or a relatively short one. Figure 5.15 includes an example of a matching low associated with short-term downtrend and short-term uptrend that follows. These swing trades are modest in price movement, but the reversal signal is clear.

Figure 5.15: Matching low

The matching high has a similar configuration, but with opposite direction and color. It occurs at the top of an uptrend and appears as two consecutive sessions closing at the same high. This anticipates reversal and a new downtrend.

Matching high: A bearish reversal consisting of two white sessions with matching closing prices, which sets up a new bearish price move.

Figure 5.16 identifies the top of the uptrend with a matching high pattern. This sets up a string and rapid downtrend of more than twenty-five points in a two-week period.

Matching high

Figure 5.16: Matching high

Key Point: The matching move is rare, but when it appears, it sets up a strong likelihood of a reversal.

A directional change is also found in the "three stars" signals. The bullish version is called three stars in the south. It involves three black sessions. The second trades below the range of the first, and the third trades complexly within the real body range of the second session (it is engulfed).

Three stars in the south: A bullish reversal signal with three black sessions. The second trades below the first, and the third is engulfed entirely within the range of the second session.

An example is found in Figure 5.17. The uptrend is set up by the pattern, which meets the criteria in every respect. It occurs at the bottom of a downtrend. Session two trades lower than session one. Session three trades within the range of session two. And finally, the pattern sets up a reversal and uptrend.

Three stars in the south

Chart courtesy of StockCharts.com

Figure 5.17: Three stars in the south

The opposite, three stars in the north, establishes the top of an uptrend. The second white session ranges higher than the first, and the third session's real body trades entirely within the real body range of the second session.

Three stars in the north: A bearish reversal signal with three white sessions. The second trades above the first, and the third is engulfed entirely within the range of the second session.

Figure 5.18 includes an example of an exceptionally strong three stars in the north. The strength is derived from the gap between sessions one and two and the long body in the second session. Once the third session appeared and traded within the range of the preceding real body, a downtrend occurred rapidly, moving six points in less than two weeks.

Three stars in the north

Figure 5.18: Three stars in the north

Ladders and "Major" Reversals

A variation of consecutively colored signals that set up reversals is found in the ladder patterns. These have very specific requirements and do not appear frequently. The ladder bottom is a bullish reversal with four consecutive sessions. The first three are black and each trades lower than the previous session. Next, price gaps to the upside and a white session form. This is the completion of the reversal signal.

Ladder bottom: A reversal pattern beginning with a series of black candles trending down, a gap moving up, and a final white candle.

Figure 5.19 contains an example. The downtrend was brief but strong, and it ended with the final black session, the gap, and a white session. This completed the reversal. The resulting uptrend, like the preceding downtrend, was very brief.

Ladder bottom

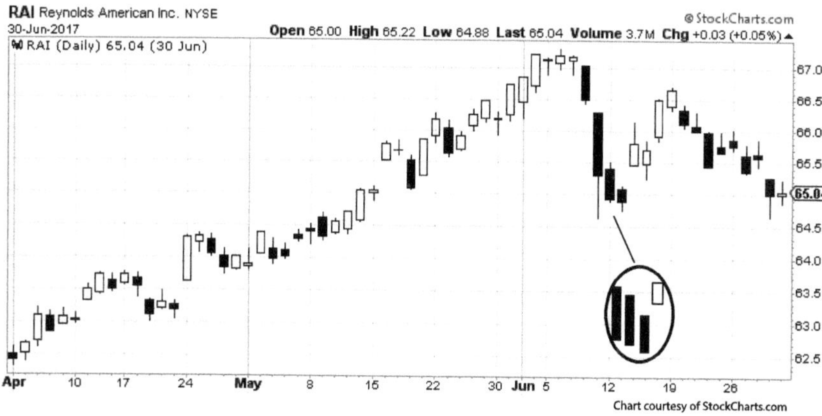

Figure 5.19: Ladder bottom

A ladder top is a bearish reversal requiring the same criteria, but in opposite color and direction. A series of consecutively higher white sessions leads to a gap and a black session, setting up the downtrend.

Ladder top: A reversal pattern beginning with a series of white candles trending up, a gap moving down, and a final black candle.

Figure 5.20 contains an example. The highest session is a near *doji* and, for purposes of completing the ladder top, is counted as a final bullish session. It is followed by a downward gap and a black session. The resulting downtrend starts out slowly but picks up momentum within two weeks.

Figure 5.20: Ladder top

Two additional reversal signals are the bearish major *yin* and bullish major *yang*. These are subtle compared to other signals and are easily overlooked in chart analysis. The major *yin* is a bearish reversal consisting of two white sessions, the second gapping higher, and a black session that closes within the range of the first session's real body.

Major yin: A bearish reversal of three sessions: two white sessions gapping upward and a third black session closing within the range of the first session.

For example, in Figure 5.21, a very brief uptrend concludes with the development of a major *yin* (bear). This is considered a mild reversal because the uptrend had barely begun. Even so, after three sideways-moving sessions, price gapped much lower and ended up nearly ten points lower in the following month.

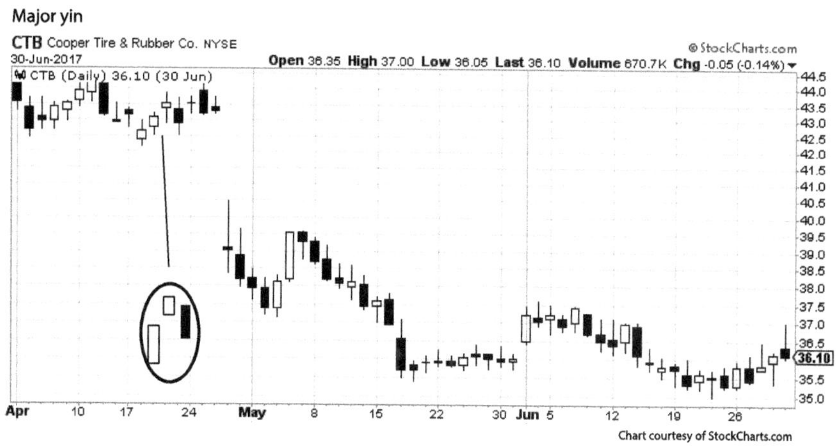

Figure 5.21: Major yin

A major *yang* (bull) is the opposite, providing a bullish reversal. It begins with two black sessions, the second gapping below the first. Finally, a white session closes within the real body range of session one.

Major yang: A bullish reversal of three sessions: two black sessions gapping downward and a third white session closing within the range of the first session.

Figure 5.22 contains a typical example of the major *yang*. The downtrend concluded with a long black candlestick and a gap downward to a second black session, then a white candlestick closing within the first session's range. This led to an uptrend. This was not an obvious signal; the major *yin* and *yang* appear with careful analysis and may not necessarily signal an especially strong reversal.

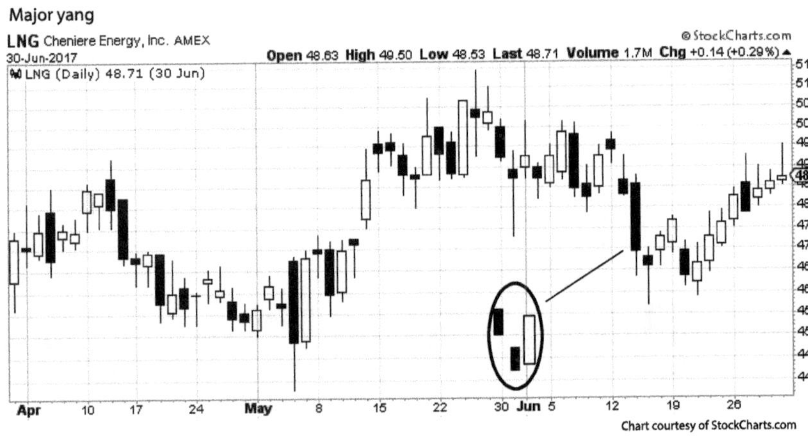

Figure 5.22: Major yang

Sakata's Five Methods

A range of price patterns serve as the origin of candlestick science and go back to eighteenth-century Japan. These original patterns did not involve specific candlesticks, which grew from the observation of price behavior.

A rice merchant from Sakata, Japan, named Honma Munehisa traded in the Dojima Rice Exchange located in Osaka. He is called the father of the Japanese candlestick. He not only observed price patterns, but also figured out a way to quickly communicate rapidly across the 380 miles between his home of Sakata and the base of the exchange in Osaka. By posting men approximately every four miles, the time for communication of market prices was cut considerably in a time lacking mechanized transportation.[vi]

This network gave Homna an edge in trading rice coupons in the market. In 1755, he published a book that described 160 rules of trading. This book, *The Fountain of Gold: The Three Monkey Record of Money*, described the psychology of traders and of the market. Homna presented the belief that the emotional sense among traders influenced prices. He could also be called the first contrarian, writing that "when all are bearish, there is cause for prices to rise."[vii]

Homna did not develop candlesticks himself, but candlestick patterns all grow out of his observed rules of trading. He developed a system called Sakata's Five Methods. These are a series of price patterns named three mountains, three rivers, three gaps, three parallel lines, and three methods. The parallel lines pattern formed the basis for the better-known white soldiers (three rising white sessions) and black crows (three falling black sessions) and the variations growing out of those signals.

The so-called Sakata Five Methods are organized not only into well-known candlesticks pointing to reversal or continuation, but also into patterns over extended periods of time. The following are descriptions of the mountains, rivers, ands gaps that grew from the Five Methods and that also formed the origins of candlestick charting.

The three mountains involves three price peaks, marking a clear level of resistance. It precedes and predicts a bearish reversal. The more prominent the slope and distinction of each peak, the stronger the signal.

Three mountains: A pattern signal marking high price resistance and forecasting a bearish reversal.

An example is shown in Figure 5.23. This is not a specific candlestick but a series of moves generating a pattern. The origin of candlesticks was based on this as the first of five Sakata Method price patterns.

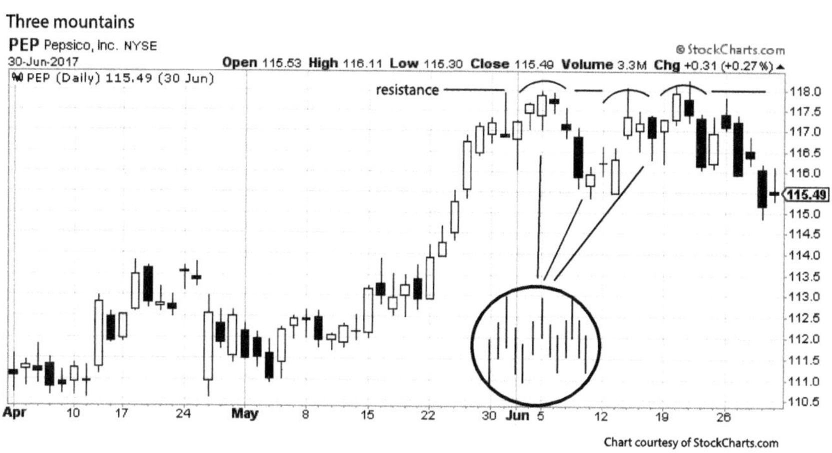

Figure 5.23: Three mountains

The opposite pattern is the three rivers. This establishes a level of support and is expected to precede a bullish reversal. Like the three mountains pattern, three rivers sets up a pattern rather than a specific set of candlestick signals. However, chart analysts and technicians will recognize the similarity between these patterns and Western practices defining price behavior in proximity to resistance and support.

Three rivers: A reversal formation consisting of a long black candle, a lower black and a short white candle closing lower (three rivers bottom, a bull formation), or a long white candle, a white higher candle, and a short black candle closing higher (three rivers top, a bear formation).

In Figure 5.24, three rivers establishes support. Whether this is defined as the bottom level of real bodies or shadows, the price limits are clearly viewed. This particular example combines several lower shadows, which adds to the strength of the signal. Lower shadows indicate a lack of sentiment to move prices lower and hold positions, further indicating a likelihood of a bullish reversal.

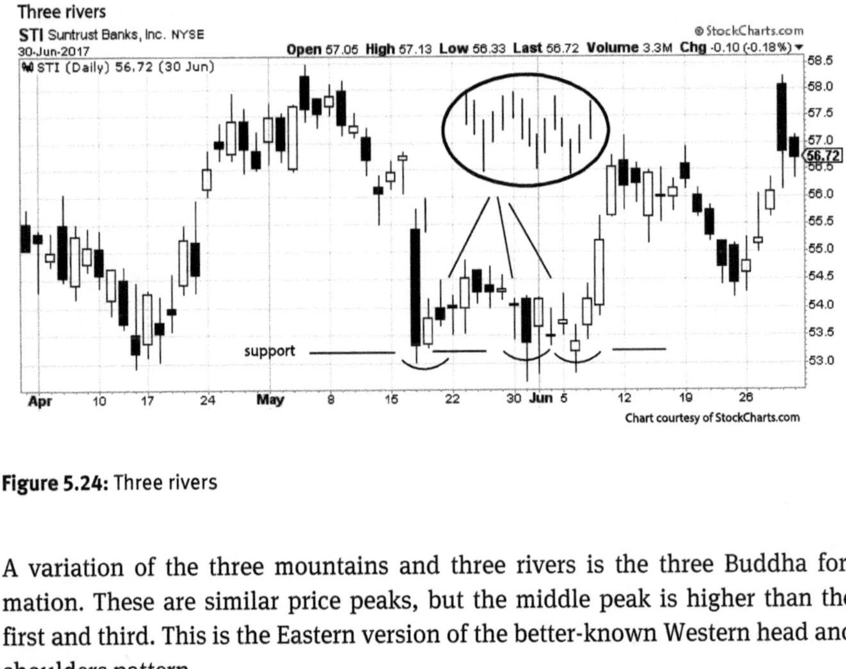

Figure 5.24: Three rivers

A variation of the three mountains and three rivers is the three Buddha formation. These are similar price peaks, but the middle peak is higher than the first and third. This is the Eastern version of the better-known Western head and shoulders pattern.

Three Buddha top: A bearish reversal signal with three price peaks, the middle one higher than the first and third; a Sakata version of the Western head and shoulders pattern.

Much like the head and shoulders, the three-part move to the upside fails to move prices higher and, as a result, predicts a reversal and bearish move to follow. For example, Figure 5.25 reveals a three Buddha top at a price high point, leading to retreat.

Three Buddha top

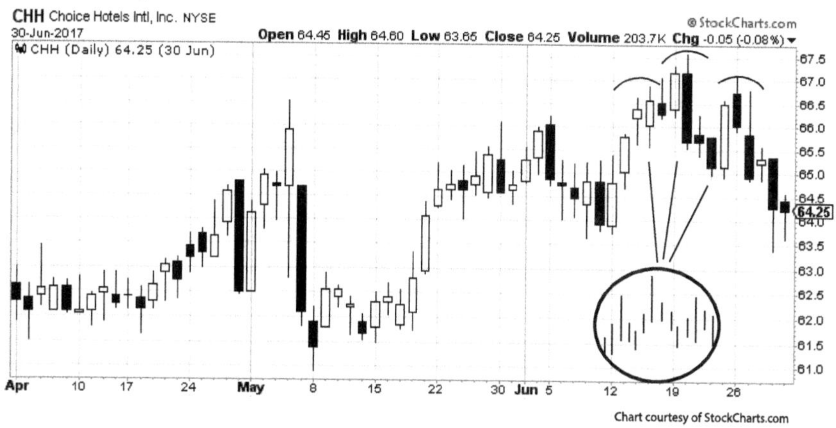

Figure 5.25: Three Buddha top

A three Buddha bottom appears on the opposite side of the chart and is similar to the Western pattern of inverse head and shoulders. This pattern demonstrates failure to move prices any lower and sets up likely bullish reversal.

Three Buddha bottom: A bullish reversal signal with three price valleys, the middle one lower than the first and third; a Sakata version of the Western inverse head and shoulders pattern.

Figure 5.26 includes a typical example of the three Buddha bottom. It appears during a downtrend, but overall it was not able to move prices lower, and the pattern concluded with a bullish reversal.

Three Buddha bottom

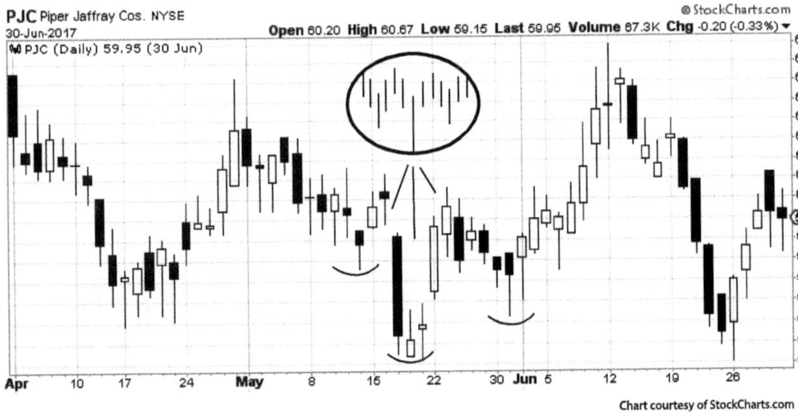

Figure 5.26: Three Buddha bottom

Another range of signals in the Sakata Five Methods is called the three gap pattern. A three gap upside is a bearish reversal signal characterized by a rapid rise in price. The repetitive gaps are warnings that price is moving too rapidly. Momentum eventually runs its course and a bearish reversal occurs.

Three gap upside: A bearish reversal pattern involving repetitive gaps, but not necessarily accompanied by specific candlestick signals. The pattern reveals excessive momentum and likely reversal to follow.

In Figure 5.27, price advanced substantially in less than two weeks. During this advance, the repetitive gaps appeared. These are known in Western technical analysis as runaway gaps, inevitably leading to an exhaustion gap. At the very top, a final gap appeared before price turned. The three signals setting up this top were very close in appearance to a bearish *doji* star. The three gaps were the typical representation of an aggressive and exaggerated price trend.

Figure 5.27: Three gap upside

A three gap downside occurs during a downtrend and also exhibits a runaway gap pattern. The strong move itself may also demonstrate directional strength but lacking retracement. This is a sign of a high likelihood of strong reversal to follow.

Three gap downside: A bullish reversal pattern involving repetitive gaps, but not necessarily accompanied by specific candlestick signals. The pattern reveals excessive momentum and likely reversal to follow.

Figure 5.28 provides an unusual example of repetitive gapping trends. As price moved rapidly downward, the three gap downside pattern appeared, ultimately bottoming out and immediately reversing. In this example, the following bullish trend demonstrated an upside gap pattern, followed by a second series of downside gaps.

Three gap downside

Figure 5.28: Three gap downside

Key Point: Spotting reversals is not always easy. One method of gap management is to look for gaps that also fit a reversal indicator. Gaps often foreshadow a change in direction.

Gaps play a key role in identifying likely reversal points, as the preceding examples reveal. A final variety of this gapping pattern (versus specific candlestick signals) is the gap up and gap down. The after bottom gap up is a bullish reversal appearing at the absolute bottom of a downtrend. Following a period of price decline, an upside gap appears, followed by a white session signaling the beginning of a new bullish move.

After bottom gap up: A bullish reversal pattern consisting of downward movement, an upward gap, and a white session.

For example, in Figure 5.29, a brief downtrend concluded with a clear upside gap and reversal. Although the reversal point had sessions with very narrow days (often weakening the reliability of reversal signals), in this case, the gap itself added strength to the signal.

Figure 5.29: After bottom gap up

The after top gap down is the bearish equivalent. Following an uptrend, prices peak at the point of a downside gap and a new black session. This marks the beginning of a new downtrend.

After top gap down: A bearish reversal pattern consisting of upward movement, a downward gap, and a black session.

The chart in Figure 5.30 contains an example. The preceding uptrend was minimal, so strong reversal was not likely. However, the gap added strength to the indicated bearish turn. The resulting downtrend was as mild as the preceding uptrend, but the gap represented the absolute turning point in the trend.

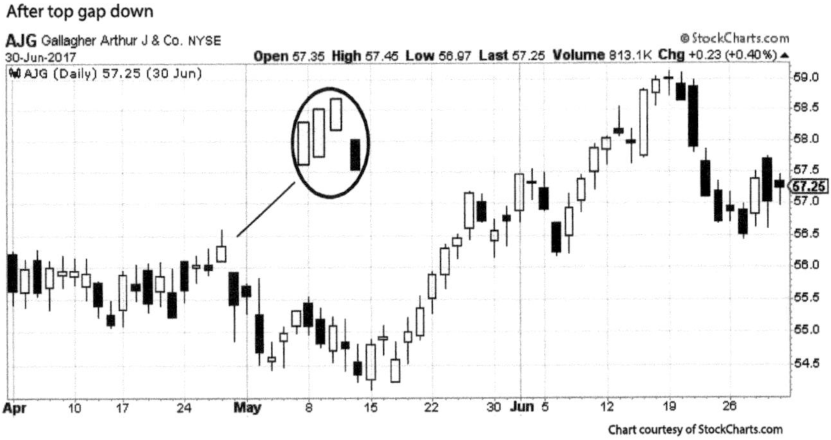

Figure 5.30: After top gap down

Price Patterns with Low Reliability

Several patterns involving candlestick signals rather than more generalized shaping tendencies often are not as reliable as some other signals. Because of this, the range of "pattern signals" should be used with caution and acted on only with strong confirmation.

The advance block, for example, is similar to both three white soldiers and three identical soldiers, but does not conform to the strict requirements for either. It consists of three consecutive sessions opening higher and closing higher, often with gaps. Some descriptions call for high upper shadows, but the lack of shadows does not reduce the value of the advance block. The most important attribute setting this apart from similar patterns is that it is not a reversal but a continuation signal.

Key Point: Finding the perfect example of a particular reversal formation is rare. The important point to remember is that if the pattern contains most of the attributes and accurately predicts a reversal, it still counts.

This is one area where candlestick science is contradictory. The pattern is very close to others that definitely serve as reversal, but it is called a continuation signal. In practice, the advance block is not as reliable as chart readers would like.

Advance block: A set of three consecutive white candlesticks, each opening and closing higher than the one before.

For example, Figure 5.31 contains two advance blocks. The first follows a consolidation period and continues the uptrend for a few additional sessions. The second marks the end of a brief uptrend but does not reverse. A third advance occurring near the end of the chart is closer in design to an identical white soldiers (see Figure 5.38), in which each session's opening price is identical to (or close to) the close of the preceding day and is a clear reversal signal. As this chart demonstrates, the advance block tends to serve as a weak signal in a weak set of trends.

Advance block

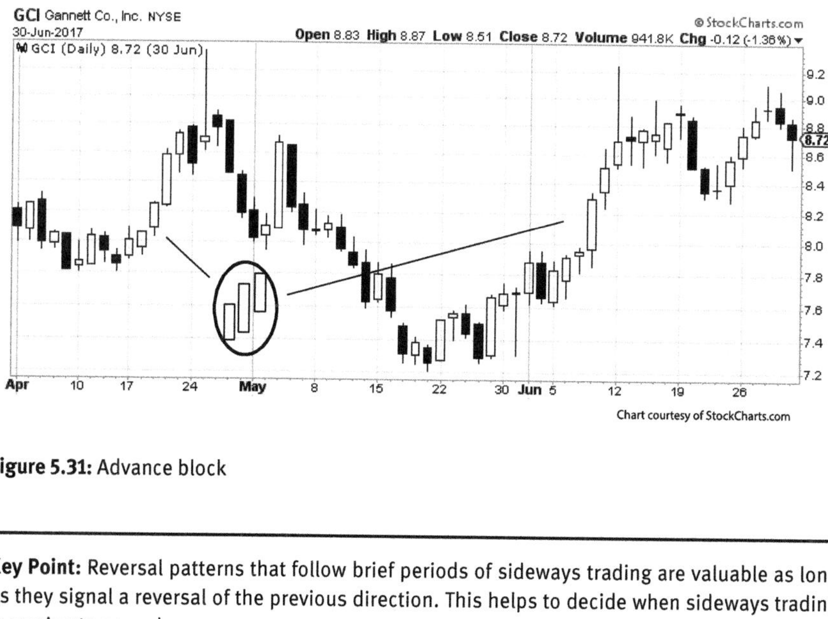

Chart courtesy of StockCharts.com

Figure 5.31: Advance block

Key Point: Reversal patterns that follow brief periods of sideways trading are valuable as long as they signal a reversal of the previous direction. This helps to decide when sideways trading is coming to an end.

The descent block is the opposite: three consecutive black sessions, each opening and closing lower. Like the advance block, the descent block is very similar to better-known reversal patterns: the three black crows and identical black crows (see Figure 5.37).

Descent block: A set of three consecutive black candlesticks, each opening and closing lower than the one before.

Figure 5.32 has an example of a descent block. On this chart, it occurs at the top of an uptrend but does not lead to reversal. In this case, it is a continuation signal, but it is not reliable and may lead to reversal in many cases. As a general observation, when a signal is not predictable, it is not useful as part of a system for timing entry or exit.

Descent block

Figure 5.32: Descent block

Another set of less reliable signals is found in a similar configuration involving gaps and a reversal day. The three gaps down involves three black sessions gapping downward and a fourth white session reversing direction. This is described as a reversal signal but often leads to continuation. As a reversal, it should appear at the end of a downtrend, but it is just as likely to occur at the top of an uptrend and act either as reversal or continuation.

Three gaps down: A set of four candlesticks, three black and gapping downward, and one white reversing direction.

For example, in Figure 5.33, a three gaps down signal is identified. It followed an uptrend and acted as a continuation signal. However, because this does not always lead to continuation and is usually described as a reversal indicator, its value is in doubt.

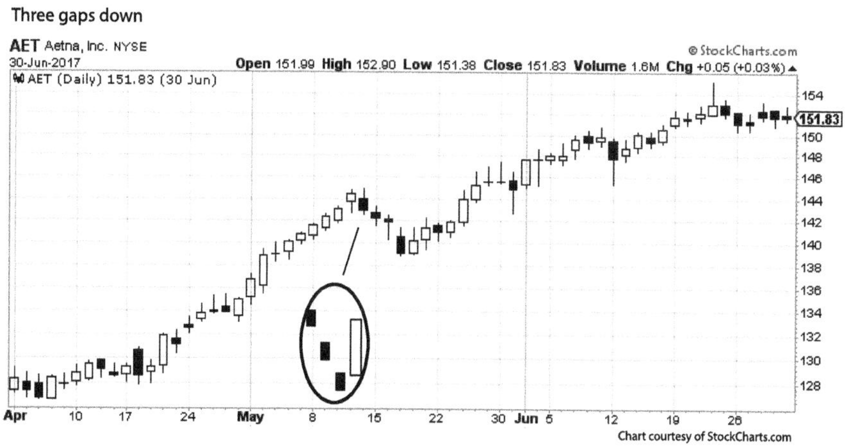

Figure 5.33: Three gaps down

The related three gaps up is also supposed to act as a reversal, but is not reliable and may be a continuation signal. As a consequence, it cannot be relied upon to predict the next price direction.

Three gaps up: A set of four candlesticks, three white and gapping upward, and one black reversing direction.

Figure 5.34 has an example of an especially strong three gaps up. It involves long white candles with gaps and what at first appears to be a reversal. However, after two weeks, the trend reverses once and again and continues upward.

Figure 5.34: Three gaps up

The deliberation pattern is another reversal signal that is not always dependable. The bullish deliberation consists of two black sessions trading in a close range, a downward gap to a third black signal, and a reversing white session.

Deliberation, bullish: A set of four signals. The first two are black and trade in close range to one another. The third session is also black and occurs after a downward gap, and the fourth session is white, moving price higher.

Figure 5.35 sets up with a reversal at the point of the bullish deliberation. Following a two-week downtrend, the pattern appears with an extra session in the form of a *doji*. The reversal and resulting uptrend last only one week.

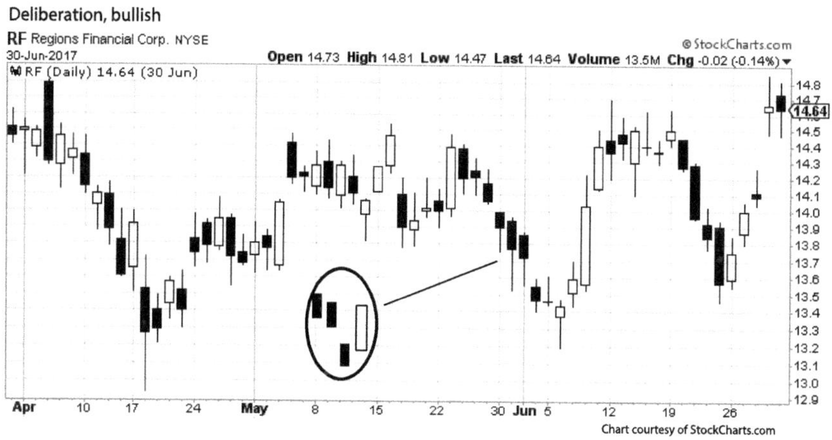

Figure 5.35: Deliberation, bullish

Bearish deliberation consists of two closely trading white sessions, an upward gap and a third white day, and then a black session signaling reversal to a coming downtrend. This is not an especially strong signal, and reversal does not always follow.

Deliberation, bearish: A set of four signals. The first two are white and trade in close range to one another. The third session is also white and occurs after an upward gap, and the fourth session is black, moving price lower.

Figure 5.36 shows an example of the bearish signal occurring at the right location, the top of an uptrend. The resulting downtrend lasted only one week and led to consolidation immediately after. This signal is difficult to spot and should be independently confirmed before entering a trade in anticipation of a reliable reversal.

Deliberation, bearish

Figure 5.36: Deliberation, bearish

Two final patterns in this group are identical three crows and white soldiers. Because each of these is similar to the advance and decline block, its reliability as a reversal signal is not high. However, these patterns are also similar to the very reliable white soldiers and black crows. The identical patterns are controversial as a result. The outcome is not consistent.

Identical three crows is assumed to act as a bearish reversal. It consists of three black sessions, with each opening price identical to or very close to the previous session's closing price. It should occur at the top of an uptrend.

Identical three crows: A bearish reversal of three black sessions. Each one's opening price is the same as or close to the previous session's closing price.

Figure 5.37 has an example. The signal moved price from a consolidation period to a downtrend, defining this as a successful signal. Even though the downtrend did not last long, it moved price for more than half the scale of the chart.

Figure 5.37: Identical three crows

The identical white soldiers is a bullish reversal expected to be found at the bottom of a downtrend. It combines three white sessions, with each opening price identical or close to the close of the previous session.

Identical white soldiers: A bullish reversal of three white sessions. Each one's opening price is the same as or close to the previous session's closing price.

Figure 5.38 demonstrates a three identical soldiers pattern breaking out of consolidation and starting a strong but brief uptrend. Confirming the reversal and adding strength to it was that the two preceding sessions formed as a bullish engulfing pattern.

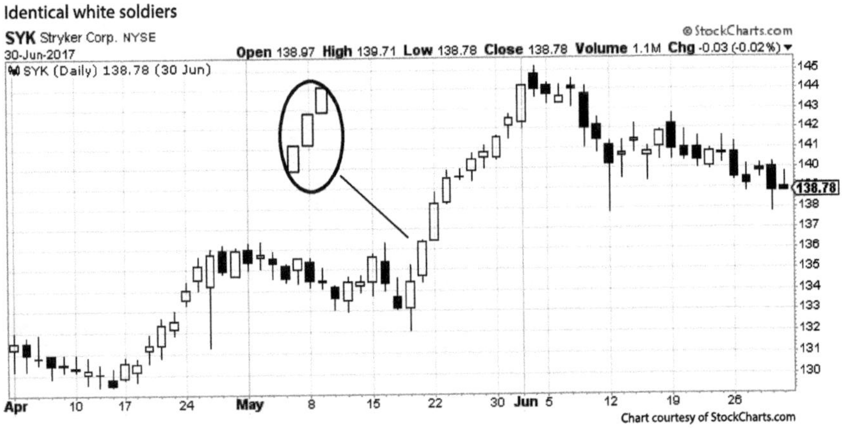

Figure 5.38: Identical white soldiers

Strong Price Line Reversals

In comparison to the uncertainty of low-reliability signals, a few patterns offer exceptionally strong reversal confidence. These are called "price lines" and consist of same-colored sessions over lengthy periods of time. The longer the period lasts, the stronger the likelihood of reversal.

The first of these is the eight new price lines. The bearish version includes eight white sessions running prices higher and leading to a strong and immediate reversal. A review of typical price charts reveals that a normal tendency is for prices to switch back and forth between white and black sessions every few days and to not run the same color for very long.

Eight new price lines, bearish: A run of eight consecutive sessions, all white and rising. This predicts a turnaround and resulting bearish trend as reaction to the unusual pattern over eight days.

Figure 5.39 presents an example of the bearish eight new price lines pattern. These are not candlesticks in the traditional sense, in which a particular relationship is seen between one or more sessions to the surrounding price behavior. In the price lines, the consistency of one direction and one color—representing eight straight days of rising prices—presents a likely reversal, which tends to occur immediately.

Figure 5.39: 8 new price lines, bearish

The bullish eight new price lines behaves in a similar manner, expected to lead to a bullish reversal. This translates to eight consecutive black sessions taking price lower and leading to a reversal and new bullish move.

Eight new price lines, bullish: A run of eight consecutive sessions, all black and falling. This predicts a turnaround and resulting bullish trend as reaction to the unusual pattern over eight days.

An example is found in Figure 5.40, but with interesting results. Price did turn to the upside, but only for two weeks. Following this was another short-lived decline and then a month-long consolidation before another brief uptrend. This pattern makes the example a weak one, demonstrating that no pattern, no matter how strong, is reliable 100% of the time.

Figure 5.40: 8 new price lines, bullish

A price lines move of ten sessions is much stronger than one of eight. The additional two sessions add substantial strength; however, as with all patterns, the resulting price behavior is not always reliable. Even so, a move of consistency over ten days is unusual. A bearish ten new price lines pattern consists of ten days, all with white real bodies, and forecasting a bearish reversal.

Ten new price lines, bearish: A run of ten consecutive sessions, all white and rising. This predicts a turnaround and resulting bearish trend as reaction to the unusual pattern over ten days.

Figure 5.41 has an example of this pattern. However, the downtrend that was expected did not materialize. The pattern concluded with a three-day bearish candlestick signal, the three inside down (a long white session, a smaller black session, and a downward move to a new black session). The combination of the ten new price lines and bearish reversal would normally result in exceptionally high confidence that prices would fall. Instead they became very narrow, trading in a range of under two points, leading to further upward movement. This example of the ten price lines failed, even with the strong candlestick reversal.

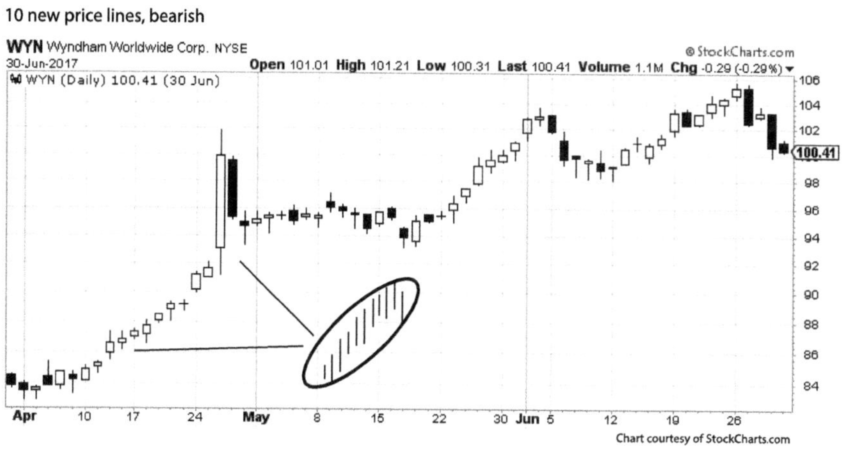

Figure 5.41: 10 new price lines, bearish

The bullish ten new price lines consists of ten black consecutive sessions, expected to lead to an upward move upon conclusion. As with the bearish version, a run of ten days with same-colored sessions is unusual.

Ten new price lines, bullish: A run of ten consecutive sessions, all black and falling. This predicts a turnaround and resulting bullish trend as reaction to the unusual pattern over ten days.

Figure 5.42 contains this pattern. It is a strong move, starting with a downside gap and a run downward. As the range leveled out at the bottom, the pattern came to a conclusion. This set up likely new support. However, prices move sideways for two weeks before the expected reaction. At that point, the bullish move occurred, recovering most of the price decline preceding the pattern.

Figure 5.42: 10 new price lines, bullish

A final version of this unusual pattern involves thirteen sessions. The bearish version involves thirteen consecutive white sessions and is expected to lead to a strong move downward.

Thirteen new price lines, bearish: A run of thirteen consecutive sessions, all white and rising. This predicts a turnaround and resulting bearish trend as reaction to the unusual pattern over thirteen days.

An example is found in Figure 5.43. Prices moving up begin with a strong upside gap and thirteen sessions going in the same direction. In this case, three of the sessions were black, but also were near *doji* configurations. In order to recognize the strength of the overall direction, counting *doji* or near *doji* sessions is acceptable as long as they do not represent a turn in the trend's direction. The final session, in fact, gapped upward strongly and preceded an expected bearish turn.

Figure 5.43: 13 new price lines, bearish

The final new price lines pattern is the thirteen sessions in a bullish move. This involves thirteen black sessions moving price lower, concluding with a turnaround and a new bullish trend.

Thirteen new price lines, bullish: A run of thirteen consecutive sessions, all black and falling. This predicts a turnaround and resulting bullish trend as reaction to the unusual pattern over thirteen days.

A nearly perfect example of this is seen in Figure 5.44. After a price peak, a downward turn contained thirteen black sessions, a move even lower concluding with a bullish engulfing signal (black session engulfed by the range of the next day's white session), and then moving to the upside. The thirteen sessions represent a strong signal, and confirmation with the engulfing signal added strength and confidence levels.

Figure 5.44: 13 new price lines, bullish

Breakaways, Strikes, and Sandwiches

A final range of signal patterns include some of the most specific and easily identified candlesticks, all containing three or more consecutive sessions. Among these is the breakaway pattern, an exceptionally strong form of reversal. The bullish breakaway begins with a strong downward move of three or more black sessions forming black crows or gaps and a final white session marking the end of the downtrend and a reversal to a bullish trend.

Breakaway, bullish: A multi-session pattern of three or more black and declining days, concluding with an upward white session identifying a reversal.

The breakaway from the prevailing trend is conclusive as long as prices do move in the direction expected. In Figure 5.45, a strong example is found in what appears at first as a modest turnaround. The small white session is a turning day and is followed a few sessions later by a wide upside gap, a month-long consolidation, and then a continuation of the uptrend.

Figure 5.45: Breakaway, bullish

The bearish breakaway begins with three or more upward-trending white sessions. These may be white soldiers or gapping patterns, but are expected to turn and lead into bearish trends. Like the bullish version, the bearish breakaway tends to provide a rare but strong reversal signal.

Breakaway, bearish: A multi-session pattern of three or more white and advancing days, concluding with a downward black session identifying a reversal.

Two examples are seen in Figure 5.46. The first came after a rapid bullish move of multiple upside gaps. This level of gapping action is vulnerable and increases the likelihood of a strong reversal. In this case, the long black candlestick that represented the last entry in the breakaway made this point. After two weeks of consolidation, the trend turned bearish. The second example also came after strong upside gapping patterns, although the bearish turnaround was not as strong. In fact, the bearish reversal lasted only a few sessions before price consolidated once again. Although this met the requirements of a breakaway, the second example was not as strong as the first.

Breakaway, bearish

Figure 5.46: Breakaway, bearish

The tendency for dynamic price moves to present confusing signals is a chronic problem for chart analysts. None of the signals provide certainty. One example is seen in the multiple-session pattern of the three line strike. This is unusual because it is expected to act as a continuation signal, but leads to reversal most of the time. As a consequence, it is not clear how to view the pattern. Going with what occurs most of the time, it should be considered a reversal pattern. The bearish reversal version begins with three white sessions and an engulfing reversal pattern. This conclusion is what strongly sets up the strike as a likely reversal.

Three line strike, bearish: A pattern of three or more white sessions, concluding with a black session that forms a bearish engulfing signal.

For example, Figure 5.47 ends an uptrend with white sessions gapping to a high, followed by a black session and setting up the expected bearish engulfing. A mild downtrend followed before prices rose once again.

Figure 5.47: Three line strike, bearish

The confusion created by this pattern makes it less useful than an analyst would expect. Because the three line strike is assumed to act as continuation but most often serves as reversal (due to the engulfing pattern that ends it), this is not a particularly reliable signal.

The bullish version contains the opposite configuration: three or more black sessions and a final white session. The last two sessions form a bullish engulfing signal and are likely to lead to a bullish reversal.

Three line strike, bullish: A pattern of three or more black sessions, concluding with a white session that forms a bullish engulfing signal.

The example in Figure 5.48 conforms to the expectation of the three line strike as a reversal signal. Several black sessions end with a white session and a strong bullish engulfing pattern, which then leads to an uptrend reversal.

Figure 5.48: Three line strike, bullish

A similar pattern clearly does provide continuation. This is the gapping play pattern. A gapping play, high price consists of white sessions, an upside gap, and continuation of the uptrend. It should occur during a prevailing uptrend to conform to the requirement as a continuation signal.

Gapping play, high price: A bullish continuation signal consisting of white sessions, an upside gap, another white session, and further movement in the same direction.

The gapping play signal in Figure 5.49 meets these criteria. The uptrend gapped higher, which often precedes a reversal. So analysts are alerted to this as soon as the gap appears. However, the white session occurring after the gap indicates continuation.

Gapping play, high price

Figure 5.49: Gapping play, high price

The gapping play, low price is a bearish continuation pattern. It consists of black sessions, a downside gap, and a final black session. This is followed by further downward price action.

Gapping play, low price: A bearish continuation signal consisting of black sessions, a downside gap, another black session, and further movement in the same direction.

Figure 5.50 has an example of a strong gapping play pattern. Although the downtrend appeared to pause in the final week of April, the development of further movement to a long black candle pointed to continuation, which occurred through the middle of May.

Figure 5.50: Gapping play, low price

Another continuation pattern is rare but exceptionally strong. The rest after battle is a pattern occurring after a strong upward move, often in the form of a gap. As with the previous set of patterns, an upside gap may predict a reversal. But when it forms into a rest after battle, it strengthens the uptrend and predicts continuation.

Rest after battle: A bullish continuation signal that follows strong upward movement. It consists of a white session followed by two smaller black sessions, likely to be followed by a continuation of the bullish trend.

A rest after battle does not have a bearish equivalent. The most important characteristic of this pattern as a continuation is the strength of the preceding uptrend. For example, in Figure 5.51, an upside gap appeared immediately before the rest after battle. The fact that trading levels did not move downward supports the prediction in this pattern that the uptrend would continue in spite of the previous gap.

Rest after battle

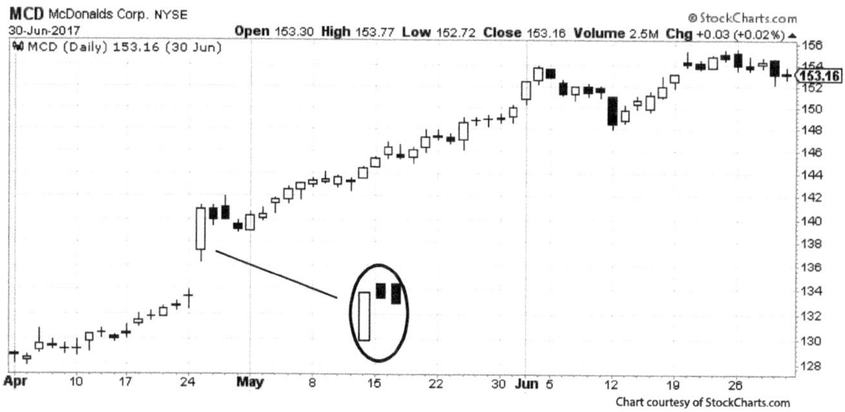

Figure 5.51: Rest after battle

A final price pattern is found in the *doji* sandwich. This is a three-session pattern with a *doji* in between the first and third. The bullish *doji* sandwich begins and ends with white sessions. This is a subtle but reliable signal acting as a reversal of the preceding downtrend.

***Doji* sandwich, bullish:** A reversal with white sessions in the first and third positions and a *doji* in between.

A bullish *doji* sandwich was found in Figure 5.52, at the conclusion of a downtrend. Price advanced to form the first white session, followed by the *doji* and a concluding white session. This was the beginning of the uptrend that followed.

Doji sandwich, bullish

Figure 5.52: Doji sandwich, bullish

The bearish *doji* sandwich consists of black sessions separated by a *doji.* It is most effective when located at the top of an uptrend, predicting a reversal and a new downtrend to follow.

***Doji* sandwich, bearish:** A reversal with black sessions in the first and third positions and a *doji* in between.

Figure 5.53 contained a strong upside gap followed by three weeks of volatility. The appearance of a delayed bearish *doji* sandwich indicated that a new bearish move was likely to follow. The new downtrend took place, but did not last long. It led to a month-long consolidation. In this example, the *doji* sandwich correctly predicted the end of the uptrend even though it was delayed, but it led to consolidation rather than an expected downtrend.

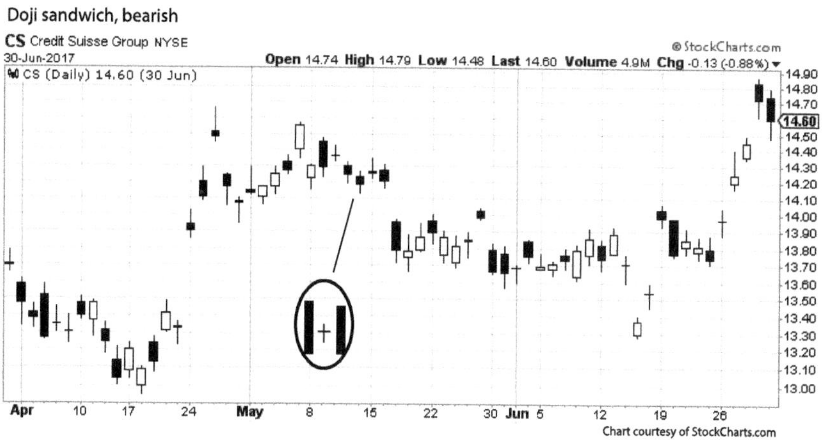

Figure 5.53: Doji sandwich, bearish

Recognizing the False Signal

As the preceding range of signals and patterns demonstrates, not all signals are reliable or consistent. Many signals do not lead to reversal or continuation as expected, and assumptions about what will occur next are subject to interpretation. It is essential to keep in mind that all candlestick signals and patterns provide a *likely* cause and effect, but can never be relied upon to act as expected 100% of the time.

Given the reality that no signals or combination of signals provide 100% accuracy, there are some elements to false signals, such as lack of confirmation or improper proximity, that provide hints:

> The majority of what are considered false signals is the mis-evaluation of the signal's potential when the confirming indicators have not aligned. Understanding that the probabilities are vastly in the investor's favor upon identifying that a good signal has appeared also incorporates the fact that it is not 100 percent foolproof.[viii]

Some general guidelines help to recognize a false or failed candlestick signal:

1. *The signal has to appear at the right place.* A bull reversal has to form at the bottom of a downtrend, and a bear reversal must appear at the top of an uptrend. Continuation has to occur during the prevailing trend direction. If these essential rules are not followed, the signal should not be taken as a reliable one.

2. *Any unexpected price movement following the pattern is suspicious.* Look for unexpected price movement after a signal, a sign that it may be false. When this occurs, defer a trade decision until the situation becomes clearer. You expect prices to rise after a bull reversal and to fall after a bear reversal. When the opposite movement occurs instead, it probably means the signal was not what it appeared to be.
3. *Look for confirmation such as evolving trends and unusually high volume to pick up false signals.* Every indicator should be confirmed, either by price movement, volume, momentum, or additional pattern development. This confirmation reduces the chance of error or misreading of signals.
4. *Reversal signals cannot serve as continuation signals.* The many formations of reversal and confirmation patterns are quite distinct. An easy trap for any technician is to decide that a reversal pattern showing up in the wrong place is actually a continuation pattern; this is not so.
5. *All signals are indicators and not guarantees.* The pattern spotted on a chart is only an indication of what might occur next, not a guarantee. The purpose of pattern analysis is to improve your accuracy in recognizing likely price movement to follow, but no one can possibly time his or her entry and exit decisions perfectly.
6. *The strength or weakness of preceding price activity matters.* As a general rule, strong price and trend activity tends to lead to strong candlestick reversal or continuation indicators. Weak price and trend activity, by the same rule, tends to lead to weak candlestick indicators.
7. *The strength of candlesticks tends to be accompanied by equal strength in confirmation.* A confirming indicator tends to match the strength of the initial signal. A strong indicator should be expected to be confirmed with equal strength, and a weak or inconclusive signal is also likely to be accompanied by weak confirmation.
8. *Strength of the candlestick signal and confirmation dictates the strength of the price behavior that follows.* Strong reversal or continuation, accompanied by equally strong confirmation signals, tends to lead to strong price reaction. Likewise, weak or less conclusive indicators and confirmation are likely to lead to weak price reaction or to reaction opposite of what is expected.

Candlesticks by themselves often lead to reversal or continuation, but these still require confirmation. Combining specific candlestick signals or patterns with traditional technical indicators is an excellent system for building confirmation and also for getting an advance indication that a reversal is underway. For this reason, building skills in chart analysis improves your ability to spot reversals as well as to spot false reversals. The next chapter expands on the importance of candlestick pattern recognition by tying in two important additional pieces of information: volume and volatility.

---

[i] Bernstein, P. L. (Winter 1999). A New Look at the Efficient Market Hypothesis. *Journal of Portfolio Management*, 25, No. 2, 1–2.

[ii] Leigh, W., Frohlich, C. J., Hornik, S., Purvis, R. L., & Roberts, T. L. (January 2008). Trading with a Stock Chart Heuristic. *IEEE Transactions on Systems, Man and Cybernetics—Part A: Systems and Humans*, 38, No. 1, 93–104.

[iii] Pan, H. (2003). A Joint Review of Technical and Quantitative Analysis of Financial Markets Towards a Unified Science of Intelligent Finance. *Hawaii International Conference on Statistics and Related Fields.*

[iv] Martiny, K. (October 2012). Unsupervised Discovery of Significant Candlestick Patterns for Forecasting Security Price Movements. *Proceedings of the International Conference on Knowledge Discovery and Information Retrieval*, 145–150.

[v] Friesen, G. C., Weller, P., & Dunham, L. (June 2009). Price Trends and Patterns in Technical Analysis: A Theoretical and Empirical Examination. *Journal of Banking & Finance*, 33, No. 6, 1089–1100.

[vi] Morris, G. L. (2006). *Candlestick Charting Explained: Timeless Techniques for Trading Stocks and Futures*. New York: McGraw-Hill, 281–282.

[vii] Nison, S. (1994). *Beyond Candlesticks: New Japanese Charting Techniques Revealed.* Hoboken, NJ: John Wiley & Sons, 14.

[viii] Bigalow, S. W. (2011). *Profitable Candlestick Trading*, 2nd ed. Hoboken, NJ: John Wiley & Sons, 237.

Chapter 6
Volume and Volatility

In addition to price movement and pattern, volume of trading and the volatility (risk) are also worthwhile indicators. Focusing solely on price trends is a mistake because changes in volume indicate changes in trading activity, and such changes often accompany or even anticipate changes in price trends. The same is true for changes in volatility levels; broadening trading ranges or repeated violations of support or resistance indicate coming price changes. Volume accompanying price analysis equates to great value in recognizing the health of a trend, even beyond price by itself:

> Traders keep a close eye on trading volume because it reflects the dynamic interplay between informed traders and uninformed traders who interact with each other in the marketplace in light of their own trading strategies and, ultimately, set market clearing prices. Trading volume is termed as the critical piece of information in the stock market because it either activates or deactivates the price movements. Stock prices are usually influenced by positive trading volume through the available set of relevant information in the market. A revision in investors' expectations usually leads to an increase in trading volume which eventually reflects the sum of investors' reaction to news. One of the most common mistakes made by the novice traders is their tendency to ignore volume and focus only on the price movements in a chart.[i]

This explanation expands on the value of candlesticks as related only to price. When combined with the equally important volume and volatility signs, candlesticks are even more effective. Changes in volume and volatility can also confirm what price patterns imply about impending trends.

Volume as a Price Indicator

Movement in price and changes in daily volume are separate matters. However, volume also serves as a key price indicator, especially when studied in conjunction with significant candlestick formations accompanied by unusual spikes in volume levels. Candlestick charts are normally presented with volume in histogram bar form on the bottom of the chart; the charts used in this book include these volume levels, with the daily level (in numbers of shares traded) shown on the bottom left of the chart.

DOI 10.1515/9781501507397-006

Key Point: Although volume and price are separate from one another, volume may serve as an important confirming indicator, especially in reversal formations.

To a pure technician, volume is one of the keys to understanding the strength or weakness of the current trend. This translates to a further understanding of how changes in volume affect the volatility (risk) within the trend. For some observers, this belief is a perception and not necessarily a reality:

> The chartist's explanation of why volume determines the health of an existing trend is as follows: rising prices coupled with high volume signifies increased upside participation (more buyers) that should lead to a continued move, whereas falling prices coupled with high volume signifies increased downside participation (more sellers). Conversely, price trends accompanied by low volume are suspect. Whether or not the logic behind this reasoning is correct is not crucial. What matters is that chartists act in accordance with this directive.[ii]

However, when volume within the trend is monitored with combined use of volume indicators and candlestick reversal and continuation patterns, the benefits become obvious. The question remains: How is volume to be used in tracking price behavior? As a general rule, volume is most useful when compared to daily price candlestick formations. Devices such as moving averages of volume are not particularly useful for most traders because, unlike price trends, volume trends are easily distorted by a few spikes. These volume spikes may have little to do with a *trend* in volume itself, so moving averages are more useful in price trends. When volume increases steadily from one day to the next, the trend serves as confirmation of a developing price trend. The confirming aspect of volume as it accompanies a price move is the best application of volume analysis. However, volume goes beyond confirmation by providing a level of intelligence concerning the way that a trader employs broader signals. This means that:

> volume provides information in a way distinct from that provided by price . . . volume captures the important information contained in the quality of traders' information signals . . . volume plays a role beyond simply being a descriptive parameter of the trading process.[iii]

This observation demonstrates that volume should not function merely as a confirming signal of candlesticks. Of course, volume confirms trends and can effectively anticipate potential reversals, but interpretation is difficult unless combined as part of a larger program of analysis. When the quality of traders' information expands to include a full landscape of signals, volume may be utilized to spot price momentum as well as to confirm (or contradict) the apparent strength of the prevailing trend.

For example, volume confirms the trend when changes in daily trading accompany price breakouts. Support and resistance are the "lines in the sand" for technicians, and breakouts are among the strongest of technical signals. However, some breakouts are the beginning of a strong trend resulting in a new price range, and other breakouts are aberrations, after which price levels will return to previously set levels. How do you know which is which? The answer is often found when a breakout is accompanied by heavy volume. This is especially likely to work as confirmation that the breakout is permanent when it follows a period of price consolidation and low volume. In an upside breakout such as this, the indication is particularly strong because an influx of new buyers supports the higher price range. In a downside breakout, heavy volume can also be significant, but it is not necessary to justify lower prices. The momentum of a resistance breakout is going to be the most important attribute of the trend and the determining factor to its permanent or temporary nature. The same momentum is not as crucial for a support breakout.

After a strong upside breakout with higher than typical volume, a fast retreat in volume levels can work as a sign of exhaustion in new buyer interest. This can anticipate a price retreat. At such times, watching candlestick patterns and exercising caution is a wise idea. The use of trailing stops or taking of some profits is advisable whenever resistance breakouts occur, but especially if volume levels retreat immediately after the breakouts occur. Remember, though, that higher than average volume is not going to be sustained indefinitely. Even in a strong price movement, volume levels are going to subside. The point here is that an immediate retreat after an upside breakout can be a warning sign.

Key Point: Spikes in volume are rarely permanent, and in a majority of cases volume will return within one to two sessions to previously established levels.

For example, in Figure 6.1, a distinctive volume spike marks a turning point. Price gapped higher at the point of the spike, and a likely retreat was marked by the *doji* star. The candlestick confirmed the likely turn indicated by the spike.

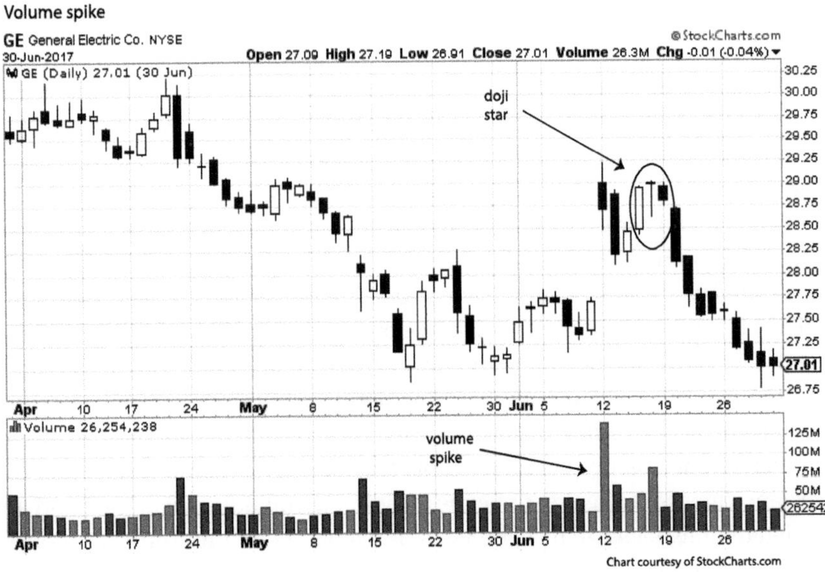

Figure 6.1: Volume spike

This example makes the point that a single-day spike in volume accompanying a breakout above resistance could signal that it is not going to last. The immediate retreat in volume was quickly accompanied by a retreat in price as well. However, volume is not a reliable indicator by itself of changes in the trading range. When a change in volume occurs, it can be interpreted based on whether higher volume remains or immediately falls away. However, the volume trend as a confirming factor is not going to be apparent in every instance.

One study reached conclusions demonstrating that volume spikes hold significance as signaling devices, often affecting price behavior after the appearance of the spike. The meaning of this was summarized in three observations:

> (a) the impact of good news on price is rapid and pronounced relative to the impact of bad news which occurs gradually and is softened; therefore (b) one-day volume spikes are more likely to precede abrupt market upturns than they are to precede abrupt market downturns; and (c) information diffusion rates and feed-forward information mechanisms, such as momentum and herding, ensure that the direction of the price change immediately preceding and accompanying the volume spike is continued for some future period.[iv]

These observations are instructive, but are by no means absolute. The observed effect of a volume spike cannot be judged in isolation, but must fit with other signals, notably those in price as reflected in candlestick (continuation or reversal). The significance of the spike is properly interpreted within the context of the preceding trend, subsequent price activity, and appearance of candlesticks on the same day as the spike.

Just as the spike indicates likely trend reversal, volume beyond the spike is also a predictor of price activity. Price breakouts may occur as volume levels increase dramatically. This trend is shown in Figure 6.2. Volume grew over a brief period of time, but no price indicators appeared until the bearish engulfing. This was a clear turning point, with the candlestick as strong confirmation of the changes in volume. Price gapped downward and continued to fall.

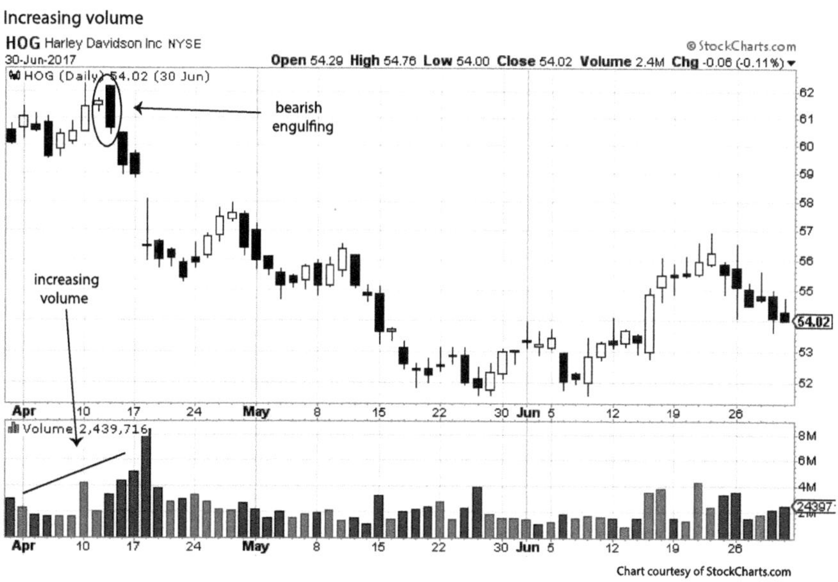

Figure 6.2: Increasing volume

A volume spike is exceptionally strong when it also marks a breakout above resistance or below support. This may be a reversal or an end to a period of consolidation. The chart in Figure 6.3 marks the end of a modest uptrend with two signals, a volume spike and a bearish *doji* star. Immediately after, price gapped power and remained in a new trading range.

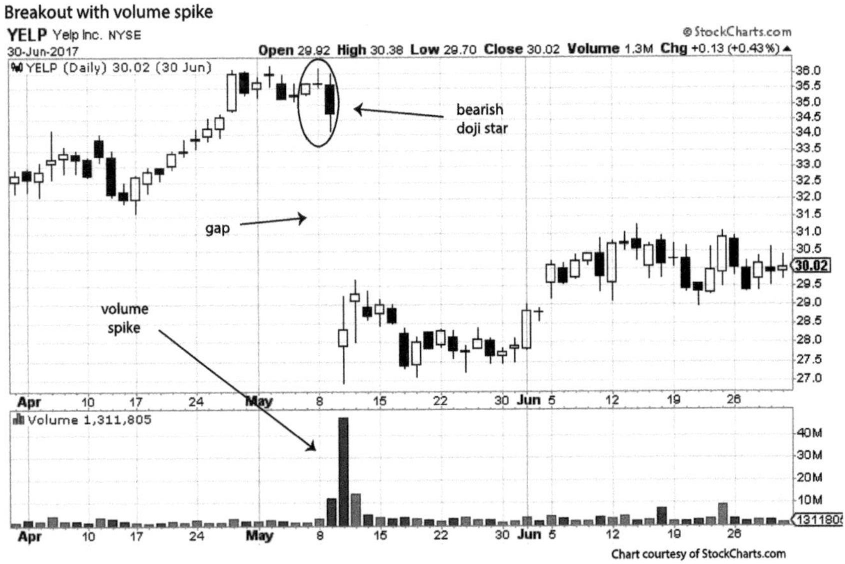

Figure 6.3: Breakout with volume spike

In any analysis of volume, the price pattern witnessed in the candlestick is the most important attribute of a trend, reversal, or breakout pattern. Volume is a useful form of confirmation as well as a method for judging the strength of the pattern. Beyond the pattern seen in volume spikes or changes in volume levels, specific indicators also provide strong indicators and confirmation.

Volume Indicators

Many volume-based indicators are valuable in conjunction with known candlestick chart patterns. These are less obvious than price movement because price is visible on charts, whereas a calculated volume trend is not realy obvious. The causes for increases or decreases in volume are not always as clear as the reasons for price trends and reversals. However, volume-based indicators provide needed confirmation for what the price candlestick formation reveals. Even among those assuming the existence of an efficient market, the role of volume is acknowledged.

The relationship between price and volume, and the role of each, relates to levels of expectation and interpretation:

> An important distinction between the price and volume tests is that the former reflects changes in the expectations of the market as a whole while the latter reflects changes in the expectation of individual investors.[v]

Reference to "individual investors" has to be clarified. This may refer not only to individuals, but also to institutions within the market. Institutional trading represents approximately 96% of all trading activity.[vi] As a result, institutional trades represent nearly the entire market, and individuals (retail investors) are able only to use the dominant volume information as an indicator of marketwide sentiment. However, large volume is not always a reliable signal of a change in buyer or seller sentiment about a company. Institutional buy or sell decisions, representing large blocks of shares, often occur near the end of a reporting period, when mutual fund management may want to clean up its portfolio to present a positive picture to shareholders. Thus a block of shares may be sold just before the end of a month to take profits, or a block might be sold right after the end of the month to defer reported losses to the next month.

> Investors have long known that mutual funds, pension funds and hedge funds roil the markets when they buy and sell en masse due to their size . . . [causing] strong return reversals in the U.S. value-weighted stock market index around the last monthly settlement day three days before the end of the month.[vii]

Key Point: Exceptionally high volume might have no actual significance, especially if it occurs near the end of the month. It might be caused by institutional investor changes in their portfolio mix.

The timing among institutional investors—accounting for up to 96% of all shares held and trading activity—can distort the picture of what is going on with a company and its stock. With this in mind, a spike in volume is one signal, but it may also be confirmed by analyzing proximity to the end of the month.

One volume trend anticipates price movement through a cumulative comparison between buy and sell days. When volume gradually increases, it indicates growing interest in the stock on the upside or growing concerns on the downside. On-balance volume (OBV) is one indicator that may indicate coming price movement. It may serve as either a confirming signal or a diverging one:

> The on-balance-volume (OBV) indicator incorporates a measure of market psychology and participation in a trend by weighing price action with its volume. The OBV can confirm the quality of the current price trend by moving in the same direction as price or warn of an impending reversal by diverging from the price action.[viii]

This indicator was developed by well-known market technician Joseph Granville. In his view, as one side or the other begins to dominate volume, it implies an emerging trend. The analysis of volume is maintained on a cumulative basis to make this analysis work. When either the buyers or the sellers tip the on-balance in one direction or the other, it signals an emerging trend in that direction as well.

On-balance volume: A cumulative indicator measuring dominance of daily trading by either buyers or sellers, used to anticipate emerging trends.

On-balance volume is an effective method for quantifying volume-based price trends. A problem with it, however, is that volume is always counted as either positive or negative, even when the difference is only slight. In spite of how closely aligned buyers and sellers actually are, even a slight edge moves the entire day into one column or the other. This potentially distorts the trend itself. For this reason, anyone analyzing candlestick pricing trends should use on-balance volume as one of many ways to double check and confirm a trend implied by candlestick movement; relying on the on-balance volume as a sole indicator or even as the primary signal may lead to some ill-timed decisions.

Key Point: On-balance volume is a useful but imperfect indicator. If a day's volume is closely mixed between buyers and sellers, even a slight edge will throw the entire day's volume into one column or the other.

An example of OBV is seen on the chart in Figure 6.4. At the point that the OBV line begins rising, price was not trending in either direction. However, OBV anticipated price movement. This was confirmed by the bullish piercing lines signal, which led immediately to a bullish price move.

On balance volume (OBV)

Figure 6.4: On balance volume (OBV)

OBV is intended as a means for tracking sentiment about stock based on whether investment is flowing in or out based on the assumption that volume leads price:

> The underlying assumption is that OBV changes precede price changes. The reason is that smart money (investment made by well-informed and sophisticated investors) are flowing into the stock, reflecting in a rising OBV. When the public starts to follow, both the stock price and OBV will surge even more.[ix]

The question for traders is whether or not OBV performs this function reliably. A problem with OBV is the potential for divergence, a price move opposite of what a volume indicator predicts. Divergence is going to occur in even the most accurate and reliable tests, whether based on daily cumulative levels of "ownership" of volume by either buyers or sellers, long-term moving averages, or other adjustments meant to eliminate spikes. This drawback to volume analysis led to two refinements, both developed by Marc Chaikin. His two major contributions to technical analysis were the Accumulation/Distribution (A/D line) indicator and money flow index (MFI).

Accumulation/distribution (A/D line): A technical indicator measuring proportionate degrees of buyer and seller volume, which acts as a momentum indicator.

The A/D indicator is calculated with the formula:

$$(((\text{closing price} - \text{low price}) - (\text{high price} - \text{closing price})) \div (\text{high price} - \text{low price})) \times \text{volume} = \text{A/D}$$

This indicator makes volume analysis more accurate than on-balance volume. Assignment of a day's volume as controlled by either buyers or sellers is more accurate after calculating the mean of prices for each day. The resulting A/D indicator is either +1 or −1.

An example of the behavior in the A/D line is found on the chart in Figure 6.5. As price continued rising, the A/D line diverged and began decreasing. This anticipated a reversal long before price signals emerged. The A/D line prediction was confirmed by a bearish engulfing signal, leading to a pause in the price trend and then a reversal.

A/D line

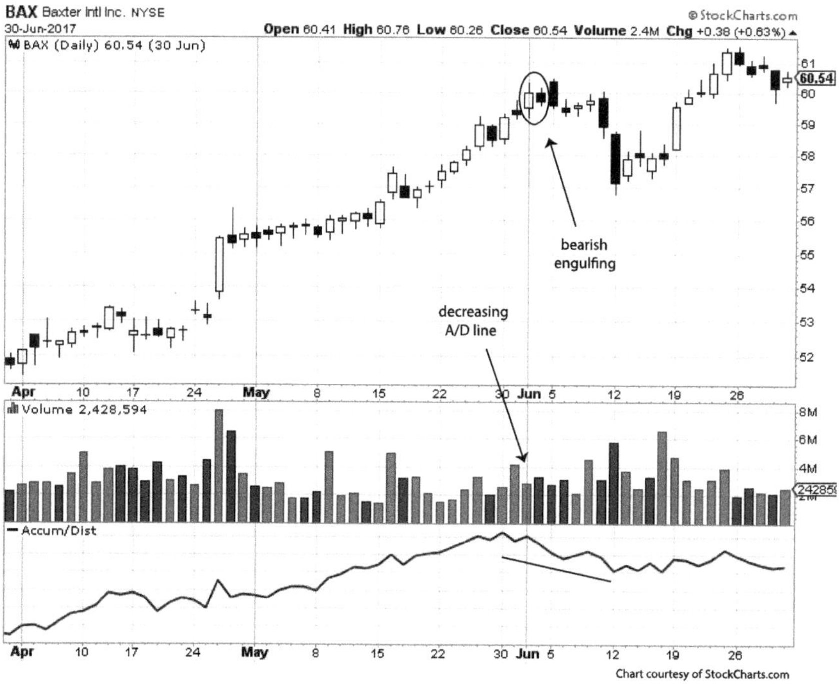

Figure 6.5: A/D line

Chaikin also devised the money flow index (MFI), which measures the strength of money flow in a stock's price. MFI tracks money flow over a twenty-one-day moving average, identifying positive (buyer) and negative (seller) flow and their net difference. This identifies the longer-term momentum in price trend.

Money flow index (MFI): A momentum indicator measuring positive and negative money flow in a stock's price over a twenty-one-day moving average, creating an oscillator ranging between 1 and 100; the indicator is also known as the Chaikin Money Flow (CMF).

Key Point: The MFI is based on a moving average and trend, and the trend reflects the net change over time between buyer and seller dominance.

Money flow is intended not only to articulate the flow of investment as part of a trend, but also to quantify perceived risk levels of investing in a particular stock.

The money flow thus represents the trend in risk evaluation within the market. In other words:

> stocks with larger positive net money flow were often considered as low-risk stocks and had a stronger possibility to increase. However, stocks with large negative net money flow were often considered as high-risk stock and had a greater probability to decrease in price. For the purpose of earning greater returns, the conflict to choose "to buy" in positive net money flows was smaller than in negative net money flows; however, this decision was severer for the "not to buy" option.[x]

The index can be compared to price trends to spot confirmation or divergence of the current trend. Price by itself may display levels of enthusiasm or lack of enthusiasm, but does not always reflect how risk perceptions come into the picture. The combination of price confirmation (or divergence) with risk perception is where money flow analysis gains in value.

Positive flow is divided by negative flow to develop each day's entry into the MFI trend, and the result is multiplied by 100. An oscillator below 20 indicates that the stock is then oversold, acting as a buy signal. When the oscillator rises above 80, the opposite conclusion results: the stock is overbought and this serves as a sell signal. MFI has a great advantage over most other volume-based price indicators because it is very easy to follow.

An example is found in Figure 6.6. In this case, MFI never moves above 80 or below 20. The lack of signal is itself a signal, indicating that the continued uptrend is not likely to reverse in the near future. Even as the MFI index approached the 80 index level, candlestick continuation signals appeared, confirming the prediction that the trend would continue. The thrusting lines and side-by-side white lines reassured traders that the prevailing bullish trend was not vulnerable to reversal.

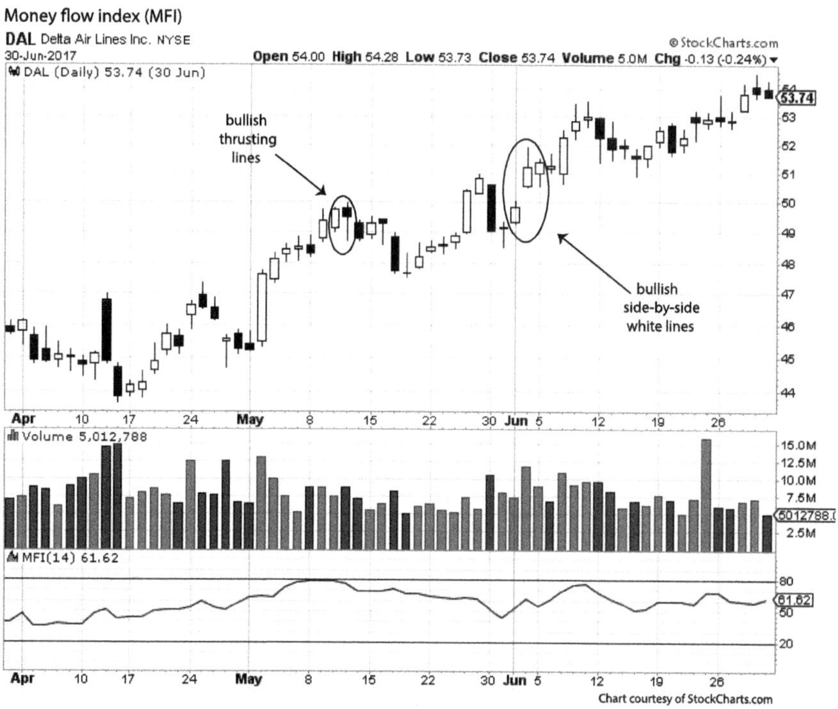

Figure 6.6: Money flow index (MFI)

Marc Chaikin also devised the Chaikin money flow (CMF) volume indicator. This tests buying and selling pressure on price and further indicates likely price direction. Figure 6.7 shows how this works. Ranging from −0.2 to +0.2, CMF measures pressure below the zero line (selling pressure) or above (buying pressure). On the chart, in early May selling pressure ended as buying pressure moved up close to the very top. This occurred while price levels were falling. The bullish piercing lines marked the end of the downtrend and reversal point. The candlestick confirmed the trend in CMF, enabling traders to anticipate the point of reversal with reliable accuracy.

Chaikin money flow (CMF)

Figure 6.7: Chaikin money flow (CMF)

On-balance volume, money flow, index and Chaikin money flow provide value in varying degrees, but should be used with caution and always in conjunction with candlestick pattern analysis. None of the volume-based signals are independently strong enough to provide adequate signals for price continuation or reversal without the price-based confirming signals found in candlestick signals.

Key Point: In a sustained uptrend, it is difficult to identify the right time to sell and take profits. This is where the CMF oscillator can be valuable and help spot whether the trend is ending or continuing.

In an ideal world, you expect to see all indicators pointing to the same conclusion; in reality, of course, you often find serious contradictions between the indicators you trust. In analyzing CMF, look for three attributes to indicate what is going on in the current trend:

1. *Is the CMF positive or negative?* Regardless of how price is acting, remember that the money flow is a moving average and this accurately pegs a positive (bullish) or negative (bearish) trend underway.
2. *How long has the current situation prevailed?* The longer the CMF remains either positive or negative, the stronger the related trend. This is especially valuable information in highly volatile markets, where price ranges have broadened and longer-term price trends have become more difficult to spot.
3. *How strong is the CMF status?* The intensity of the indicator is also a key ingredient in its interpretation. As a general rule, when the oscillator is at 0.10, it is bullish, or when it is at −0.10 it is bearish. When the oscillator moves to 0.2 it is extremely bullish, and at −0.2 it is extremely bearish. These extremes identify the likely tops and bottoms of price trends and are among the strongest of confirming signals. However, these extremes do not always appear, so rather than waiting for them, they should be treated as exceptional signals rather than signals necessary to make a move.

Key Point: The duration of a volume indicator like CMF helps you to decipher otherwise contradictory signs. How long has the CMF remained in positive or negative territory?

Testing Price Volatility

Volume tests serve as confirmation for what you observe in the candlestick signs, moves, and patterns, and help you spot changing directions in a trend as early as possible. However, volume is only half of the noncandlestick confirmation test. The other half is price volatility, or the degree and scope of change in a stock's price—in other words, the level of market risk.

The greater the price volatility, the higher your market risk. This is going to manifest in two ways. First is a broadening trading range over time; second is a tendency for price to bounce between resistance and support in larger increments and more frequently than in the past. In the technical sense, risk is based on the volatility of price and a real or perceived weakness in price support. Thus a strong support level is perceived as a safety net. By the same argument, a weak support level or one that is violated with price decline is a symptom of high-risk stock positions. For the technician, this technically based market risk is the most serious consideration in picking stocks. However, it is wise to also be aware of fundamentally based market risk and how that affects price trends.

The fundamental market risk is going to manifest in price volatility, either as a lagging indicator or—more often—preceding actual price trend changes. This is seen in many forms:

1. *Traditional form of fundamental volatility.* The tendency for a company to report volatile revenue and earnings makes it very difficult to predict long-term trends. So when profits are high one year and low the next, followed by a year of jarring net losses, how can you predict the future? This most basic version of fundamental volatility has the most direct correlation to technical price volatility.
2. *PE-caused volatility.* If the PE ratio tends to rise over time, it is also likely that prices are going to react with growing volatility. A moderate-range PE—between 10 and 20, for example—is viewed by many as a reasonable expectation and one of many ways to reduce a list of trading candidates. Once PE rises above this moderate range, the stock becomes too expensive. A bear might use high-PE stocks for short positions, but most traders prefer to make long plays on lower-PE stocks.
3. *Subtle cause and effect.* A few key fundamental tests have a direct effect on price volatility, although this is often a delayed effect. Among the most important are changes in dividend yield, debt ratio, and declining net return. The dividend yield is a sound method for judging management's cash flow control and growth plans, debt ratio identifies companies overly dependent on debt, and the net return is a key ratio even the ardent technician recognizes as crucial in stock picking. This is especially true when revenue is on the rise but net return is declining. This could be a symptom of decreasing internal controls and management effectiveness.

Key Point: Even if you believe completely in technical analysis, also keep an eye on the fundamentals. Price volatility is likely to reflect changes in financial condition, which in turn changes the stock's market risk.

Fundamental indicators are not widely believed to have an immediate impact on price volatility. Even so, in picking one stock over another, price patterns and trends are not the sole way to determine likely trading candidates. Testing volatility also makes sense.

Triangles and Wedges

Rather than trying to measure and quantify volatility using one of many formulas, it is more valuable to visualize the trading range and to observe consistency in breadth, or an expanding or narrowing trend in that range. Two patterns—triangles and wedges—are valuable in recognizing changes in volatility over time.

Triangles: Continuation patterns characterized by a narrowing trading range over time; these may be symmetrical, ascending, or descending.

There are three types of triangle patterns, all reflecting continuation of the trend by way of a narrowing trading range. First is the symmetrical triangle, which is also called a coil. In this pattern, a triangle forms with at least two lower highs and two higher lows, followed by continuation of the established trend with approximately the same breadth as that in the beginning of the triangle.

Symmetrical triangle: A continuation pattern consisting of a trading range of the same breadth in both the beginning of the triangle and the continuation.

Coil: Alternate name for the symmetrical triangle.

An example of this is found on the chart in Figure 6.8. The symmetrical triangle ends as price breadth closes. At that point, price moves strongly to the upside and forms as identical white soldiers, a strong bullish signal.

Figure 6.8: Symmetrical triangle

Although triangles are continuation signals, the symmetrical version is the least reliable. It indicates price movement but does not reveal a likely direction. In the chart, the upward price movement continues the trend set a month before, which was interrupted by sideways movement leading to the triangle.

Key Point: The symmetrical triangle confirms patterns, but confirmation of the existing direction is unclear; this is why more reliable reversal signals are just as important.

The symmetrical pattern is a clear continuation and it is found in both bullish and bearish trends. In comparison, other types of triangles are either bullish or bearish based on their shape. The ascending triangle is a bullish pattern consisting of a consistent price level at resistance and a rising support level.

Ascending triangle: A bullish triangle characterized by a level resistance and rising support level.

The ascending triangle in Figure 6.9 contains the required elements, a rising support level combined with level resistance. Making it even stronger is the repetitive appearance of bullish continuation signals, consisting of three in neck signals.

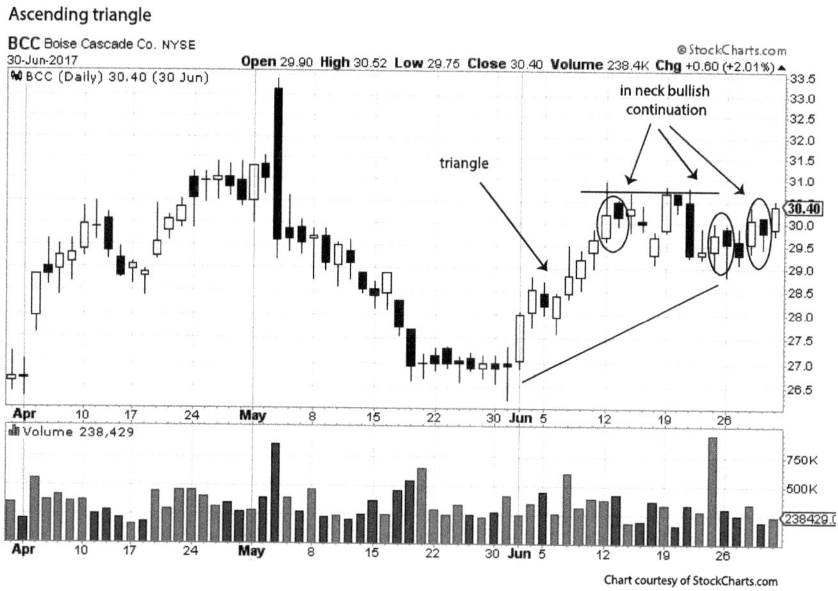

Figure 6.9: Ascending triangle

The same tendency works in a bearish trend. The descending triangle contains a steady level of support with declining resistance. An example is found in the chart in Figure 6.10.

Descending triangle: A bearish continuation pattern consisting of steady support price and declining resistance.

Figure 6.10: Descending triangle

The downtrend was expected to continue based on the triangle. This was confirmed by a bearish in neck signal occurring as the triangle narrowed to its conclusion.

Like the continuation patterns of triangles, wedges are reversal patterns characterized by narrowing trading range. However, the directional indicator is the opposite. A rising wedge is bearish and a falling wedge is bullish.

Wedge: A reversal pattern in one of two shapes: a rising wedge is bearish and anticipates a reversal from the existing uptrend to a downtrend, and a falling wedge is bullish, anticipating a reversal from the existing downtrend to an uptrend.

A rising wedge is bearish because, although prices are moving, their narrowing (wedge) formation anticipates a coming price decline. An example is found in the chart in Figure 6.11.

Rising wedge

Chart courtesy of StockCharts.com

Figure 6.11: Rising wedge

As prices continued rising in the strong bullish trend, the range narrowed, leading to a reversal signal, the bearish *doji* sandwich. This accurately predicted a bearish reversal, which occurred one week later.

The falling wedge is bullish, although placement of the signal often puzzles a chart reader. For example, in Figure 6.12, a falling wedge appears as prices decline. However, the decline was not over. It first moved into a large downward gap, a bullish piercing lines signal, and a volume spike. Only after this series of downward moves did a reversal take place, and it was mild and short-lived.

Falling wedge

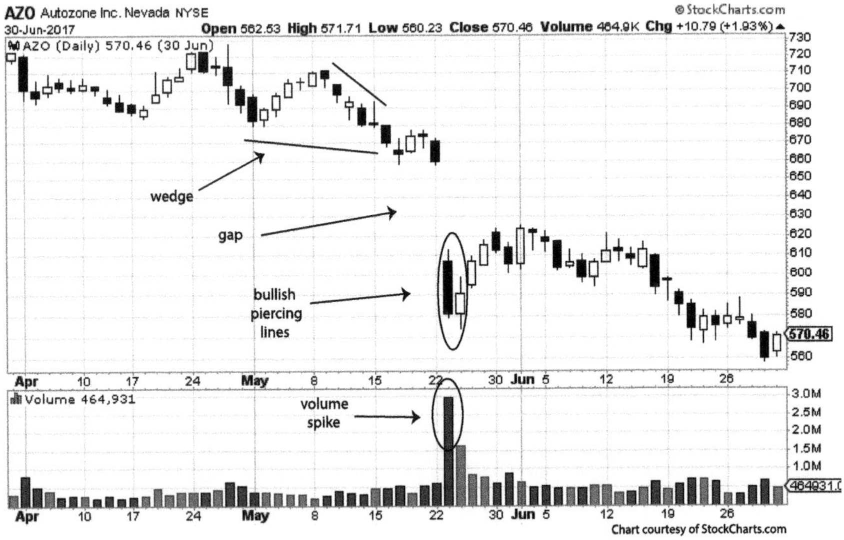

Figure 6.12: Falling wedge

Key Point: A wedge does not have to be extreme to properly identify a coming reversal. Many examples prove that even a slight wedge movement is adequate to foreshadow the change; however, placement often is not what you would expect.

In all of the triangle and wedge examples, changes in the breadth of the trading range define either continuation or reversal. These examples of volatility as a confirming indicator with candlestick analysis are most useful when reviewed in line with other technical signals (such as on-balance volume and CMF and, most of all, as confirming signals of related candlestick moves and patterns).

A problem in both triangles and wedges is that a very slight adjustment in the lines can convert a triangle into a wedge, and vice versa. Since the meaning of each is opposite, this points out the weakness in triangles and wedges. An ascending triangle is a bullish continuation, whereas a rising wedge is a bearish reversal; a descending triangle indicates bearish continuation while a falling wedge is a bullish reversal.

The similarity between triangles and wedges is troubling and points out the need for strong confirmation. Relying too much on these patterns makes you vulnerable to confirmation bias. If you believe price will either continue or reverse, you can easily find a triangle or wedge to suit that bias. Some traders avoid reliance on these price patterns for this reason. However, they serve a purpose as contributors to an overall chart analysis, but caution is advised because of the confusion that may arise due to the similar shape but opposite indication involved.

Any charting system, including candlesticks, is going to put forth false signals on occasion. The value in developing and employing a system is not to eliminate errors, but to reduce them. The result, making well-timed decisions more often, is the desirable outcome. Analysis based on both volume and volatility is valuable because it provides additional confirmation to signals you pick up from observing candlestick signs, moves, and patterns. Spotting weakening trends or continuation signals may clarify what short-term candlestick patterns reveal or seem to reveal.

This combined application of candlesticks and other indicators helps create a powerful system for entry and exit set-up signals. The next chapter explores this point further.

---

[i] Mubarik, F., & Javid, A. Y. (2009). Relationship between Stock Return, Trading Volume and Volatility. *Asia Pacific Journal of Finance and Banking Research*, 3, No. 3, 1–17.
[ii] Westerhoff, F. (2006). Technical Analysis based on Price-Volume Signals and the Power of Trading Breaks. *International Journal of Theoretical and Applied Finance*, 9, No. 2, 227–244.
[iii] Blume, L., Easley, D., & O'Hara, M. (March 1994). Market Statistics and Technical Analysis: The Role of Volume. *The Journal of Finance*, 49, No. 1, 153–181.
[iv] Leigh, W., & Purvis, R. (2008). Implementation and Validation of an Opportunistic Stock Market Timing Heuristic: One-Day Share Volume Spike as Buy Signal. *Expert Systems with Applications*, 35, 1628–1637.
[v] Beaver, W. H. (1968). The Information Content of Annual Earnings Announcements. *Journal of Accounting Research*, 6, 67–92.
[vi] Boehmer, E., & Kelley, E. (2009). Institutional Investors and the Informational Efficiency of Prices. *The Review of Financial Studies*, 22, No. 9, 3563–3594.
[vii] Schoenberger, C. R. (April 6, 2015). The Dark Magic of Month-End Trades. *The Wall Street Journal.*
[viii] Zeigenbein, S. (2011). A Fuzzy Logic Stock Trading System based on Technical Analysis. *All Regis University Theses*, Paper 474.
[ix] Tharavanij, P., Siraprapasiri, V., & Rajchamaha, K. (2015). Performance of Technical Trading Rules: Evidence from Southeast Asian Stock Markets. *SpringerPlus*, 4, 552.
[x] Wang, C., Paulo, V., & Ma, Q. (2015). A Neuroeconomics Analysis of Investment Process with Money Flow Information: The Error-Related Negativity. *Computational Intelligence and Neuroscience*, Article ID 701237.

Chapter 7
Buy and Sell Set-Up Signals

A long-term investor will probably find candlestick patterns interesting, but at the same time might not use them to time short-term trades. In comparison, a trader who relies on candlesticks to time entry and exit decisions is going to rely on candlesticks (as well as traditional technical analysis and volume indicators) to *swing trade* in stock. The swing trader is anyone who wants to make moves in and out of positions to take short-term profits resulting from price spikes (in both directions) and the tendency of the market as a whole to overreact to news.

Swing trade: A trade with a short time in a position, entered after price spikes or percentages above the norm of movement. The purpose is to time short-term profits by trading contrary to the market tendency.

Swing trading is not appropriate for every investor or trader. Portfolio managers, for example, may be constrained to trade in a particular manner and to focus on a "buy and hold" strategy. Conservative investors may also find short-term trading strategies less desirable. Finally, the level of holding (dollar amount as well as number of shares) will dictate whether or not swing trading is appropriate:

> Intuitively, traders with various volumes of shares behave differently and play different roles at affecting stock price. For example, traders with large shares prefer position trading whereas traders will less shares usually pursue swing trading or even day trading.[i]

The decision to swing trade is part of a larger observation of market behavior. Contrarian investors and traders are more likely to find appeal in swing trading due to the nature and tendency of the market itself. The swing trader rightly observes that the market exaggerates the importance of all news. This includes company-specific economic news, domestic and international economic developments, and political change. In other words, everything affects markets, but traders drive prices too high following good news and too low following bad news.

The natural "swing" in price occurs when the overreaction creates buy and sell opportunities and reverses the direction. This normally occurs within two to five trading sessions after the spike in price.

DOI 10.1515/9781501507397-007

Key Point: The key to short-term swing profits is recognizing overreaction in price to both good and bad news.

Traders rely on moving averages for the same reason. Short-term price movement is chaotic and the result of numerous cause and effect drivers. Whenever a dominant factor creates an exaggerated price movement, the swing trader makes a move, buying on price declines and selling (either selling an existing position or selling short) after prices have risen. Everyone has seen examples of this price tendency. Analysis of moving averages, and in particular of the slope of change in the average over time (the trendline), has led some analysts to identify clear relationships between the averages and price. This applies even though moving averages are lagging indicators.[ii]

The role of moving average (MA) has to be cast as one set of indicators among many. For the swing trader and contrarian, MA helps define a "normal" trading range and spot moments when price deviates from it. At such times, a swing away from the norm is likely to occur soon after due to exaggerated price behavior following news.

For example, analysts have estimated that a company will report quarter earnings of seventeen cents per share, but actual results come in at sixteen cents. The stock loses four points on the day of the announcement, but recovers three points over the following two days. This type of price overreaction is common. It dispels the efficient market hypothesis convincingly. An "efficient" market would react logically and reflect little if any movement on a specific day.

In fact, the cited efficiency refers not to markets in general, but to the way in which all publicly known news is taken into account in pricing. The true flaw in the efficient market theory is that it makes no distinction between actual and true news (such as earnings or announcements of mergers) and rumor or gossip. All "news" is treated with the same level of efficiency, and therein lies the flaw in this theory.

The tendency with unexpected news is to experience a two- to five-day set of gyrations in either direction or in both directions in turn. The net effect of news is realized over the entire swing. So a one-cent disappointment in earnings might justify a one-point drop, while actual price movement consists of a jarring four-point drop followed by a three-point reversal.

Rather than an efficient market, the short-term chaos in price reaction demonstrates that the market is driven by two primary emotions. When good news arrives, *greed* takes effect and drives prices up beyond a rational level. When bad news is announced, *fear* dominates and drives prices down too far. Swing traders are able to stand back from these short-term overreactions and recognize that they are extreme. So as contrarian investors, swing traders buy on price declines (knowing that prices are likely to recover) and sell on price increases (knowing that prices are likely to retreat).

The inefficiency of markets exploited by contrarians is found in the tendency among analysts to be overly optimistic in both estimates of earnings and in stock recommendations. A clear bias toward "buy" recommendations over "sell" is part of this problem. However, for proponents of the efficient market theory, the obvious contradiction of the way stock prices behave augments the great advantage contrarians have over the herd mentality of the market:

> Optimism in stock analysts' recommendations contribute to market inefficiency in the equities market. This puts into question the information role of stock analysts and their usefulness to the investing community. In light of the private information contained in analyst recommendation reports, it is intuitive to think that stock prices would become more efficient in the presence of analyst recommendations.[iii]

A believer in efficiency will naturally be puzzled by the often glaring contradictions between assumed efficiency and actual performance. More than anything else, as contrarians know, markets are extremely inefficient, especially in the swing trading window of three to five days. Contrarians exploit inefficiency by ignoring the prevailing market emotions of greed and fear and relying instead on cold, pure logic.

Contrarian investor: A trader or investor who recognizes that markets overreact to news, and who makes buy and sell decisions in a direction opposite to the prevailing trend.

Key Point: Two ruling emotions—greed and fear—cause virtually all of the short-term price movement in the market, followed immediately by correcting price changes. Knowing this is the key to finding entry and exit points.

The well-known price spikes that are typical of price movement, notably in volatile markets, create reaction swings, providing swing traders with a great opportunity. At these times, candlestick signs, moves, and patterns are valuable in improving timing and confirming the best timing of entry into and exit from positions.

Price Spikes and Reaction Swings

A price spike is any change in price above or below the established trading range. Although a spike may signal the beginning of a new trend, it is expected to be followed by a return to the previous range. If a large price move does not lead to a return to the previous range, it is not a true spike. This realization points out the advantage to using spikes as set-up signals for short-term profits.

One definition of an "efficient" market claims that "real stock prices equal the present value of rationally expected or optimally forecasted future real dividends discounted by a constant real discount rate." However, this definition does not work because

> measures of stock price volatility over the past century appear to be far too high—five to thirteen times too high—to be attributed to new information about future real dividends . . . . The failure of the efficient markets model is thus so dramatic that it would seem impossible to attribute the failure to such things as data errors, price index problems, or changes in tax laws.[iv]

Spike: A sudden price move above or below the trading range, which is followed by a return to that range within a few trading sessions.

The failure of the academic model of efficiency highlights the advantage of trading on spikes. Traders who buy after a downward spike to sell after an upward spike are responding to technical inefficiencies that disprove the theory of fundamental efficiency that has never worked in the chaos of the market.

When a spike is also accompanied by large increases in volume, it signals a change in trading range. However, many spikes also occur without any noticeable change in the typical level of trading. When volume does not spike along with price, this usually means that the spike has no lasting importance. In fact, it often occurs that prices spike with no change in volume *until* the price returns to previous levels. When this occurs—price spike with no change in volume, followed by a return to previous volume levels and a price spike—it signals that price is not moving to a new range. Swing traders can take advantage of these short-term adjustments and overreactions by viewing the false signal spike as an entry signal. On the downside, it works as a buy signal (or a signal to close out a previously opened short position), and on the upside, it serves a signal to sell short (or to close previously opened long positions).

For example, the chart in Figure 7.1 shows a departure from the bullish trendline with price gapping downward. The exceptionally long black candle is accompanied in this case by a very prominent price spike. Once this occurs, prices resume the bullish move and trend upward once again. This is an example of a spike representing a temporary move and not a breakout in the established price direction.

Price spike

Chart courtesy of StockCharts.com

Figure 7.1: Price spike

In this case, the spike did not lead to an immediate return to the established range but instead to a longer-term adjustment. Volume also spiked, providing a strong signal that no breakout was underway. Instead this was a puzzling price reaction to an earnings report. On May 11, the company beat earnings estimates, setting up a positive earnings surprise. Overall weakness in projections for future revenue and earnings level led to the decline, but the price bounced back quickly in spite of negative estimates for the future.

Key Point: A price spike is most significant when volume also spikes. However, a volume spike occurring after a price spike is also noteworthy.

A completely different situation evolved in the chart in Figure 7.2. This chart reveals a very large price gap with two candlestick reversal signals (identical white crows and morning star). The spike occurred with an upside gap and a session with a large upper shadow (indicating weakness among buyers and predicting a price retreat). This was confirmed by the bearish engulfing signal, leading to a downward gap. The downtrend faltered in mid-June and appeared to be turning, but a new reversal occurred with the bearish evening star.

This busy chart reveals how candlesticks work along with gaps. For swing traders, this set of price gaps and candlesticks presented a rich opportunity for swing trades.

Price spike and gap

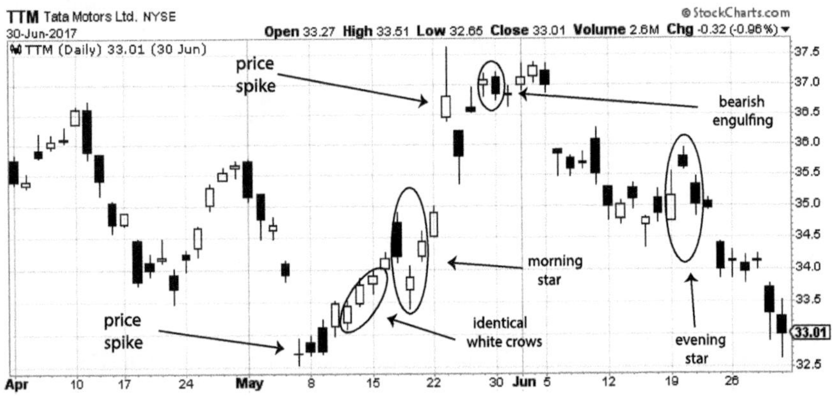

Chart courtesy of StockCharts.com

Figure 7.2: Price spike and gap

Another important price pattern is the reaction swing, a rapid turn in price direction accompanied by strong candlestick reversal signals. The tendency for price after a big move is to retrace to the previous range, whether or not a price or volume spike is part of the pattern.

Reaction swing: A tendency for short-term prices to return to an established trading range following a price spike.

The causes of reaction swings may be far more complex than the well-known swing following earnings surprises. A broader positive or negative sense among investors and traders further determines how reaction swings occur. The observation is offered that

> investors swing between being optimistic and being pessimistic in their interpretation of the new information driven by not only the prevailing market uncertainty and sentiment but also by a significant number of firm-specific characteristics. Pessimism prevails when uncertainty is high, sentiment is weak and the information is being disseminated by companies that are lowly-valued, have high risk, are thinly traded and/or are small cap stocks. However, investors swing to being optimistic when one reverses some or all of these factors. The conclusion that we draw is that risk, uncertainty and the attitude of investors combine to determine how the markets react to new information and this flows through to asset valuations.[V]

The reaction swing—whether caused primarily by current news or by broader investor sentiment—is easily recognized when it takes place in an isolated trading day; however, it can also occur in a series of trading sessions. For example, Figure 7.3 contains a chart with a scaling of only 1.5 points but a high degree of volatility, including two strong reaction swings. The first one follows a brief downtrend and is identified with a morning star. This reaction swing is unusually strong due to the long white session in the third position of the signal. On the other side, a bearish reaction swing is marked by an equally strong long white session in the first day of the bearish dark cloud cover. This was confirmed immediately by the bearish engulfing signal.

Reaction swing

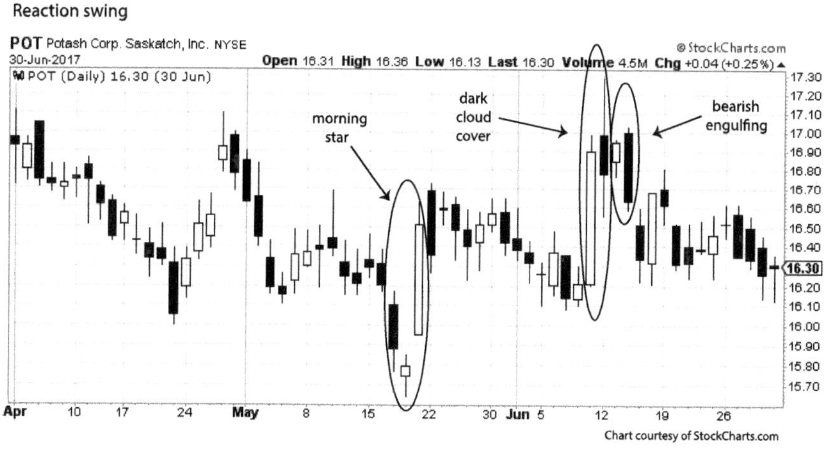

Figure 7.3: Reaction swing

The reaction swing is often convincing and offsets the uncertainty found when reversal signals are weak or unconfirmed. The strength of the signal forecasts equal strength in the price movement to follow.

Key Point: Recognizing the uncertainty of what will happen next is just as valuable as a clear reversal signal. Uncertainty is an indication to stay out of positions until the picture clears up.

The uncertainty of price action during and after a price spike can lead to false signals, a time when additional confirmation such as volume trends is valuable. Another useful indicator is the occurrence of a new high or new low in prices on a fifty-two-week basis. A spike may occur at such a time. If price has been trending downward and concludes with a downside spike at the fifty-two-week low, that may be a strong signal that the downtrend is ending. If this confirms what you see in the candlestick pattern and volume of the same time, it works as a very good entry indicator. The same is true on the upside. As a stock's price reaches its fifty-two-week high, experiences an upside spike, and also has exceptionally high volume, it works as a short-side entry signal or as a sell signal for previously entered long positions.

Percentage Swing Systems

Adhering to a candlestick-based system accompanied by volume and other indicators is perhaps the most reliable method of timing entry and exit from positions. An alternative is to rely on percentage swing systems, or systems signaling entry or exit based on the degree of price movement away from the previous trading range.

Percentage swing system: A method of timing entry and exit based on the percentage by which price moves above or below the previously established trading range.

The problem with the percentage system is that it is fixed and is not based on the patterns of candlesticks. The relative strength or weakness of an evolving candlestick price trend may not be supported in an inflexible percentage of change; it is more likely that strength or weakness in price movement is going to be reflected in candlestick patterns, even when only a small percentage of change has occurred. The percentage system works in varying degrees, at times giving out an entry or exit signal at the wrong time. Its best application occurs when the percentage of price change is supported by candlestick reversal signals.

For example, Figure 7.4 forecasts a downward move with the three inside down candlestick pattern. Although the preceding uptrend was mild, the reversal was strong, consisting of a large gap and a long black candlestick. Further confirmation was found in the 20% decline in price.

Percentage of change system

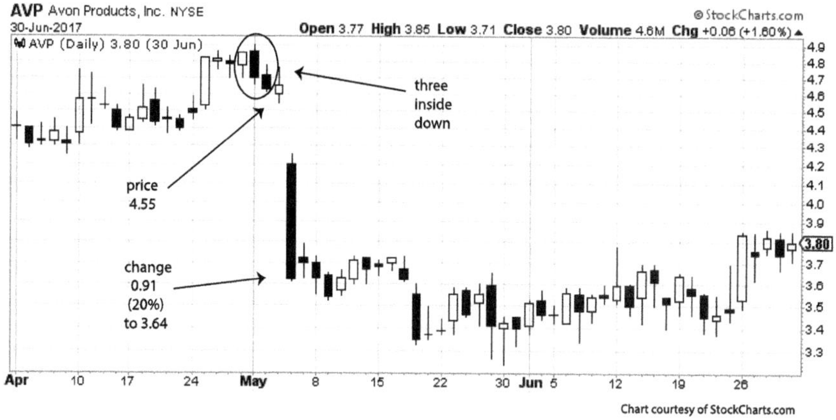

Figure 7.4: Percentage of change system

The use of this system is based on a predetermined percentage to signal a trade. However, by the time the change occurred, it was too late to exploit it. Price settled into a two-month consolidation period.

This is one of the problems with percentage-based systems. Signals are often recognized too late. If you waited for the 20% decrease in price, you would enter this position *after* growth. A contrarian point of view after this growth would be to sell rather than to buy. Both decisions—buying after the downtrend or selling—would have been wrong in this case. A stronger signal to confirm a bullish stand is the combination of the candlestick formation with gaps and exceptionally high volume.

These data can be distorted with little effort through distortions of market activity. For example, a "pump and dump" tactic creates large percentage moves in some instances, especially with the use of online chat rooms and message boards. In the typical pump and dump, a trader invests in a security and then enters online rooms to generate interest, often in the form of rumor and prediction of big price increases. If this works, the price of the security is driven up, at which point the trader sells shares and earns a profit, while other traders are stuck with overvalued shares. The SEC describes this illegal activity on their website:

> "Pump-and-dump" schemes involve the touting of a company's stock (typically small, so-called "microcap" companies) through false and misleading statements to the marketplace. These false claims could be made on social media such as Facebook and Twitter, as well as on bulletin boards and chat rooms. Pump-and-dump schemes often occur on the Internet where it is common to see messages posted that urge readers to buy a stock quickly or to sell before the price goes down, or a telemarketer will call using the same sort of pitch. Often the promoters will claim to have "inside" information about an impending development or to use an "infallible" combination of economic and stock market data to pick stocks. In reality, they may be company insiders or paid promoters who stand to gain by selling their shares after the stock price is "pumped" up by the buying frenzy they create. Once these fraudsters "dump" their shares and stop hyping the stock, the price typically falls, and investors lose their money.[vi]

The practice is artificial and distorts systems such as percentage-based predictive timing. The level of discussion online also tends to be overly bullish, also distorting what otherwise might be a measured and analytical attribute of any system.

> Even after controlling for news in print media, we find evidence that the message boards reflect the views of day traders. At daily frequency an increase in the number of messages predicts a subsequent increase in trading volume and volatility; particularly marked is the surge in small size trades. We also find that trades increase with the bullishness of posted messages, while trades decrease with greater agreement among message posters.[vii]

Key Point: Entry and exit based on percentage systems works at times, but not consistently. No matter how promising the approach sounds, timing is better with a focus on candlestick trends and not on price movement percentages.

A percentage change system can be used as a confirming signal to candlestick patterns (further confirmed by additional technical indicators such as volume tracking signals). It can also be applied in a contrarian manner. For example, if price moves down 20%, that could be seen as a sign of a coming correction. In the example provided, that would not have worked.

Short-Term Gapping Behavior

A more reliable timing system than percentage change is based on tracking a stock's "true range," or the analysis of price movement between days rather than in an isolated single-day range. In the typical daily trading range, the previous day's activity is completely ignored. This is the most popular method, but it ignores what is often extremely valuable information.

True range: A stock's trading range within a trend rather than a single trading session. It includes the previous session's closing price and the current session's price movement.

Even considering the potential advantages of combining two or more days to create a "true range" of activity in a security, the practice is vulnerable to confirmation bias. It often is the case that a desired conclusion can be reached by combining trading activity over time, setting up artificial signals. One of the basic tenets of candlestick analysis is that each session stands alone as part of a broader price trend, and signals develop from session to session. When this concept is adjusted by combining periods, it destroys the consistency of comparison between sessions of the same duration (trading days, for example). An observed range is not necessarily identical to the true range, so price, and volatility, may both be distorted by application of true range:

> The properties of the range-based estimator . . . depend on the level of trading activity. In particular, when there are only a few trades per day, the observed range can be far from the true range of the underlying price process and, as a result, range-based volatility estimates can substantially deviate from the true volatility.[viii]

Key Point: It is amazing how different the trend looks when changes between days are taken into account. It clarifies the trend and points out the flaw in myopic review only of session-specific action.

True range consists of the previous session's closing price, carried through to the current session's price movement. In this analysis, you seek the otherwise invisible gaps that often take place between days. The obvious gaps are easy to spot. The range of a candlestick's trades gaps from day to day. But another type of gap may be equally significant. It is the overnight change between prior close and current open. This gapping trend can occur in a number of configurations, which are summarized in Figure 7.5.

Overnight gapping trends

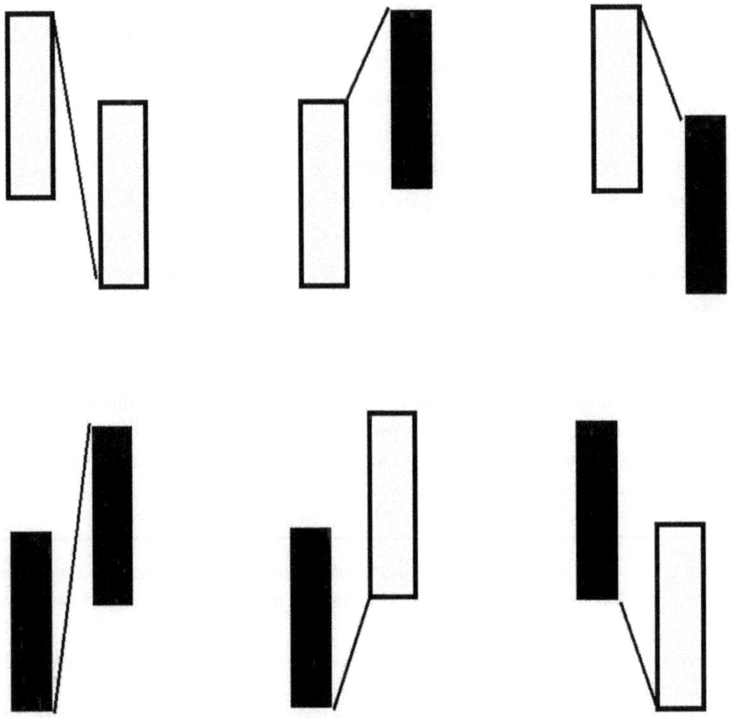

Figure 7.5: Overnight gapping trend

Gapping trend: Any trend involving price gaps, especially between trading sessions in which the gaps are not immediately visible.

The real bodies in all six of these gapping sessions overlap between days. This means that the overnight gapping trend is invisible. If you only look at each day's open and close, you will not notice this important gapping trend. Gaps themselves set up some of the most reliable reversal signals. The idea behind this is that excessive gapping action represents exaggerated or excessive price movement. When this occurs, a reversal is likely.

Gaps, however, do not always provide exceptional signaling value. Some studies have concluded that many patterns (including gaps) are strong indicators, but others have disagreed:

> Regarding the ability of predicting future prices through pattern recognition methods, there are numerous studies which provide evidence that there exist patterns with predictive capability that can indicate the potential of getting profits. On the other hand, there are studies that reject this evidence and support that price patterns have no value or capability to produce trading profits.[ix]

The point is that gaps, like all price patterns, have to be viewed in a larger context of price behavior, signal proximity to resistance or support, and confirmation. An example with repetitive gapping price activity is shown in Figure 7.6. The upward move begins with the bullish reversal signal, piercing lines. A sixteen-point bullish trend takes place over the next two weeks, but is characterized by three consecutive gaps. Forming a bullish reversal, the three gap upside. The last gap is invisible, but the final black session opens with a gap above the previous close. The reversal is confirmed by the dark cloud cover.

Gapping trend anticipating price reversal

Figure 7.6: Gapping trend anticipating price reversal

Key Point: A visible gap is easy to spot, but it is not always the entire picture. Gaps are revealing when the true distance between open and close from one day to the next reveals the gap's real extent.

Another example of the gapping trend is seen in the chart in Figure 7.7. Once again, a three-gap upside set up the likely reversal. This was confirmed by the bearish three outside down, which led to a long black session and further downward moves. By late May, all of the gains in the gapping uptrend were reversed. This demonstrates the vulnerability of any trend that moves too rapidly, especially with gapping price behavior.

Figure 7.7: Excessive gaps and reversal

This chart displays a series of repetitive gaps during an uptrend, followed by a strong and very sudden reversal. A series of gaps are likely to mean that price moved too far in one direction; a reversal should be expected. This trend led to a strong reversal. An astute chartist would have recognized that the upward price gaps were a danger signal.

Anticipating the Trend During Consolidation

Entry and exit set-up signals help anticipate coming price direction, whether reversal or continuation. A swing trading strategy is especially effective when playing with price movement caused by the institutional investor. The individual (retail) investor has an advantage in two respects. First, the majority of price movement and its cause and effect belong to the institutional investors. Second, the individual can move quickly in and out of positions without having to worry that a big block trade will influence the price of a security. Institutional investors have to act slowly and cautiously because of their influence on stock prices.

This reality points to a clear advantage held by individuals over institutions. You are able to move in and out of positions by trading on the emotions that rule the market. Most trades take place based on reaction to institutional influence. This is why greed (on the way up) and fear (on the way down) are the driving forces behind the majority of individual stock trades, executed by "the crowd" that as often as not is misinformed and that times trades poorly. If you are able to put aside the tendency to trade based on emotions, you stand an excellent chance of improving your entry and exit timing.

Key Point: Individuals can move quickly and easily in and out of positions. This is an advantage over the large institutional investor who cannot move large blocks of shares as readily.

Swing trading is a system based on exploiting the very short-term price trends resulting from the emotions dominating the market. Traders adhering to this system focus on a short list of stocks with desirable attributes: moderate volatility, strong technical signals, and a tendency to track the market closely (thus when the indicators rise, so does the stock, and vice versa). This is known as beta. The overall market has beta of 1, so a stock that also has a beta of 1 is tracking the market exactly.

Beta: A measure of how closely a security moves with the market. Beta of 1 indicates exact movement with the larger market; beta under 1 indicates low responsiveness. Beta above 1 is a sign of greater risk than overall markets.

A swing trader working with a short list of favored stocks trades emotions of the market in a two- to five-day range, rather than trading stocks based on fundamental merit. A swing trader may initially select stocks based on the strength of fundamentals as part of the selection criteria, but timing entry and exit requires recognition of candlestick patterns, unusual volume spikes, changes in volatility, and proven technical indicators.

By trading emotions instead of stocks, entry and exit timing is likely to improve vastly because you acknowledge the overreaction of price based on the greed and fear that are present at all times in the market. The only respite comes during periods of sideways price movement. Swing traders, in fact, rely on an uninformed and overreacting marketplace to identify opportunities. As a swing trader, you interact with market forces by knowing when other traders are ready to give up shares of stock too cheaply or to buy shares from you that have become too expensive. It does not come naturally to many people to make decisions based on rational, calculated observation. Many traders time their moves emotionally and as a gut reaction, and this is a great advantage to the analytical swing trader.

The pauses between uptrends and downtrends—periods of consolidation—occur because buyers and sellers are more or less in agreement about two points. First, the relatively narrow trading range appears to be reasonable for the moment. Second, no one knows which dynamic trend (bullish or bearish) will take place next. The belief that consolidation is merely a pause between trends is incorrect; consolidation is itself a trend moving sideways. The emotion dominating this sideways price period of consolidation is uncertainty. Few people are content with knowing that buyers and sellers agree on price. It is preferable to recognize when one side or the other is in command.

Consolidation: A period in which a narrow trading range is in effect and little if any movement occurs. This is likely to occur in between upward or downward trends and reflects uncertainty in the market about future price direction.

In some periods of consolidation, it is not uncertainty but confusion that rules price. It may also mean that most technical traders do not know how to read the trend, so both buyers and sellers wait out the market. This is where reading candlestick moves and patterns can help you to get a jump on the next trend.

Consolidation presents an exceptional opportunity for chartists who know how to read candlestick signals. A *reversal* does not refer only to price direction but to changes in trends as well. So the most well-known reversal is from bull to bear or bear to bull. However, a reversal from either of these to consolidation should also be acknowledged as prices stop moving and plateau. Finally, reversal also applies to a breakout from consolidation to a bullish or bearish trend.

For example, Figure 7.8 contains an example of how this form of reversal works. Following a two-month consolidation trend, a failed breakout below support led price back into range. A bullish piercing lines signal was the first sign of a likely bullish breakout. Such signals are known to occur at the point of a failed breakout, pointing to likely movement in the opposite direction. Within two weeks, a strong bullish breakout appeared with a very strong bullish reversal signal, the window rising.

Breakout from consolidation

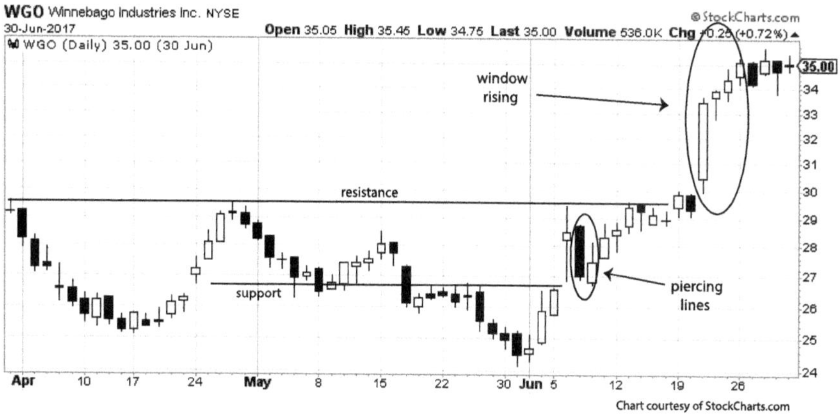

Figure 7.8: Breakout from consolidation

Chartists who adhere to the belief that consolidation is only a pause between dynamic trends miss an opportunity. These chartists also believe that a signal is not possible because there is no trend to reverse. However, once traders accept the argument that reversal applies to trends, not only to price, they will find ample opportunities to anticipate breakout. The combination on this chart of the failed breakout below support and the bullish piercing lines would have been able to spot a likely bullish breakout.

Breakouts would be difficult to spot without the visual character of candlestick indicators. It helps overcome a traditional statistical bias in analysis, making issues such as breakouts easier to recognize:

> Technical analysis is primarily visual, whereas quantitative finance is primarily algebraic and numerical. Therefore, technical analysis employs the tools of geometry and pattern recognition, and quantitative finance employs the tools of mathematical analysis and probability and statistics. In the wake of recent breakthroughs in financial engineering, computer technology, and numerical algorithms, it is no wonder that quantitative finance has overtaken technical analysis in popularity—the principles of portfolio optimization are far easier to program into a computer than the basic tenets of technical analysis. Nevertheless, technical analysis has survived through the years, perhaps because its visual mode of analysis is more conducive to human cognition, and because pattern recognition is one of the few repetitive activities for which computers do not have an absolute advantage (yet).[X]

This feature allows an analyst to spot breakout and, by also studying the strength or weakness of accompanying signals, to determine whether the price pattern is more likely to succeed or to fail. However, even with the best signals and confirmation, many indicators, even strong ones, may end up being false and could mislead a trader rather than help to improve timing.

The False Indicator

Every trader seeks a reliable set of indicators to improve timing of both entry and exit. Knowing what signals mean requires skill in pattern recognition. The stronger the reversal signal, the better your timing will become. Swing traders have to be concerned with two issues. First, they want to get the most from the swing trade, which means knowing when an apparent signal is false and no action should be taken. Second is to know when to close the current position and whether to wait out the trend or perform a true swing.

You can use candlestick moves and patterns to not only identify a short-term trend, but also to decide how strong or weak the signal is. Some signals are quite strong and are confirmed by candlestick developments, volume changes, and other technical patterns. Others are tentative or contradictory. Identifying the difference further improves your timing in entering and exiting the swing trade. There is a point in every trend in which the "last gasp" of price movement is apparent. This is easily recognized in hindsight when you look back to see what signals were there just before the price turned. It is not as easy to spot these signs at the time. The key is to seek combinations of signals that confirm one another. However, it is also crucial to realize that some signals provide false indicators.

Key Point: Confirmation is the key to chart analysis and timing of both entry and exit. Candlestick patterns combined with other technical indicators improve your interpretation of trends.

Observing changes in price and volume at the same time is a rudimentary but reliable method for identifying likely reversal. However, this is not foolproof. Instances of false indicators point to the importance of strong confirmation and also to the acknowledgment that no signal is 100% reliable. In some cases, even the best reversal signal will turn out to be false.

Key Point: A simple observation of changes in price and volume together is one form of confirming technical information that usually points out exactly which direction price is heading next.

False signals are common and may recur in a single chart. This is one attribute of technical analysis, and candlestick patterns may fail as easily as any other form of price reversal. For example, the chart in Figure 7.9 contains four specific false signals.

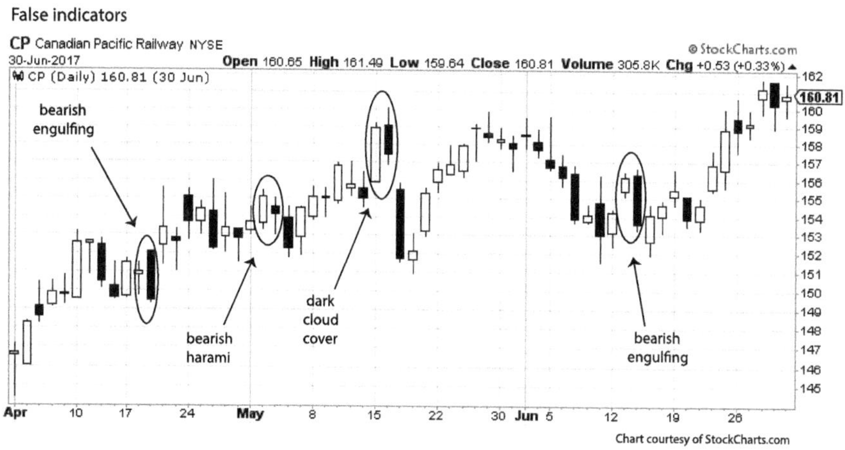

Figure 7.9: False indicators

The engulfing pattern is considered one of the strongest reversals and is among the most reliable. However, the first one failed to produce a bearish price move. As price continued moving upward after the engulfing signal, a second bearish reversal, the *harami*, appeared. This also failed to produce a bearish move even though it would be considered confirmation of the engulfing. As price peaked, the dark cloud cover was the strongest, most convincing, and bearish reversal signal on the chart. Although price declined for the next two sessions, a bearish trend could not get established. Finally, another bearish engulfing signal predicted a downward move, but instead price continued moving upward.

The repetitive bearish failed signals would be discouraging to a trader relying on signals and confirmation. However, this simply makes the point that in some instances, candlesticks do not lead to the price behavior that they predict.

A closely related problem is that of weak response. There is no guarantee that a reversal will be long lasting, even with the strongest of reversal signals and confirmation. This is one reason that swing traders prefer limiting their trade duration to a small number of sessions. A reversal may last weeks or months or it may last only a matter of days.

For example, in Figure 7.10, an exceptionally strong set of reversal signals and confirmation at first appears to promise a strong downtrend; although a downtrend occurred, it lasted only through one gap, then consolidated for two weeks and finally reversed and led to a new uptrend.

Repetitive price gaps

Figure 7.10: Repetitive price gaps

The initial three-gap upside points to an excessively quick trend, which is expected to retrace and give back some of the price gaps. In fact, the potential for a bearish move was confirmed twice, first by the dark cloud cover and then by the bearish engulfing. All of these signals are strong, especially when they occur in close proximity. But the predicted bearish trend lasted for only one gap and signal, and consequently the set of bearish signals combined to yield a false indicator.

The lesson in all of this is that reliability of candlestick signals is high when confirmed, but never absolute. The way to guard against loss in events such as this is to diversify the amount of capital at risk among several different trades and to utilize a consistent level of investment without taking exceptional risks. A great flaw in trader thinking is to become convinced that a set of signals is so strong that reversal is certain. With that mindset, a large dollar amount is placed into a trade. When the strongly confirmed signals end up to have been false, a large loss results. This demonstrates that resisting a tendency toward greed (and on the other side toward panic) is a wise form of self-discipline.

Another example of how a combination of signals may be false is shown in Figure 7.11. Here, repetitive price gaps broke from consolidation and moved price from the bottom of the chart to near the top. Once price stabilized, the bearish *harami* cross pointed to high likelihood of reversal. However, this did not occur, and for the remainder of the period shown, price moved into a new consolidation, moving gradually upward.

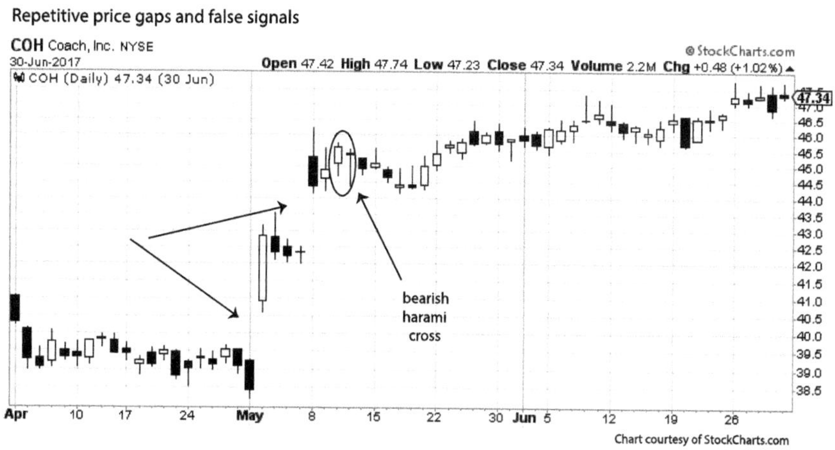

Figure 7.11: Repetitive price gaps and false signals

The instances of failed signals are rare, but they occur, and that is the point. You need to protect exposure to false signals by limiting the amount of cash placed into single trades. This is why swing traders tend to prefer using options rather than shares of stock for short-term trades. The highly leveraged long option allows control of 100 shares of stock for a very small percentage of the cost, often as low as 3% (thus an options trader gets the same price activity for a $100 stock for only 3% of the cost of 100 shares [$10,000], or $300 per option).

Key Point: The risks associated with false signals are mitigated by using leverage gained with long options, reducing exposure while producing the same result as that of 100 shares of stock.

Support and Resistance in the Swing Trade

The confirmation of signals in the isolation of a few trading sessions can be revealing, but it always makes more sense to analyze the emerging pattern in a larger context. How does the apparent signal conform with (or contradict) established support and resistance levels?

Trading is expected to remain within the established trading range. When a breakout occurs, prices tend to quickly retreat as the breakout fails and is reversed. The exception is a breakout that remains permanent. The new range is going to be tested and a tendency is for one side or the other to overextend, requiring a range correction immediately afterward. This general rule of thumb helps to further determine whether a signal or combination of signals is exceptionally strong or suspiciously weak.

Key Point: It is reassuring when prices remain in the established trading range. Breakouts are exciting and unavoidable, but they introduce more risk and more uncertainty.

The trading range, bordered by resistance at the top and support at the bottom, is the visual summary of supply and demand for a company's shares. Swing traders generally operate within the trading range, with prices bouncing between resistance and support and presenting short-term trading opportunities. A conservative-leaning swing trader may close out positions when prices go through a breakout, recognizing that any number of scenarios can play out. For the "range-bound" swing trader, this is a safe hedge against the possibility of making an expensive mistake by misreading the signals. What may work reliably within an established trading range could present falsely during and after a breakout period. After a breakout has taken place (as many of the previously presented charts display), false signals may also appear.

Combining candlestick moves and patterns with the position in a trading range (or, more to the point, when prices go through a breakout), you will be able to judge buy and sell set-up signals more accurately. In studying candlestick patterns in both cases—those resulting in breakout and those with price remaining range bound—you can judge the strength of support and resistance and better determine the significance of a trend.

For example, Figure 7.12 shows how a subtle indicator of potential breakout below support led to a fast price decline. The bearish *doji* sandwich not only added a hint of coming price movement, but also took price below support in the third session. Although this move was slight, the *doji* sandwich was confirmed immediately by the second bearish signal, the meeting lines. The gap that followed was proof of the success in the bearish breakout.

Support and breakout

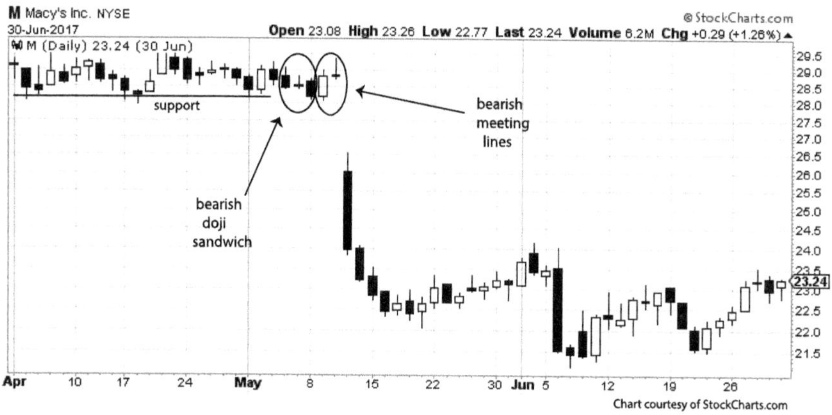

Figure 7.12: Support and breakout

In this case, the signals confirmed a likely movement below support. However, even within a trading range, the indicated signal is not always reliable as confirmation. It is possible that conflicting and contradictory signals will develop at times, adding to uncertainty, at least until a stronger set of signal and confirmation appears.

Key Point: Some technical signals contradict one another as price bounces back and forth within the trading range. At such times, seek a strong candlestick-based development to anticipate a price breakout.

Breakout above resistance follows a similar pattern as breakout below support. In Figure 7.13, resistance rose gradually until the strong bullish reversal appeared in the form of three white soldiers. This led to a higher move with no signs of a retreat back to previous trading range levels.

Figure 7.13: Resistance and breakout

Even with strong signals of breakout, the price move may fail. There are no assurances even with strong signal and confirmation. For example, in Figure 7.14, a gradually declining resistance suddenly ended when prices gapped higher. This was short-lived, however, and an offsetting bearish signal, three black crows, pointed to a likely return to the previous trend of slowly falling resistance.

Figure 7.14: Failed breakout

The analysis of candlestick patterns is a sensible trading system when combined with other technical indicators and, equally important, when reviewed in the context of basics like the trading range and the existence of double or triple tops and bottoms, head and shoulders formations, gapping patterns, and other well-known technical chart developments. However, technical analysis combines art with science and at times is elusive. The search for absolute guarantees about the next price move inevitably leads to an understanding: Candlesticks are among the most reliable of technical indicators but, like weather forecasting, they are vulnerable to inaccuracy and unexpected failures. However, those using candlesticks along with other indicators should expect to see improved timing in entry and exit, but never at 100%.

In the next chapter, the discussion of technical indicators is expanded to explain how to effectively improve swing trading techniques with candlesticks and other signals.

---

[i] Sun, X., Shen, H., & Cheng, X. (2014). Trading Network Predicts Stock Price. *Scientific Reports*, 4, 3711.

[ii] Neftci, S. N., & Policano, A. J. (1984). Can Chartists Outperform the Market? Market Efficiency Tests for "Technical Analysis." *Journal of Futures Markets*, 4, No. 4, 465–478.

[iii] Guiliani, J. M. (2012). Is Analyst Over Optimism Creating Price Inefficiency in the Stock Market? *All Graduate Plan B and other Reports*, Paper 171.

[iv] Shiller, R. (1981). Do Stock Prices Move Too Much to Be Justified by Subsequent Changes in Dividends? *American Economic Review*, 71, 421–436.

[v] Bird, R., & Yeung, D. (2011). The Relationship between Uncertainty and the Market Reaction to Information: How Is It Influenced by Market and Stock-Specific Characteristics? *International Journal of Behavioural Accounting and Finance*, 4, No. 2.

[vi] Securities and Exchange Commission (SEC), at https://www.sec.gov/fast-answers/answerspumpdumphtm.html, retrieved August 24, 2017.

[vii] Antweiler, W., & Frank, M. Z. (2004). Is All that Talk Just Noise? The Information Content of Internet Stock Message Boards. *Journal of Finance*, 59, No. 3, 1259–1294.

[viii] Sassan, A., Brandt, M. W., & Diebold, F. X. (June 2002). Range-Based Estimation of Stochastic Volatility Models. *The Journal of Finance*, LVII, No. 3., 1047–1091

[ix] Goumatianos, N., Christou, I., & Lindgren, P. (July 2014). Intraday Business Model Strategies on Forex Markets: Comparing the Performance of Price Pattern Recognition Methods. *Journal of Multi Business Model Innovation and Technology*, 2, 1–34.

[x] Lo, A. W., Mamaysky, H., & Wang, J. (August 2000). Foundations of Technical Analysis: Computational Algorithms, Statistical Inference, and Empirical Implementation. *The Journal of Finance*, LV, No. 4, 1705–1765.

Chapter 8
Swing Trading with Candlesticks

In the last chapter, finding buy and sell set-up signals made the point that distinct patterns emerge to help improve trade timing. This approach—short-term trading based on the tendency of markets to overreact to both good and bad news—is widely known as swing trading. However, far from a "sure thing," even the strongest patterns and best forms of confirmation give out false signals at times. Recognizing the subtle differences between breakout or reversal and the coincidental movement of price and shapes of candlesticks are skills developed with time and practice.

Swing trading is based on the belief that it is possible to beat the averages of the market by applying logical, recognizable signals and price patterns, exploiting the emotional tendencies in the larger market. To those who believe in the efficient market hypothesis (EMH), this is a worthless endeavor. A truly efficient market would offer no opportunities to gain an advantage. In the real world of practitioners, trading with real money, EMH is disproven time and again.

> The efficient market hypothesis (EMH) is a cornerstone of financial economics. The EMH asserts that security prices fully reflect all available information and that the stock market prices securities at their fair values. Therefore, investors cannot consistently "beat the market" because stocks reside in perpetual equilibrium, making research efforts futile. This flies in the face of the conventional nonacademic wisdom that astute analysts can beat the market using technical or fundamental stock analysis.[i]

This chapter is based on the concept that EMH refers to how information is efficiently taken into account in price; however, it makes no distinction between valid and true information, versus rumor and false information. The approach here is to explore this practical view by describing technical tools to expand swing trading and timing of entry and exit. This is based on the effective use of candlestick signs, moves, and patterns, the one-, two-, and three-day indicators representing the essential insights gained through candlestick analysis. In fact, candlestick signals are viewed by many as containing attributes strengthening the belief that it is possible to identify methods for outperforming the average market. Part of that has to do with the often irrational practices among traders, tending to rely on gut reaction and impulse rather than on logic. This has led to "the increasing popularity of technical analysis with practitioners and the growing evidence that investors do not always act rationally, have caused academic finance to take another look at technical analysis."[ii]

DOI 10.1515/9781501507397-008

A Swing Trading Overview

The "swing" involved with swing trading is usually described solely as movement of price between high and low levels. These levels are likely to be found within the trading range bordered by resistance and support. These swings take place between two and five days, although short-term trends can last longer as well. Entry and exit signals consist of popular patterns and developments, including the appearance of consecutive directional candles. These candlestick trends are defined as a series of days with higher highs and higher lows (uptrend) or lower lows and lower highs (downtrend). The second popular swing trading signal is the narrow range day (NRD), better known among candlestick chartists as a *doji*. The third of three strong signals is an unusually high volume spike. In combination, these basic swing trading patterns are the core of a timing strategy.

However, finding a "perfect" signal or combination of signals is not always an easy task.

> Under the technical school of thought trading rules are developed by studying historical market data to find trends that investors can exploit. These market trends tend to appear when certain features (narrow range, DOJI, etc.) appear in the historical data. Unfortunately, these features often appear only in partial form, which makes trend analysis challenging.[iii]

The difficulty of finding perfect swing trade set-up signals points to the need for confirmation in the form of candlesticks and other signals. Combinations of the basic swing signals are exceptionally strong indicators of reversal. So when a short-term candlestick trend concludes with a *doji*, it is possible that the price direction is about to change. The *doji* combined with a volume spike is even stronger. It means that all trading for the day took place within a very small range and that volume was high.

Key Point: Swing trading signals require confirmation before being acknowledged as definite entry or exit indicators. Confirmation is the key element to identifying an action point.

These are the well-known indicators used by swing traders. Because trading is done on the swing, there are a few variations of the technique, and these are worth examining:

1. *Entry only at the bottom.* The most conservative swing trader avoids shorting stock. This trader believes shorting to be far too risky to include in a strategy. As a result, only bottom-swing, long-side transactions are made. An en-

try signal is looked for at the bottom of a downtrend and an exit is looked for at the top.

The advantage to bottom-only entry is that it restricts activity to long positions, making it a lower-risk approach. The disadvantage is that it misses half of the opportunities inherent in swing trading. The swing trader knows that overreaction within the market takes place not only after a downtrend, but also after an uptrend. So in exchange for less risk, the long position swing trader takes part only in reversals of downtrends. In markets that are overbought and due for downside correction, there are going to be many missed opportunities.

2. *Entry only at the top.* An exceptionally bearish swing trader believes that the market is generally overbought and due for downside corrections. Accordingly, this trader views uptrends as aberrations in the longer-term bear market. Distrustful of any uptrend, the bear-oriented swing trader—like the bottom-only long trader—misses half of the swing trading opportunities. The top-only trader shorts stock when uptrends show signs of reversal or buy put options to play the market in the same way but with less risk.

   The major advantage to this approach is that when the bear is correct, the short-term downtrends tend to be rapid and extreme. So a bear swing trader is likely to earn many short-term profits above those of the swing trader entering at the bottom for short-term uptrends. The major disadvantage is that the bear trader only trusts half of the swing opportunities and uses shorted stock in a high-risk strategy or uses long puts while not also using long calls at the bottom.

3. *Entry and exit at the same time on both sides.* The flexible swing trader is not concerned with long-term market trends, but focuses on exploiting overreaction by other traders. This trader recognizes that short-term price movement is emotional and often irrational, and fast moves represent short-term opportunities on both sides of the trade. As a result, this swing trader enters a long stock position at the bottom of a downtrend and exits at the top. Using the same point of view about uptrends, reversal signals lead to short entry at the top and closing the position at the bottom. The dual approach can be employed on a single stock or on different stocks going through varying trends. For example, one issue may be bottoming out at the same time that another is going through a strong uptrend.

   The advantage to swing trading on both sides is that it enables you to take part in market overreaction in both uptrends and downtrends. It can also be employed on a range of stocks at the same time, but undergoing a variety of different price trends. The disadvantage is that playing both sides of the swing doubles risk exposure. It also requires shorting at the top if stock positions are employed in the strategy instead of long puts.

Swing trading in its highest form involves entry and exit at both sides of the swing. The flexibility allows you to trade based on current conditions and the exaggerated movement of price so often experienced. It can also apply to a single stock. In that case, a reversal signal involves two transactions: closing a current swing position in one direction and opening another at the same time. Thus as an uptrend signals a reversal, a long position is closed and replaced with a short position, and as a downtrend concludes, the short is closed and replaced with an offsetting long position.

A related issue for swing traders is the cost involved, the brokerage fees charged upon entry and again upon exit. With this in mind, a minimal level of return is not acceptable unless trading takes place in volume. This requires that traders set goals based on the net outcome after brokerage fees.

> Although ignoring short-term signals' predictive information is wasteful, the cost-to-benefit ratio of trading on such information may not appear to make sense at first glance—after all, paying $10 for $3 of expected revenues is not good business if you try to trade on this information alone.[iv]

With increasingly lower costs charged today by online brokers, the trading cost is a shrinking concern. Even so, it cannot be ignored in calculating breakeven points and net rate of return.

Key Point: Many swing trade action points involve both exit and entry; however, this also doubles your risk. A poorly timed double move equals twice the potential loss.

The use of short positions makes profitability more attainable while also increasing the risk. Adding in the brokerage cost places more pressure on what is required to exceed breakeven and avoid loss. If the timing is wrong or the two-part transaction is made in response to a false signal, you not only lose the opportunity for further profits in the first position, but you stand to lose more in the replacement position as well. For this reason, it makes sense to isolate uptrends and downtrends between two or more different stocks. When a current trend ends, the position is exited. Reentry does not occur in that issue until a new signal emerges. This is a more prudent course than a close-and-open reverse swing position. However, depending on the strength of the reversal indicator, it makes the most sense to keep an open mind about the strategic and risk approach and to apply a strategy that makes sense at the time. This requires astute analysis of confirmation signals as well as awareness of the entry and exit indicator in the context of the longer-term trading range and other technical signals.

For the candlestick chart analyst, the swing involves more than just the price trend. This may seem contrary to widely accepted definitions of swing trading, but realistically, swings also occur in trading range, moving averages, and technical indicators. Analysis in short-term trends is based on price along with nonprice indicators (like volume spikes). However, if you combine these well-established indicators with an in-depth analysis of candlestick signs, moves, and patterns, you realize that it is not just price movement but the strength or weakness of that movement that defines improved timing for entry and exit in a swing trade.

Key Point: Spotting a dual entry/exit point requires confirmation from additional technical signals beyond candlestick patterns.

Quantifying Price Movement with Candlesticks

Candlesticks are not just part of a set-up; they are visual summaries of entry and exit strength or weakness. You need the visual aid because it displays *all* of the attributes in a glance. Beyond the visible uptrend and downtrend so readily acknowledged as it occurs, the collective signals beyond price are visible as well, confirming the initial visual clues. When you look backward at a chart you can see what occurred and it is obvious. However, in the moment a trend is far less certain. For example, an uptrend involving twelve days of strong movement is going to end somewhere. However, after the third, fifth, or seventh day of the trend, how do you know when the move is weakening? Price movement can be quantified with observation of collective technical trends beyond price alone. The candlestick moves and patterns are the primary indicators, but at the time you watch a trend develop, you need more.

Key Point: Treating candlestick patterns as primary indicators is a good starting point; however, you also need to rely on nonprice technical signs.

Candlesticks along with confirming signals are effective in spotting trend development and in determining both reversal and confirmation. However, this is not a 100% accurate method but only a way to improve outcomes above random levels:

> It is extremely difficult or almost impossible for any mathematical formula to predict the next move probabilistically with an acceptable accuracy.
>
> By assuming that market trend is just a random variable, one simple method has been proposed called Trend Following (TF). Instead of doing any prediction, it simply rides on the trend and generates signals of buy or sell by following the long-term moves. Traders who use this approach can use current market price calculation, moving averages and channel breakouts to determine the general direction of the market and to generate trade signals.[V]

The analysis of price patterns within trends has to include both candlestick and noncandlestick signals. Two examples make the point that in addition to analysis of the candlesticks, other signals can and should be brought to the table. The overall analysis is vastly improved by their inclusion. The first example is the chart in Figure 8.1.

Multiple reversal signals, example 1

Figure 8.1: Multiple reversal signals, example 1

The nonprice signals add great value to timing. Both the overbought momentum in relative strength index (RSI) and the initial decline in on-balance volume

(OBV) anticipated and even predicted a bearish turnaround. This initial nonprice forecast was confirmed as the uptrend leveled out and the bearish engulfing pattern appeared. Further confirmation was seen in the bearish inside down signal. This chart contains many strong signals, including those appearing before the reversal occurred. A trader observing the combination of signals would have been able to time a bearish swing trade perfectly.

A similarly well-defined reversal was signaled in Figure 8.2 at two separate points. Both combined volume spikes with price signals.

Multiple reversal signals, example 2

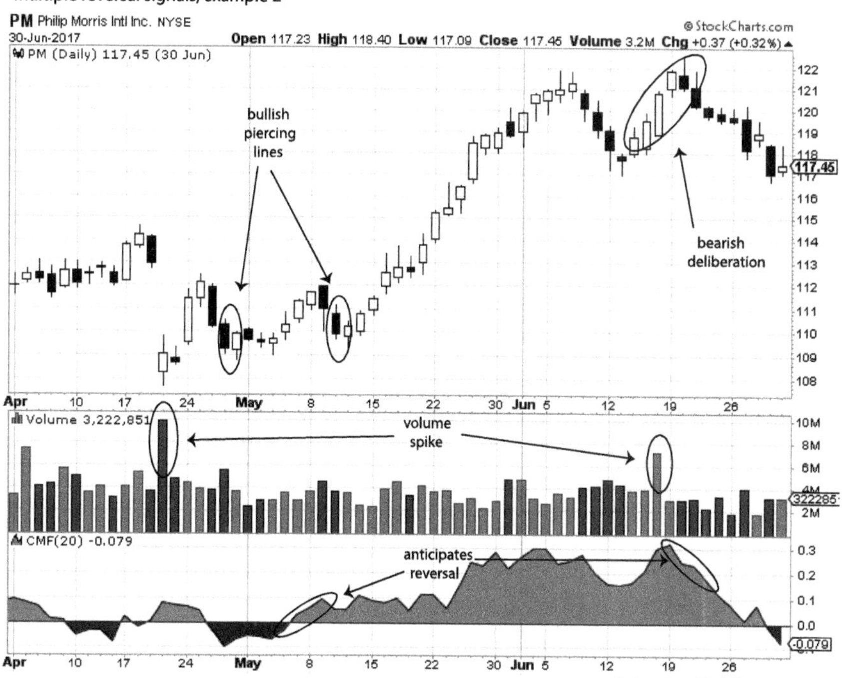

Figure 8.2: Multiple reversal signals, example 2

The number of confirming signals in this example combined price and nonprice formations and forecast reversal accurately. The first volume spike appeared more than a week before the first of two bullish reversal signals. The piercing lines signals occurred nearly two weeks apart, typical of a delayed reaction that a patient trader has to expect. The final confirmation of reversal was found in the volume signal from CMF, when the negative status moved into positive territory.

The second reversal was anticipated by another volume spike as the bearish deliberation appeared. The spike occurred even before the gap that defines deliberation. Final bearish reversal was again confirmed by CMF as the peak in the index began a sharp decline well in advance of price reversal.

Key Point: Finding many signs confirming entry or exit is reassuring. But if you do *not* find such signs, that is just as valuable because it tells you to *not* act.

Given the value in signal and confirmation, especially when combining price and nonprice signals, traders can time their decisions well. However, often overlooked is the benefit of moving average (MA) and its convergence and divergence. Even though MA is a lagging indicator, thc pattern formed with two different MA lines may define crucial points of reversal in a current trend.

In a rapidly developing price pattern, the lag factor can throw off the analysis of MA related to price. The rapid development of an average with extremely volatile price movement can provide false indicators. This is one of many reasons for employing two MA lines with different time periods, but it does not overcome the lag problem.

> The moving averages have a major deficiency. They are mainly a "lagging" indicator. Moving averages, because of their mathematical construction (averaging prices over some prior periods), lag behind the current price. In financial markets, where the price moves very fast, this lag affect will affect identifying trading opportunity in correct time.[vi]

The lag factor demonstrates why MA has to be utilized as confirmation and combined with other signals. It is not reliable in isolation, as it is merely a reflection of past price behavior. However, when added to current signals, notably candlesticks, it may confirm the likely next phase in the trend.

The Importance of Convergence and Divergence

Besides the easily spotted confirmations from technical price and volume changes, the trends in moving averages are useful in recognizing changes to price patterns. The concepts of convergence and divergence help in identifying longer-term price direction and degrees of strength or weakness in those trends.

In fact, the movement on average toward or away from one another may predict more meaningful signals. Even a lagging indicator brings order to the complexity of price developments, and the more volatile that price movement, the more valuable the role of convergence and divergence to confirm to other signals and to aid in timing of trade decisions.

> Technical analysis is based on the use of technical stock market indicators that are configured according to a set of parameters. These indicators are the mathematical calculations that day traders use in their charts in order to anticipate the price evolution. The complexity of the indicators may vary from one indicator to another. Some indicators are performed using simple formulae and are easy to understand while others use some complex structures and need a large number of input variables. The performance of the indicator does not necessarily depend on its complexity. Traders use indicators in two main ways: to confirm price movement, and to form buy and sell signals.[vii]

Convergence/divergence: The tendency for two long-term moving averages of price to move toward one another (converge) or away from one another (diverge).

Convergence signals a reduction in price volatility or the pending conclusion of a primary trend (bull or bear). Divergence signals increasing volatility and a growing trading range or the beginning of a new primary trend.

Primary trend: The overall price direction in the market, either bull (upward) or bear (downward). Within each primary trend, offsetting secondary trends occur.

Trends may develop in confusing and chaotic moments. Even when a strong primary trend reversal appears to be developing, market observers may disagree as to whether it is a reversal to a new primary trend or only a secondary trend. To some, the solution is to automate all of the available data to provide a means for well-timed trades:

> Stock market forecasting includes uncovering market trends, planning investment strategies, identifying the best time to purchase the stocks and what stocks to purchase. There has been a critical need for automated approaches to effective and efficient utilization of massive amount of financial data to support companies and individuals in strategic planning and investment decision making.[viii]

However, even the most sophisticated automated system is no substitute for chart analysis by a knowledgeable trader. History has revealed that increasing the size of data pools and automating the analysis have not generated reliable fixes for timing of decisions. Because of the many variables involved, automation is not the answer. The individual trader can gain as much from visual analysis and reliance on signal and confirmation. Spotting price behavior *within* a primary trend is based on analysis of candlestick signals for short-term reversal or continuation, aided by many other signals. Among these, the use of moving averages is an effective tool for spotting the nature of trends, both primary and secondary.

There are many ways to calculate moving averages; in charting, the most popular combined averages are two-hundred-session and fifty-session lines. Chartists may be more concerned with the current trend than with the primary trend, recognizing that short-term price movement is where significant swing action generates profit points. With short-term trends as well as intermediate time periods, convergence and divergence play a different role than that associated with changes in the primary trend. Tracking the primary trend, convergence and divergence are seen as signals of coming long-term change. For swing traders, the importance of convergence and divergence is more immediate and short-lived.

Key Point: The convergence and divergence of two moving averages is a powerful trend signal; however, it is a lagging and confirming indicator rather than an immediate action point.

This reliance on patterns, including convergence and divergence in MA, requires that traders believe in predictability of price to a degree. Price is not always repetitive, even though technical analysis is based in part on recent historical price trends (such as those expressed through MA analysis). As a result, analysis combines the patterns and behavior of price as well as attributes among traders.

> Chartism is based on the assumption that trends and patterns in charts reflect not only all available information but the psychology of the investor as well. Analysts who use charts look for graphical cycles and repetition of patterns to discern trends. The rules derived from the analysis of charts are often subjective and, as such, chartism is considered more of an art than a science. This is primarily why it has not been possible to define chart patterns with mathematical rigour.[ix]

This insight is profound. It is easy for traders to believe that their analysis is based purely on the reliable patterns and trends visible on the chart and to overlook the role of their own set of beliefs concerning price behavior. This combined attribute of chart analysis is strongly correlated with convergence and divergence, with crossover a key element. Crossover occurs between two averages or between a moving average and price.

A lot of analysis is devoted to positive and negative crossover points. This is based on the difference between the level of a moving average either above or below its moving average; however, swing traders can make use of the same crossover points to confirm candlestick-based indicators. In fact, the candlestick indicator is often visible well before convergence or divergence occurs. With this in mind, the trend *toward* crossover is just as important as the crossover itself. When moving averages begin to converge, it confirms what candlestick patterns predict concerning reversal.

Some general observations can be made concerning moving averages in pairs (a two-hundred-day and fifty-day MA used together) and the relationship between the two. An additional series of observations can be made about the proximity and trend between moving averages and price:

1. When the shorter MA is above the longer, the trend is bullish.
2. When the shorter MA is below the longer, the trend is bearish.
3. When an MA remains lower than price levels, it signifies an uptrend.
4. When an MA remains above the price levels, it signifies a downtrend.
5. When the MA crosses the price (above in an uptrend or below in a downtrend), it signals a reversal.

Two important additional points: Because moving averages are lagging indicators, these trends are best used as confirmation of the candlestick pattern. Second, when tracking the relationship between MA and price, contradiction may be observed. When this occurs, look for convergence as a signal of a change in the price trend.

An example of convergence leading to crossover and then to confirmation is seen in Figure 8.3. The bearish *harami* would not be a strong signal by itself, but it marked the point of crossover between the two MA lines. Even so, price declined only minimally. The strong downward move occurred only after two dark cloud cover reversal signals.

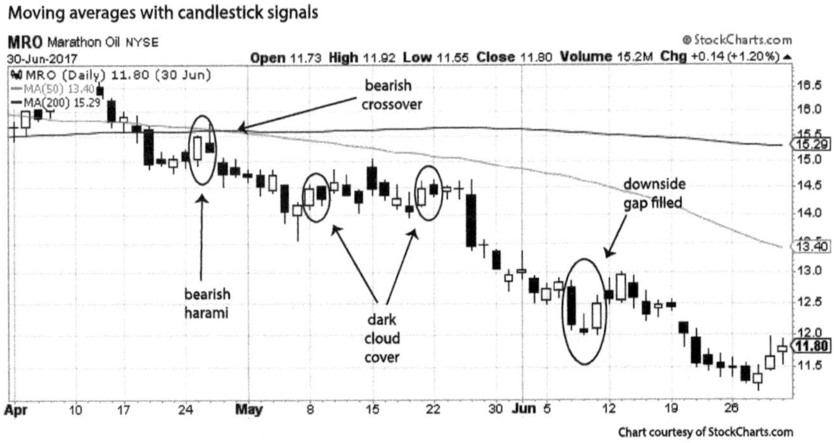

Figure 8.3: Moving averages with candlestick signals

The final signal, the downside gap filled, was a bearish continuation, adding strength to the downtrend and predicting more decline in price. This chart demonstrates that even with numerous candlestick signals, price reaction is not always immediate. The time from the initial bearish *harami* to the beginning of the downtrend was two months.

Collectively, the price, candlestick patterns, and MA lines all provide strong signals throughout this chart, even though the delay in price reaction was confusing. Swing traders relying strictly on candlestick patterns might have been uncertain at several points in this chart. The converging MA lines anticipated the downtrend but did not indicate how long it would take to develop. The relationship between change in trend and crossover in the MA lines was apparent in hindsight.

Key Point: The MA trends confirm previous entry or exit points. They are most useful when the convergence or divergence trend takes place where candlestick entry or exit is observed immediately *before* crossover.

Primary Trends and Candlestick-Based Entry or Exit

Timing of entry and exit is the key to swing trading. Recognition of a short-term trend is fairly easy, but knowing (a) when a reversal is coming and (b) when a continuation pattern is underway are more elusive interpretive skills. Although swing trading is invariably based on very short-term trends, the primary trend at the time defines the character and duration of a short-term trend that appears within that longer-term trend.

In a bullish primary trend, by definition the short-term upward price moves are likely to be longer lasting and cover a greater number of points than the opposite downtrends within the broader uptrend. In a bearish primary trend, the opposite is true: short-term downtrends are going to move faster and cover more points, and offsetting short-term uptrends will be weaker and of shorter duration. This general observation is important intelligence for swing traders. Awareness of the primary trend helps to judge the character of current price behavior and to improve timing even more than you can by relying on specific signals in the chart patterns.

Swing traders relying on the many entry and exit signals found in short-term price movement, notably in candlestick signs, moves, and patterns, can overcome the dilemma every trader faces. How do you know when a directional change in price is a swing trade or a primary trend reversal? How can you tell when a strong single-day movement is a sign of continuation or exhaustion? In many instances, the signals are not conclusive and you need to rely on judgment and even hindsight. Swing traders are wise to follow one general rule: When you cannot read the signal, get out and stay out until the picture clears. If you are already in a position and the signals are unclear, refer to the primary trend. If you are in a bull market and an uptrend is underway, chances are good that a conflicting signal to the upside means continuation; in a bear market, a conflicting signal to the downside means continuation.

Key Point: Perhaps the best rule for swing trading is: When you are not sure of a signal, stay away. Don't act until the signal is clearer.

An example of how a swing trade occurs within a primary trend is seen in Figure 8.4. The downtrend is interrupted by the bullish engulfing. The swing trade moves up rapidly over two weeks, concluding with the bearish meeting lines reversal.

Short-term trends within the primary trend

Figure 8.4: Short-term trends within the primary trend

This combination of primary and secondary or swing trades is a healthy price pattern. A trend that moves in one direction without offsetting price movement becomes increasingly vulnerable to sudden and extreme reversal. The role of the short-term trend is to settle the disagreements between buyers and sellers. In a downtrend, the short-term uptrend indicates that some traders viewed the initial price as a bargain; in an uptrend, a retracement or short-term downtrend represents profit taking. These offsets strengthen the primary trend.

Even so, visual signals are not easy to interpret given a tendency for misleading signals to develop. Many different methods have been used by traders to manage trends and interpret apparent reversal signals as they emerge.[x]

The most effective way to manage short-term offsets is by locating strong candlestick reversal signals. Traders are frustrated by the seesaw action of stocks in back-and-forth movement. The lack of a specific trend could be confusing, but swing trades are likely to be most effective at times when a primary dynamic trend is lacking. For example, in Figure 8.5, the initial uptrend led to a month-long period of movement offsetting the primary direction. However, clear candlestick reversals pointed to swing trading opportunities as long as the primary trend had paused.

Short-term trends with strong candlestick signals

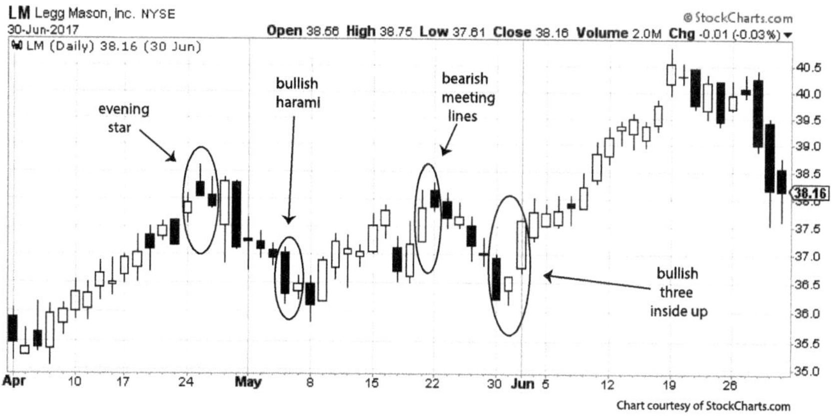

Figure 8.5: Short-term trends with strong candlestick signals

The evening star occurred at the top of the primary trend in April. A two-week bearish move followed, with its end marked by a bullish *harami*. Two weeks later, the bearish meeting lines pointed to a second bearish downtrend. It lasted only one week before the bullish three inside up signaled resumption of the primary trend.

On this chart, the short-term trends could be characterized as interruptions. In fact, however, the seesaw action represented a plateau in the primary trend and was a healthy signal for continuation. Traders have to be given the opportunity to take profits (at the peak) or enter with recognition of bargain price levels (at the short-term valley).

Among the many confirming signals, one factor is the price pattern occurring within a larger primary trend. This not only keeps the primary trend healthy in terms of buyers and sellers, but also indicates the likelihood that price will, in fact, continue upward once the plateau is complete. After a plateau, price may either reverse or continue in the same direction. In the chart in Figure 8.6, the stock price had been rising strongly until it plateaued, forming consolidation between $175 and $185. However, a continuation signal identified the point at which the previous uptrend resumed and began once again moving to the upside.

Figure 8.6: Price direction confirmation within a primary trend

The two instances of windows rising strongly pointed to continuation. However, each played a different role. The first, in May, indicated a breakout from the consolidation plateau; the second, seen in June, indicated even more bullish movement. In fact, in the two months after the period in this chart, price advanced an additional 40 points.

Set-Up Criteria and Action Points

Every chart watcher seeks a reliable entry and exit signal. However, swing traders may not always be aware that the characters of entry and exit signals are not always identical. If they were, you would assume that a proper indication would always tell you to exit one position and, at the same time, enter another. For example, if you have bought shares at the bottom of a downtrend, what happens when the resulting reversal and uptrend concludes? You would expect to acknowledge the exit signal and sell shares, but then go short in anticipation of another downtrend.

Key Point: Be sure to identify the difference between concurrent exit/entry signals and exit signals alone, which are often followed by a period of consolidation.

In some situations, the end of the trend does not signal reversal, but consolidation. If price movement will be sideways for an extended period, it could hint that once prices move again, it will be in the opposite direction. However, it is equally possible that prices will continue in the same direction following a pause in the trend. In this case, an exit set-up signal is *not* also an entry signal for the opposite price movement.

This development of a consolidation trend is caused by changes in volatility based on declining interest among buyers and sellers. This settling down of supply and demand explains why consolidation is often described as a time of agreement between the two sides or as uncertainty as to what will occur next. As long as buyers and sellers are in agreement about the current trading range, the perception of bargain pricing or overpricing is lacking. It often follows a distinct pattern. A trend begins with high interest among buyers (uptrend) or sellers (downtrend), causing early trend volatility. As price agreement replaces the period of high volatility, consolidation follows. This declining volatility, as a result, represents an exit signal in the same way that accelerating volatility at the beginning of the trend represents an entry signal. This tendency is observable in price patterns, when

> higher volatility coincides with the early stages of chart pattern development and declining volatility with the later states. This has a logical basis: A more active market attracts and supports more participants, and hence more gross supply and demand—or total investor interest—than does a less active market. Any sudden changes in supply and demand in a less active or "quiet" market can result in sharply higher or sharply lower quotes due to a sheer lack of available buyers or sellers.[xi]

In this sense, entry and exit signals are quite different, especially if based on emerging levels of volatility. In other instances, notably swing trades, entry and exit signals are likely to be far more similar in design and significance. The similarities between entry and exit signals reveal that in many cases entry and exit are identical—but not always. When you see *exit* you do not always see *entry* indicated at the same time. A comparison between the sets of signals makes this point, notably when two or more of the signals occur together:

entry signals

end of the trend via a narrow range day (NRD), also known as a *doji*
reversal candles such as long-legged *doji*, spinning top, or *marubozu*
high volume
gapping patterns near beginning of the trend
technical indicator changes, such as MA convergence and cross-over

exit signals

end of the trend lasting three sessions or more via different-colored candles

long-legged *doji* or spinning top, especially in conjunction with a *marubozu*
gapping pattern including intraday gaps, near the end of the trend
technical indicator changes, such as MA divergence

Many of the signals are similar or identical; the key is to find confirming indicators of the same directional forecast, either entry or exit (or both). But the differences may be subtle. For example, price gaps are among the strongest of swing trading signals. Some points to remember:

1. Intraday gaps often are invisible. The importance of gaps is often missed because they take place between sessions. The difference between yesterday's close and today's open might include overlapping real bodies, but significant gaps as well.
2. Gaps occurring after a trend is established and moving in the same direction may signal exhaustion and an impending end to the trend, thus providing an exit signal. One of the strongest signs that the current short-term trend is coming to an end is a gap in the trend direction. This is not easy to distinguish from a continuation pattern, which is why you need to confirm the indicator with other candlestick or technical measures, notably basic signs like support and resistance, head and shoulders, or top/bottom repetitive tests over an extended period. The exhaustion signal often follows tests or stops right at the border of the trading range.
3. Gaps occurring at or near the beginning of a trend and moving in the trend direction may signal that the new trend is genuine and will continue; thus this serves as an entry signal. When you see one trend end and another begin, gaps can take on a different meaning than exhaustion. A continuation gap is most likely to take place at or near the beginning of the trend. So if an uptrend starts out with a gap close to support or a downtrend starts with a gap near resistance, traders may accept the premise that the trading range provides "movement room" for the trend to develop. Given separate technical confirmation, gaps at the beginning of a trend are strong indicators supporting the current price direction.

Key Point: Price gaps, including those between trading sessions, tend to be strong signals, but depending on where they occur within the trend and within proximity to the support or resistance levels, they can have different meanings.

These have to be generalizations because for every rule of charting, you can find the notable exception. However, gaps are often present when entry signals are not found at the same point as exit signals. In some instances, exit stands alone without the requisite entry signals, and it may be followed by either continuation of the previous trend or a reversal. For example, in Figure 8.7, a movement reverses a consolidation period followed by a continuation signal.

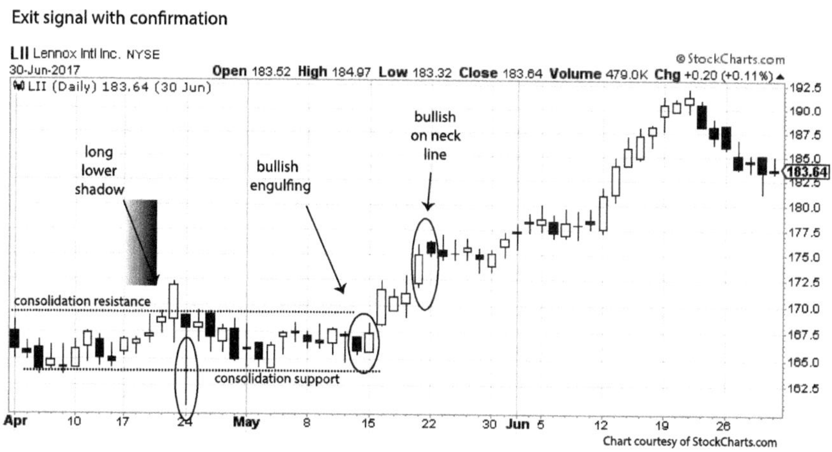

Figure 8.7: Exit signal with confirmation

Note that during the period of consolidation, price did not fall below support. The initial forecast of exit from consolidation occurred with the exceptionally long lower shadow in late April. Although breakout did not occur for another three weeks, the failure of price to move lower was a forecast of an upside breakout. The bullish engulfing marked the end of consolidation. This is an example of a reversal applied to the trend rather than to price direction. The reversal was from consolidation to an uptrend.

Soon after the breakout, traders had to face a prospect of failure and retreat into the consolidation range. However, this concern disappeared quickly with the continuation signal as the form of a bullish on neck line. As expected, subsequent price direction was upward.

An established trend will not always continue in the same direction after a pause. Some consolidation plateaus are followed by strong reversal trends, and there is no way to know in advance which outcome will follow. So an exit signal without the requisite entry signal requires waiting out the consolidation before moving, based on the fact that price could move in either direction. By the same argument, even the strongest of breakouts can fail, with price returning to the previous trading range. For example, Figure 8.8 provides an example of a large gap after a bearish engulfing, with price moving far below support. This may appear at first as a strong breakout likely to succeed, but the exceptional size of the gap was a concern because, as a general rule, gaps tend to fill.

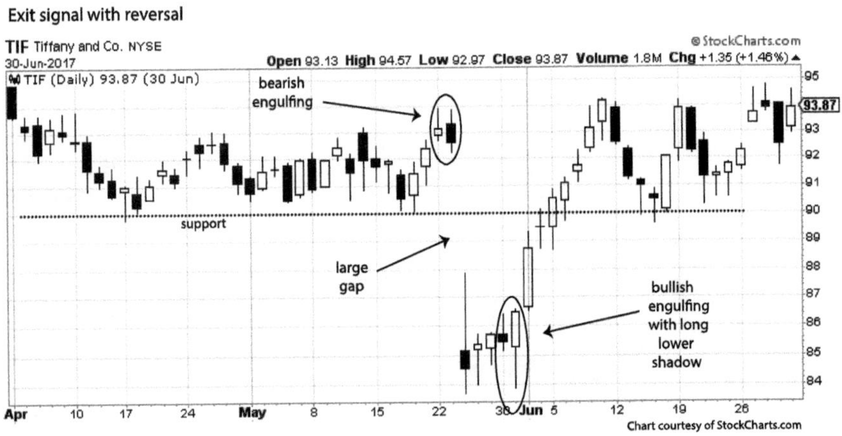

Figure 8.8: Exit signal with reversal

The initial exit signal (bearish engulfing) was confirmed at first by the downward gap. However, only a few sessions later, an offsetting bullish engulfing signal indicated a failure in the breakout. This was especially strong as a reversal indicator based on the long lower shadow in the second day. As predicted by this second signal, price immediately jumped higher, returning to the previous range above support.

This overall pattern revealed how resistance and support add strength and predictability to the trading pattern. In the period before and after the failed breakout, support held strongly and the real bodies of sessions never moved below that support level. The exception was found in the eight sessions that broke out below and quickly failed, with price returning to the established consolidation range. The resistance level of $94 and support of $90 were established and reestablished throughout this period. During the failed breakout, the immediate reversal and strong upward gaps revealed the strength of the support price.

Key Point: Gaps found during a breakout and moving back toward the previous range are among the strongest signals that the breakout will fail.

This chart also serves as a good example of how traditional technical indicators can work nicely with confirming candlestick patterns. The failed breakout below support may have been enough for a chartist to call the reversal; when support is tested in this way, it often precedes a strong uptrend. However, it does not always occur. The candlestick signal at the bottom of the breakout was not only a strong indicator on its own merit (especially with the uptrend gaps that followed), but also confirmed the strength of the previously established consolidation trend.

Selling Short in Swing Trades

Swing traders have to be aware that entry and exit coexist at times, but not always. There are times when exit is clear, but entry has not yet emerged. Swing traders face another dilemma, however: to trade both sides of the swing, they need to be able to go not only long at the bottom, but also short at the top.

A great number of traders, probably a majority, avoid short selling due to the complexity, cost, and risk involved. Shorting stock is not a moderate strategy; as a consequence, many swing traders seek entry at the bottom and exit at the top, but avoid the other side of the swing cycle. When you short stock, you have to borrow shares from your broker and then sell them. As long as the short position remains open, you have to pay interest to your broker for the borrowed shares. You face considerable risk as long as you are short; if you time the entry incorrectly and stock prices continue to rise instead of falling, you lose. Eventually, you may need to cover the short at a loss. In the ideal trade, prices do fall and you can cover at a profit.

Some swing traders limit their long-side risk by employing fewer than one hundred shares of stock. You can swing trade with a smaller number for very little added cost, so this makes sense. However, shorting fewer than one hundred shares of stock might not be possible. It is understandable that short sellers will avoid shorting for all of these reasons. However, there is a practical and affordable alternative: using options for downside swings and using options to swing trade.

Key Point: The risk, cost, and complexity of selling short restrict many swing traders to working with uptrends only. This means they miss out on one-half of all swing trading opportunities.

Rules of the options market are particularly complex, and no one should employ options strategies without experience and practice. However, for those who do understand options, their use for swing trading is flexible and actually reduces risks. A *put* is an option granting its owner the right (but not the obligation) to sell one hundred shares of an underlying stock. So instead of selling short, you can *buy* a put and accomplish the same swing trading posture. As the stock's price declines, the put's value increases. This is one of the rare instances in which it makes sense to buy puts that will expire in less than one month. Under most strategies involving long options, you need to keep positions open long enough for price changes to develop, meaning you have to pay for *time value* as well. But in swing trading, you expect a trend to develop over as little as three trading sessions.

Every option gives you control over one hundred shares of stock. With this in mind, there are many possible swing trading combinations you can use on both sides of the swing. These include:

1. Buying calls at the bottom and buying puts at the top.
2. Selling calls at the top and buying calls at the bottom. (This is a practical system, especially when you also own one hundred shares of the underlying stock, so that the short call is covered, making this a very conservative strategy.)
3. Selling puts at the bottom and buying puts at the top. (Selling puts is higher risk than buying, but as one possible swing trading strategy, shorting the put produces cash income; when the signal is exceptionally strong for an uptrend, the risks are mitigated.)
4. Selling puts at the bottom and selling calls at the top. (This is a completely credit-based strategy, meaning you earn money on both sides, further reducing the price-spread risk. If you own one hundred shares, the short call risk is very low.)

Options make swing trading very flexible, but for much lower costs. Long options cost only a fraction of the one hundred shares they allow you to control, as little as 5 to 10% of the price for one hundred shares. However, long positions also limit risk. You can never lose more than the relatively small price of the option. With their low cost, you can diversify among several different stocks at the same time using options in place of stock as a swing trading mechanism.

Key Point: Swing trading with options instead of stock improves flexibility and diversification while reducing risk. However, no one should consider using options in any strategy unless they completely understand how they work.

The complexity of options and their selection criteria demand a lot of study. Risk levels vary greatly between long and short positions and depending on whether or not those short positions are covered or uncovered. Another risk factor is the price distance between the fixed strike of the option and the current price of the stock. In other words, there are many risk considerations to keep in mind when trading options. They are exceptionally powerful tools for swing trading leverage, but should be used only by seasoned options traders.

Whether you trade in shares of stock or option contracts, the entire system for timing of entry and exit relies on your skill in spotting and using *trends*. This is the subject of the next chapter.

---

[i] Leigh, W., Frohlich, C., Hornik, S., Purvis, R., & Roberts, Tom. (2008). Trading With a Stock Chart Heuristic. *IEEE Transactions on Systems, Man, and Cybernetics*, Part A, 38, 93–104.

[ii] Marshall, B. R., Young, M. R., & Rose, L. C. (2006). Candlestick Technical Trading Strategies: Can They Create Value for Investors? *Journal of Banking & Finance*, 30, 2303–2323.

[iii] Greenwood, G. W. , & Tymerski, R. (December 2008). A Game-Theoretical Approach for Designing Market Trading Strategies. Computational Intelligence and Games.

[iv] Israelov, R., & Katz, M. (September/October 2011). To Trade or Not to Trade? Informed Trading with Short-Term Signals for Long-Term Investors. *Financial Analysis Journal*, 67, No. 5, 23–36.

[v] Fong, S., Tai, J., & Si, Y. W. (May 2011). Trend Following Algorithms for Technical Trading in Stock Market. *Journal of Emerging Technologies in Web Intelligence*, 3, No. 2, 136–145.

[vi] Mitra, S. K. (July 2011). Usefulness of Moving Average Based Trading Rules in India. *International Journal of Business and Management*, 6, No. 7, 199–206.

[vii] Fayek, M. B., El-Boghdadi, H. M., & Omran, S. M. (April 2013). Multi-Objective Optimization of Technical Stock Market Indicators using GAs. *International Journal of Computer Applications*, 68, No. 20, 41–48.

[viii] Devi, B. U., Sundar, D., & Alli, P. (November 2011). A Study on Stock Market Analysis for Stock Selection: Naïve Investors' Perspective using Data Mining Technique. *International Journal of Computer Applications*, 34, No. 3, 19–25.

[ix] Acar, E., & Satchell, S. E. (1997). A Theoretical Analysis of Trading Rules: An Application to the Moving Average Case with Markovian Returns. *Applied Mathematical Finance*, 4, 165–180.

[x] Liao, S., Ho, H., & Lin, H. (2008). Mining Stock Category Association and Cluster on Taiwan Stock Market. *Expert Systems with Applications*, 35, 19–29.

[xi] Chesler, D. L. (Winter–Spring 2000). Volatility and Structure: Building Blocks of Classical Chart Pattern Analysis. *MTA Journal*, 35–44.

Chapter 9
Spotting Trends and Using Trendlines

Candlesticks provide intelligence on two levels. First, they help you determine what is happening at the moment and what price direction is likely in the next handful of trading sessions. Second, they provide insight to the current trend—its strength or weakness, likelihood of continuation or reversal, and duration.

Candlesticks can be used by themselves to time entry and exit. However, they are even more powerful as timing tools when viewed in a larger context of long-term chart analysis. Swing traders, for example, acting as contrarians, are likely to rely on very short-term trends and expect three- to five-day price movement followed by reversal. The process of finding and acting on entry and exit set-up signals is continual and is based on an observation that most traders overreact, causing prices to move too far within a limited time span:

> A popular view held by many journalists, psychologists, and economists is that individuals tend to overreact to information . . . that stock prices also overreact to information, suggesting that contrarian strategies (buying past losers and selling past winners) achieve abnormal returns.[i]

This belief is well founded in most cases, especially in a swing trading strategy based on contrarian observations. However, it does not address the problem of managing and timing longer-term trends. Some trends continue in one direction for weeks or even months. This is especially true when stocks have remained within an extended sideways trading pattern for weeks at a time, leading to breakout and establishment of a new dynamic trend. The pressure on prices to move upward or downward becomes pent up at such times and could lead to an unusually long and unbroken trend. In uncertain markets, swing traders will note that greed and fear dominate short-term price movement and are probably augmented as trends continue. However, these times may also create uncertainty so that price suddenly breaks away from the sideways trend and moves in a bullish or bearish surge.

As long as continuation signals are found in candlestick formations, it is possible to ride a trend in the established direction. However, it is also difficult to accurately judge the meaning of some candlestick formations in such long-term trending patterns. This is where additional confirmation tools are required. Candlesticks only work well when prices go through typical short-term waves of change. When momentum is exceptionally strong, candlestick formations require more confirmation than ever. The best confirmation is achieved by com-

DOI 10.1515/9781501507397-009

bining candlestick formations with continuation or reversal signs found in trendline analysis.

The many technical indicators popularly used by chartists to identify price trends certainly have value as timing tools, but when they confirm what the candlesticks reveal, their accuracy is increased significantly. Even when momentum is stronger than interim technical signals, the process of signal and confirmation is crucial for accurate timing of entry and exit.

Candlesticks remain a primary early indicator of what is going on in the pattern. The formations come in three distinct types. The single candlestick of significance (such as the *doji* or *marubozu*) is a sign. A two-stick series like engulfing patterns and the *harami* is defined as a clear reversal move. And finally, a candlestick formation of three candlesticks like three white soldiers or the morning star sets up a pattern for likely reversal. Collectively, the visual price patterns of candlesticks contribute to trend timing, but candlestick formations are not trends. A *trend* is the direction in which prices move and is distinguished by momentum and either strengthening or weakening movement over time. Candlesticks do not identify trends, but do spot continuation and reversal, especially within a current trendline.

Identifying the Trendline

A trend is a well-known phenomenon in stock prices. Those prices—whether seen in individual stocks or in market indices—tend to continue moving in an established direction for a period of time before it stops and reverses. This tendency of *reversion to the mean* is a statistical reference. It tells you that when prices move away from their longer-term average, the tendency is for price to revert and move back toward the mean. The value in trendline analysis goes beyond merely identifying the direction of a trend; analysts may also draw conclusions about the strength of a trend through observing the slope of its trendline:

> A trendline is drawn below an apparent up trend or above an apparent downtrend. As more troughs touch the trendline without violating it, the technician may place more confidence in the validity of the trendline. The angle of the trendline indicates the speed of the trend, with steeper lines indicating faster appreciation (or depreciation).[ii]

Key Point: No trend continues forever. Eventually, the current direction stops and begins moving back toward the longer-term average.

Reversion to the mean: A tendency for prices to reverse course and move back toward their longer-term average.

Not every trend moves at the same rate or lasts the same period of time. Anyone who has studied chart patterns over time knows that the faster price moves beyond its trading range, the more likely it is to exhaust that trend and revert. Fast price movement is seen in repetitive price gaps, breakouts, and higher than average volatility. You are also likely to see an increase in unusual candlestick signs such as longer than average days, consecutive *doji* moves, and misleading or contradictory signals. Those are signs that trends are concluding. The simple realization that no trend is going to last forever can be put to good use by looking for changes in an established trendline.

The statistical observation expressed in reversion to the mean tells you that prices *tend* to track with averages. So when you are observing price in conjunction with a two-hundred-day and a fifty-day moving average, you assign great importance to the distance between price and the two averages. The statistical rule tells you in addition that the greater the distance that price moves away from the mean, the higher the chances that reversion will soon occur.

This is not just a theory; it is also a reality. It is easily observed in a series of coin tosses, for example. You know that there is a 50/50 chance of either heads or tails coming up. However, every toss is independent, so there is no assurance that a trend will develop. Even so, if the toss comes up "heads" eight times in a row, you know that the 50/50 odds have wandered substantially away from the average. For that reason alone, you would expect to see "tails" come up soon. Every toss is independent, but the odds of tails are still at 50/50.

The theory of reversion to the mean tells you that no trend will continue indefinitely. Eventually, every trend ends and turns back toward the moving average levels. This is inevitable because stock prices, like all *trends*, rely on interaction between buyers and sellers, the two moving forces behind price. If price moves too high, stockholders will seek an exit and will sell. If prices move too low, traders will seek a bargain price and will buy. This unending interaction shows up in a series of trendlines. These are not difficult to spot and, in fact, are among the most basic but valuable of continuation signals. They may consist of:

1. *A weakening or breakdown of the line.* The most visible sign is a change in the direction of the trend, which is expressed in a violation of a trendline. As long as the line continues moving upward with evolving support or resistance, the trend continues. However, eventually price is going to reverse, even slightly. This is often a sign that the trendline is concluding. However, because short-term price movement is always chaotic, you need confirma-

tion from other technical indicators or from candlestick patterns indicating reversal.

A trendline is a powerful tool because it tracks evolving support or resistance. As price levels rise or fall, they often tend to remain within the same breadth of trading, making the trading range easily definable. The range is rarely stationary. The tendency is for price trends to generally move while the distance between resistance and support moves as well, but without expanding or contracting. When the trading range changes as price levels evolve, triangles, wedges, and pennants form and take on significance separate from the trendline. When such indicators counter the trendline direction, it may provide early signs that the current trend is narrowing and will soon stop and reverse direction.

Key Point: Trendlines make support and resistance visible even when the trading range is evolving as part of a long-term trend.

---

2. *Candlestick formations that anticipate reversal.* The best-known and most visible types of candlestick formations signal reversal. Confirmation of this occurs in several ways. One way is a reversal indicated by one candlestick sign, move, or pattern, followed immediately by another that also anticipates reversal. A second confirming sign is a violation of the trendline, even a small or momentary one. You expect to see trendlines hold consistently. Any drop below an ascending support level or a rise above a declining resistance level is a subtle but important warning sign that the whole trend may reverse. This is similar in strength to the better-known head and shoulders pattern, which tests resistance or support and then sees prices move in the opposite direction.

   Another way that candlestick formations are confirmed is through outside changes like volume spikes, consecutive price gaps, or important reversals in CMF and other technical indicators. Converging or diverging moving averages further support what the candlestick formations anticipate. There is no shortage of potential conforming signs in support of what the candlesticks tell you. Unfortunately, there may be so many that you observe both confirming and contradictory signs at the same time. When this occurs, you may rely the most on what two indicators reveal: candlestick formations and the signs in the current trendline.
3. *Other technical changes.* In so many trendline indicators, you find confirmation through not only the specific candlestick formations, but also through

what longer-range technical indicators emerge. For example, a trendline may be characterized by a strong movement culminating in numerous price gaps. These may be reversal gaps that warn you of the reversal before the trendline itself turns around. This may occur when momentum of the trend carries price to the level of being overbought or oversold. When momentum trumps other technical signs, it may shield the impending reversal from view. At such times, look for technical signs in the form of volume indicators, moving average convergence and divergence, and repeated but unsuccessful tests of resistance and support. These may all occur even as the trendline appears to be holding steady.

Pay special attention to tests of resistance and support. One of the widely observed "rules" of chart analysis is that trading always remains within the trading range . . . until it breaks out of the trading range. In other words, resistance and support are truly the "lines in the sand" of trends, and once a breakthrough takes place, it may signal a fast change in price or may exhaust and reverse the "rule" of resistance and support for a long period of time before price breaks out. The breakout is a red flag that price is going to move rapidly, but you may not be able to tell in which direction. This is where the trendline, supported by candlestick formations, can be the most revealing.

Key Point: The breakout signal is difficult to interpret; it may signal a strong price movement away from the previous range, or impending reversal back into range. At such times, the trendline determines which price direction dominates.

A distinction should be made between the trend and the *trendline*. They are not necessarily the same, even though they usually are seen at the same time. The trendline is a readily seen, visible straight line connecting a series of ascending or descending price levels. The trendline is normally drawn just above price levels in declining resistance or just below price levels in rising support. A study of trendlines often anticipates a change in direction or weakening of the current trend. In technical analysis, a broadening or narrowing trendline (known variously as the triangle, wedge, or pennant) signals either a strengthening of the current trend or its conclusion.

Trendline: A series of straight lines bordering the highest and lowest point in a current price trend.

For example, Figure 9.1 tracks a clear uptrend with the trendline drawn below price. The rule for trendlines is simple: It continues until interrupted by price. In this example, there were no such interruptions.

Figure 9.1: Rising trendline

Several aspects of this chart are noteworthy. In late May, continuation of the uptrend was signaled by a change in the CMF line from below the zero line to above. In spite of the price decline following the gap to the upside, the CMF movement predicted that the bullish move remained strong. This signal persisted until the end of August, when CMF suddenly moved strongly downward, predicting possible reversal to follow.

The same basic rule applies during a downtrend. Figure 9.2 began downtrend as prices peaked in late May. The very strong bearish thrusting lines signals appeared twice, predicting continuation. The trendline was brief but tracked a strong downtrend. It also revealed when the downtrend ended, at the point that the declining trendline was interrupted by a rising price. The downtrend's end was confirmed by the strong bullish reversal, the three inside up.

Falling trendline

Figure 9.2: Falling trendline

Key Point: Trendlines provide a context for defining price movement and orderly trend continuing. The end of the trendline is invariably confirmed with candlestick formations, often very strong ones.

The point here is to show how trendlines appear and are marked. Also note how clearly the beginning and end of each reversal was marked.

Trendlines and Confirmation Signals

A trendline helps to locate and confirm reversal points in the trend. In fact, when a trend begins to weaken, the accompanying end to the trendline may be better visual proof of a coming reversal than many other, more popular indicators. When you see that the existing trendline is confirmed by candlesticks providing the same clues (bullish formations in a bullish trendline and bearish formations in a bullish trendline), it is an excellent form of information that the trend is continuing. When you see emerging opposite indicators such as bearish candlesticks in a bullish trendline or bullish candlesticks in a bearish trendline, it is an early sign of reversal.

Key Point: When trendlines are compared with candlestick indicators, it is much easier to determine whether the current tendency is toward continuation or reversal.

For example, in Figure 9.3, a rather strong trendline (meaning a steep slope) was predicted in advance by the OBV move to the upside. At the point that the OBV advance stopped, the price also reversed, peaked once again, and finally moved to the downside through the end of June.

Weakening uptrend with strong trendline

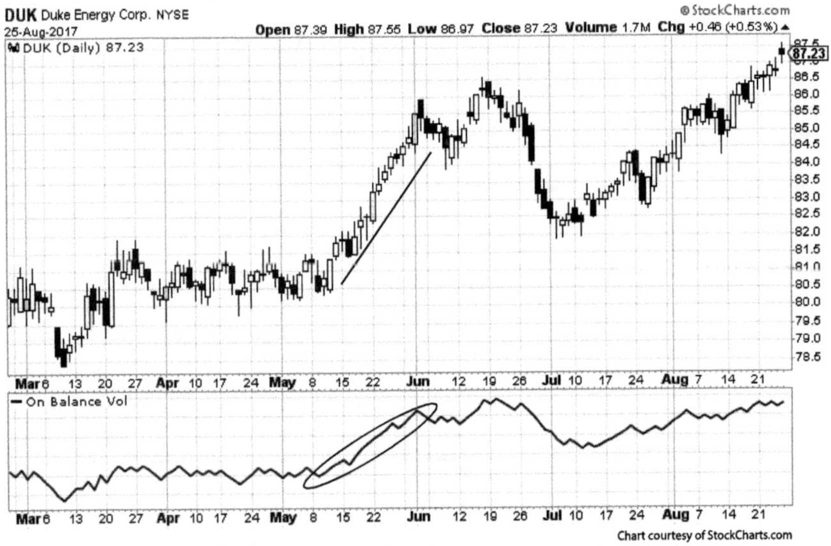

Figure 9.3: Weakening uptrend with strong trendline

The same type of confirming signals are found in downtrends as well. The long-term downtrend in Figure 9.4 was confirmed by CMF remaining for the most part in the territory beneath the mid-line index value of zero. An early indication of the downtrend's ending came between June 19 and June 26 when CMF momentarily moved above the mid-line. Although this predicted a short-term reversal, the downtrend resumed in August.

Weakening downtrend with strong trendline

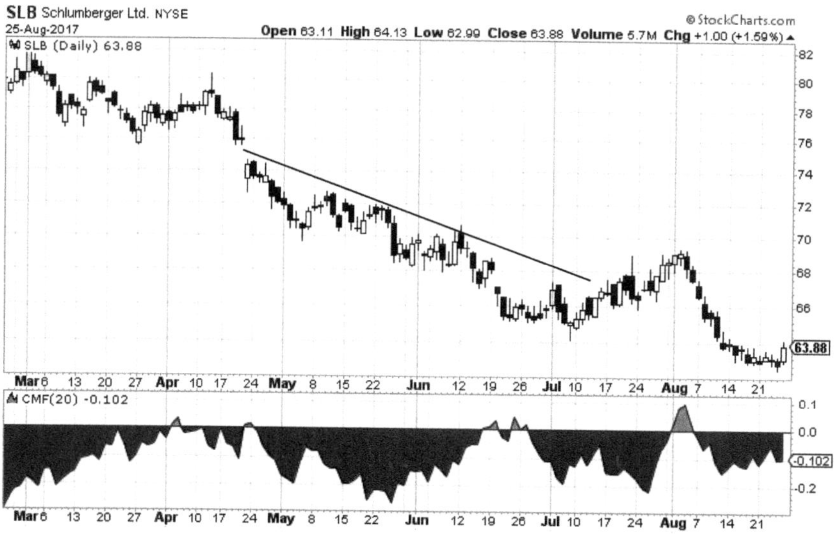

Chart courtesy of StockCharts.com

Figure 9.4: Weakening downtrend with strong trendline

The point to these examples is that different types of signals work well together, even in the lack of strong candlestick reversal or continuation. The trendline, by itself, tells only part of the story. Indicators such as OBV or CMF also tell only part of the whole. But combined together, the signaling strength is greatly improved.

Key Point: Even a subtle indicator—like an isolated shadow at the top or bottom of the trend—ends up being the best indicator of a strong reversal. When confirmed by a change in the trendline, the reversal can be quite strong.

The trendline does not have to be especially strong to confirm continuation of the trend or, equally revealing, to point to the weakening of that trend. Trendline duration can be further confirmed by commonly appearing bullish or bearish candlestick formations that indicate continuation. These include neck lines, thrusting lines, or meeting lines confirming patterns in either direction and ongoing moving averages without signs of impending convergence. Reversal patterns include gaps, MA convergence, changes in CMF or on-balance volume, exceptional volume spikes, *doji* patterns (especially consecutive *doji* days), and large gaps indicating exhaustion of the trend.

Applying Moving Averages to Candlestick Analysis

A trendline is easily visible on most charts. However, some charts also demonstrate exceptional volatility, making it impossible to use price alone to understand whether the current price is in a continuation mode or about to reverse. In these instances, you can use moving averages—and especially a visible converging pattern—to augment price analysis.

For example, in Figure 9.5, price moved upward but with several short-term trends and retracements. Drawing a trendline and adhering to the rule that the line ends once it runs into a price move would have resulted in several short-term trendlines and no clear direction, in spite of the clear long-term bullish move.

Key Point: Some trends are hard to read or even impossible to spot. At such times, a study of moving average lines can be the best indicator or confirmation available.

Figure 9.5: Trend with MA confirmation

In place of a trendline, this chart has an overlay of a fifty-MA moving average. The MA tracks support effectively, remaining below price during most of the chart and identifying the upward movement. The interim retracements are easily identified, but none violate the MA line. This reveals the strength of the trend.

In using MA in place of the more rigid straight lines of the trendline, the guideline should be that identification of the trend itself is the underlying purpose. As far as reversal is concerned, the best method is to look for candlestick signals as well as traditional Western technical signals in price, volume, and momentum. Because MA is a lagging indicator, it can predict change, but is not effective as a primary signal. If you wait for crossover to occur, you often are too late to take advantage of the directional indication.

Observing convergence between two signals is an effective system for MA advance warning of possible change. As lines of two MA signals begin to converge, it often precedes crossover and reversal. As long as the primary reliance is on candlesticks, this is a useful monitoring device, a method for keeping track of a trend and looking for declining momentum and plateau effects, ultimately leading to reversal. Anticipating reversal requires strong confirmation from candlestick patterns. At the point of reversal signals and confirmation, expect to see a weakening of the trend, even a sudden reversal.

Key Point: Convergence and divergence are excellent confirming signals, but they should not be relied on as the sole means for timing entry or exit.

The moving averages may be further confirmed by another technical indicator: the reaching of a new high or new low price based on the last fifty-two weeks. The marketwide indicator is used to support the existing trend. As new highs increase, the signs are bullish, and as new lows increase, the signs are bearish. However, when a new high or new low is seen on an individual stock, it has to be analyzed in context, based on several factors:

1. *Comparison to the overall market.* When the overall trend is firmly set, stocks may tend to follow suit, even if the individual technical indicators are weak or contradictory. However, this tendency is also most likely to be adjusted once traders realize that the market momentum has created an overbought or oversold condition in the stock.
2. *Placement within the current trend.* The trend and trendline are the most revealing portions of price momentum and movement. Candlestick formations are short-term and serve to pinpoint reversals (or continuation) in the trend itself. So when a stock's price reaches a fifty-two-week high or low, it has to be judged in the context of the existing trend. Has the trend topped or bottomed out with the fifty-two-week price level? Is the trendline still strong or is it weakening?
3. *Sustainability of the record price level.* Trends eventually reach an end, known among traders as exhaustion. So the big question for the new high or new low point is whether it can be sustained or not. The combined visual signals of trendline and candlestick formations will define the sustainabil-

ity of the current price level, whether at the top or at the bottom of the fifty-two-week history.

4. *Proximity to resistance and support of the new price and of recent price movement.* Some stocks remain within a clearly defined trading range over many months, while others maintain the same breadth of range while price levels evolve, either upward or downward. Thus a new top might not violate resistance and a new bottom might not be below support. In these cases, proximity to the borders of the trading range without a breakthrough imply that the range is likely to continue holding. When the new high or new low is a price breakthrough, you need to refer to trendlines and candlestick formation as well as confirming technical signals to determine whether the breakthrough will continue or reverse and fill.
5. *Frequency of new high or new low.* Is this the first time in fifty-two weeks that a new high or low price level has been reached? That would be significant. However, if price levels are evolving, it is possible that a new fifty-two-week record is being set repetitively. The fifty-two-week price record is itself a moving average. If the stock's price is going through a long-term bull or bear trend, you may see numerous record high or low prices. Identifying the number of new price records is one way to articulate the significance of the indicator.
6. *Recent price volatility of the stock.* If a new high or new low shows up in a stock with low volatility, that is probably far more significant than for a stock with high volatility. By definition, high-volatility stocks have to be expected to continually violate previously set trading ranges. The problem is that in these situations, identifying an emerging trend is difficult, even with strong candlestick formations and short-term trendlines. Higher-volatility patterns make all forms of analysis more difficult. The good news is that even the most volatile stocks eventually settle down and begin to conform to widely recognized technical "rules" and trends.

The Channel Line

The trendline is simple, but at the same time visually powerful. However, it tracks only one side of the trading range, rising support in a bull market or declining resistance in a bear market. A variation of the trendline occurs when both sides of the trading range move dynamically but without a change in the breadth of trading.

This means that price is on the move, but the distance between resistance and support does not change. This is called a channel line.

Channel line: A variation of the trendline in which resistance and support move together but without a change in the breadth of trading.

In those instances when a trend occurs within a channel line, the indication is exceptionally strong. Continuation of the trend is easily identified, and so is the end point. Inevitably, the channel line ends in the same way as the trendline: price reverses and interrupts the line itself. This occurs in support during an uptrend channel and in resistance during a downtrend channel.

For example, in Figure 9.6, a two-month uptrend was exceptionally rapid and strong, but had a trading range of only 1.5 points. The consistency of this breadth of trading during a time of rapid bullish movement meant the trend would continue as long as price advanced. That trend ended in the last week of July, when price topped out and began to decline.

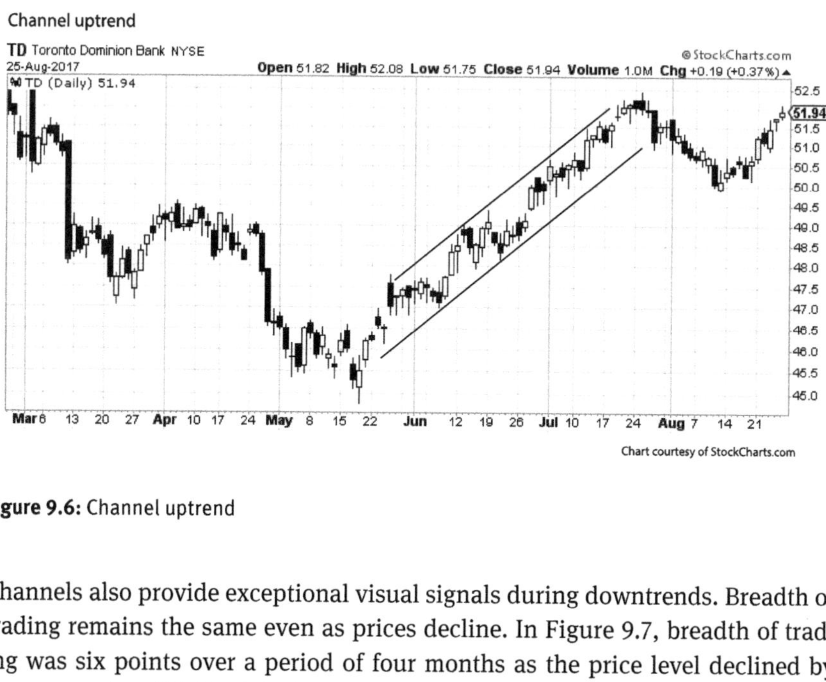

Figure 9.6: Channel uptrend

Channels also provide exceptional visual signals during downtrends. Breadth of trading remains the same even as prices decline. In Figure 9.7, breadth of trading was six points over a period of four months as the price level declined by fourteen points. Within this downtrend, several retracements to the upside took place, but the channel did not conclude until price rose to interrupt its progress in mid-July.

Channel downtrend

Figure 9.7: Channel downtrend

The channel, like the trendline, is a simple indicator that applies only in cases of strong but narrowly defined trading breadth. It will not apply in most charts, where price tends to seesaw too quickly to establish a longer-term trend. However, where it is found, it indicates strength in the trend. During these moments, continuation candlestick signals bolster confidence in the trend, and candlestick reversal signals may forecast reversal yet to occur as the channel comes to an end.

The many ways that signals are recognized and confirmed invariably point to the value of candlestick signs, moves, and patterns as a primary and leading source for reversal and continuation. However, candlesticks are only the first step in locating the point at which entry and exit make the most sense. You still may benefit from additional technical indicators to confirm what candlesticks predict. The next chapter studies many of the technical indicators that are most useful as confirmation of trends first seen in candlestick formations.

---

[i] Jegadeesh, N., & Titman, S. (March 1993). Returns to Buying Winners and Selling Losers: Implications for Stock Market Efficiency. *The Journal of Finance*, XLVIII, No. 1, 65–91.
[ii] Neely, C. J. (September/October 1997). Technical Analysis in the Foreign Exchange Market: A Layman's Guide. *Review, Federal Reserve Bank of St. Louis*, 23–38.

Chapter 10
Technical Indicators

In preceding chapters, candlestick signs, moves, and patterns were described and shown on stock charts. Throughout, the concept of confirmation was emphasized as essential to the proper reading of candlesticks. Among the many forms of confirmation, traditional technical indicators are the best tools you can use.

The "technical" realm combines many different types of signals. Besides candlesticks, traditional Western technical price patterns are well known and include head and shoulders, double tops and bottoms, breakout above resistance or below support, triangles and wedges, and dozens of lesser-known signals. In addition to price, technical signals are also found in volume, moving averages, and momentum oscillators. However, because charting and, more broadly applied, technical analysis itself are a combination of science and art, there can never be absolute certainty about what will happen next.

The power of this range of technical indicators is not in certainty, but in the application of price patterns and confirmation to improve the instances of well-timed entry and exit. Candlesticks lead this effort, and related signals for reversal and continuation, when strongly confirmed, raise confidence levels as high as can be expected, given the chaotic nature and unpredictability of short-term price behavior.

In fact, uncertainty expresses the imperfection of all technical analysis and emphasizes the need for confirmation in order to avoid poorly timed trades. An observation is made that

> technical analysis can be profitable when informed traders make systematic mistakes or when uninformed traders have predictable impacts on price. However, chartists face a considerable degree of trading uncertainty because technical indicators such as moving averages are essentially imperfect filters. . . . Consequently, technical trading may result in erroneous trading recommendations and substantial losses.[i]

Losses resulting from mistakes, made either by "informed" or "uninformed" traders, are not avoidable; however, with reliance on strong signals and equally strong confirmation, those losses can be managed and mitigated.

DOI 10.1515/9781501507397-010

The Value of Confirmation

For the purpose of using candlesticks as timing tools, perhaps the most important technical concept is *confirmation*. The idea is that no single indicator is reliable, on its own, to clearly and specifically tell you when to enter or exit a position.

No combination of indicators provides a guarantee either. However, when you see an initial indicator and a confirming one, that increases confidence that the implied meaning is true and correct, whether reversal or confirmation. One aspect of confirmation rarely discussed is the significance of the *lack* of signals. For example, when prices are moving sideways—times in between clear trends when neither buyers nor sellers are in control—the proper indication is to wait on the sidelines until a clear pattern or signal begins to emerge. Thus the lack of signals itself "confirms" that the proper action is to take no action, but instead to wait.

The lack of a specific signal may be cited as evidence that candlestick charting and other forms of technical analysis are not reliable and cannot be used effectively. The longstanding conflict between the world of practical trading and the world of academia is well summarized in the following passage:

> Technical analysis uses past prices and other trade statistics, such as volume, to predict future prices movements. Proponents of technical analysis believe that these data contain important information about changes in investor sentiment and that the reaction to news is a gradual process which allows trends to develop. Despite its widespread acceptance and adoption by practitioners, technical analysis has been described . . . as an "anathema to the academic world."[ii] This is due to its conflict with market efficiency, one of the central pillars of academic finance.[iii]

The challenge, then, for everyone relying on technical analysis is to recognize the *facts* concerning how technical analysis is applied in the trading world. The conflict between the two sides will not disappear, even with evidence of candlestick chart effectiveness. A trader should not give up and accept the inevitability of claims that markets are efficient and cannot be beaten.

As the author cited above noted, technical analysis is an "anathema to the academic world," which can be taken in two ways. First, technical analysis may be viewed as a distraction from the claim of inefficiency; second, it may be acknowledged as proof that efficiency is a theory alone, but one disproven by signals, specifically by the strength of candlestick signals and confirmation.

Candlestick signs, moves, and patterns provide a clear advantage to the trader, creating the strongest possible indicators about the state of a trend. One technical strategy where confirmation has a particular focus is swing trading.

Swing traders rely on the combined indicators found in short-term trends (the clearest candlestick versions of which are three white soldiers or three black crows), narrow range days (also known as one of the forms of the *doji*), and volume spikes. These are the three primary indicators and confirmation signals swing traders rely upon. However, swing trading would be very rudimentary if restricted to only these limited signs. In fact, in a majority of instances, a swing trader will be fortunate to find two of the three signs (trend, NRD, and volume spike) together at the same approximate time. They are fortunate to find two of the three.

Swing trading is based on the ancient basis for candlestick trading and discovery of patterns strongly favoring a particular price movement within three to five days:

> In keeping with Honma's philosophy, most of the reliable patterns ("no confirmation necessary") are expected to be the patterns that occur over a three-day (or longer) period. The rationale for this is that a manifestation of trading strategies that occurs within a shorter period may not reflect accurately the changing balance of supply and demand, but rather a momentary change in sentiment.[iv]

This is where candlestick analysis enriches the analysis of chart patterns and improves timing of entry and exit. The set-ups are expanded to dozens of candlestick signs, moves, and patterns, each containing degrees of strength as to what they indicate. Many are clearly bullish or bearish, and some depend on placement on the chart. Because there are so many different candlestick formations, two or more such formations may confirm one another. In some of the examples in preceding chapters, for example, chart examples were provided showing consecutive candlestick formations in which both pointed to reversal.

Candlestick indicators are further confirmed by noncandlestick signs, notably volume spikes along with candlesticks, especially when reversal is anticipated. Gaps also serve as a very important price trend and some gaps are invisible. To appreciate the complete meaning of gaps, you need to not only spot the spaces between real bodies from day to day, but also between one day's closing price and the next day's opening price. Even though the ranges overlap, a gap may often be found between days, which may confirm continuation or reversal, depending on what else has appeared on the chart. These are generalizations without any doubt, but they point out that technical analysis provides real value. Even proponents of the efficient market hypothesis have to admit that technical indicators provide value even though it contradicts the closely held theory: "The fact that a market statistic widely used in technical analysis can provide information about relative under- or over-valuation is surprising and is difficult to reconcile with existing theoretical work."[v]

Facts persist, however. Volume, for example, plays an important but often overlooked role in the signaling of coming price changes. Use of indicators is not only the question status or direction within a confirming signal, but also the strength or weakness of the indicator itself, relative to price. For example, as a continuation indicator during a bull trend, you may note that a volume signal indicates a negative reversal to follow. However, if it does not remain negative for very long, that tells you that the existing trend is likely to continue. The failure of a negative signal to persist may provide confirmation that the current bull trend will continue.

Additional technical indicators are provided in this chapter. However, before proceeding, one of the most important of these indicators needs to be emphasized: the trendline. Remember, the *trend* is the direction of price, and the *trendline* is an indicator that tells you when the trend is beginning to weaken. You can confirm continuation of a trend in many ways, including candlesticks, volume, moving averages, and other technical indicators. However, the trendline is one of the early warning signs. It is drawn under an uptrend, tracking rising support, or above a downtrend, tracking declining resistance. Once the straight line of the trendline begins to fail, it is highly likely that the trend will stop and perhaps reverse in the near future. In numerous examples of charts under analysis, you will find this to be true time and again. As with all indicators, nothing is guaranteed, but trendline study is one of the most reliable confirming indicators, especially when a reverse is also signaled in the candlesticks.

Any confirming indicator takes on additional value when it appears in a set of two—or even three—additional signs. In other words, when you see a candlestick formation that indicates reversal, finding a single confirming sign is encouraging. When you find two or more confirming signs, it is even better. No one should rely solely on candlesticks (or on any other technical indicators) as their only method for entry or exit timing. Candlesticks are the foundation for a timing program, but they need to be confirmed before taking action. The quality, consistency, and reliability of the indicators you use to time trading decisions are going to improve timing overall. You will never get 100% of your trades pegged to the perfect entry or exit, but you will improve your rate of well-timed decisions when you rely on confirmation.

A Review: Technical Analysis Basics

The patterns recognized on charts often anticipate what will occur next. It is not merely the pattern, however. It is not enough to simplify the process by expecting price to reverse just because it has continued in one direction for several weeks, for example. You need to be able to recognize signals in the candlesticks and combinations of candlestick days, in volume spikes, in a weakening of trendlines, and in well-known tests of resistance and support.

Technical analysis is intended as a means for improving entry and exit timing. This requires the ability to move in and out of positions rapidly and often. For this reason, a widespread belief that technicians are speculators pursuing high-risk trading strategies is not always justified. In fact, proper application of candlestick analysis with a range of confirmation methods can lead to the development of a *conservative* trading strategy. As contradictory as this might seem, it could make more sense than the more traditional buy-and-hold strategy used by value investors.

As the trading cycle becomes more rapid, average holding periods of long positions have been shrinking in recent years. This does not mean that investors are becoming less risk averse; however, it does mean that with improved information and technical systems, higher-volume trading is becoming recognized as a viable alternative to simply buying and holding stock. Figure 10.1 summarizes the average holding period of stock between 1920 and 2017. The period peaked in 1942 at ten years; more recently, the average holding period has declined to below two months or less.

The change makes sense. For example, you will be better off moving in and out of positions as a swing trader if a stock continues trading in a four-point range over twelve months than you would be to just buy shares and wait. As a swing trader, you have several technical advantages:

1. You can earn numerous short-term profits.
2. Potential losses are limited to what may be a relatively small investment level for each swing trade.
3. The activity can be spread or moved among many stocks, which is quite difficult for round lot stock buyers whose available capital is limited.

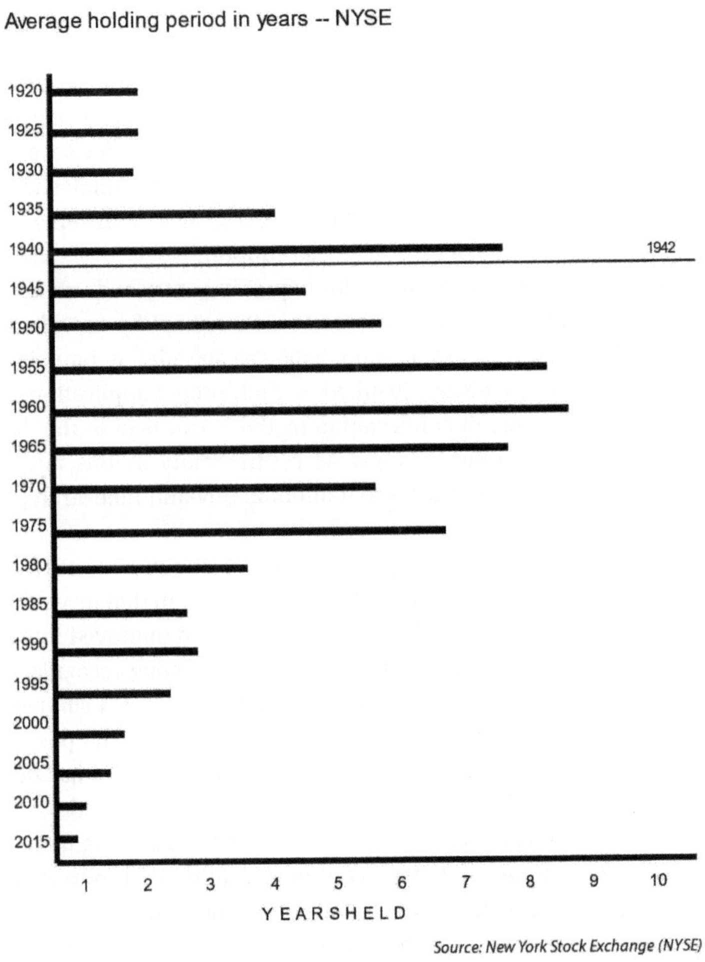

Figure 10.1: Average holding period in years—NYSE

The purpose of technical analysis is not to guarantee 100% success, but to improve your odds of accurately timed entry and exit—based on recognized signals and confirmation within the price movement and its strength or weakness. The fact that patterns occur repeatedly and predict price behavior accurately is a reflection of how well technical analysis works. Even so, acknowledging that price patterns do certainly lead to profitable trading, academic opinions may want to rationalize this reality based on factors other than the simple reality that technical indicators work:

> While many technical trading rules are based upon patterns in asset prices, we lack convincing explanations of how and why these patterns arise, and why trading rules based on technical analysis are profitable . . . . We point to the importance of confirmation bias, which has been shown to play a key role in other types of decision making. Traders who acquire information and trade on the basis of that information tend to bias their interpretation of subsequent information in the direction of their original view.[vi]

Confirmation bias does play a role in behavior among traders, but it does not explain why technical analysis works much of the time. Technical analysis is not magic and does not offer a secret formula for success. However, within the broad classification of technical analysis, you will find many "indicators" that have no practical application to price cause and effect. Some indicators are just coincidence. For example, you may not expect to profit by making trading decisions based on the width of annual tree rings, winners of annual sports championships, or four-year presidential winners or even approval ratings. This is controversial, however, because many nonmarket factors such as political policies directly affect the economy. However, the controversy is whether or not you can safely rely on esoteric indicators. If you are willing to perform the hard work of analysis, you can master a few technical basics, including candlestick formations, and apply these to timing decisions. In fact, contrary to the assumptions in the article cited above, other studies have concluded that even within academia, a shift in opinion has been underway for many years, moving toward acceptance of technical analysis as a means for generating better-timed entry and exit:

> Technical trading rules have been used in financial markets for more than a century. Numerous studies have been performed to determine whether such rules can be employed to provide superior investing performance. By and large, recent academic literature suggests that technical trading rules are capable of producing valuable economic signals.[vii]

The best forms of analysis simply make sense and are easily understood. The use of indirect social or political trends is not consistently reliable, and neither are some exceptionally complex technical formulae. Many forms of technical analysis are more academic than practical, so it makes sense to distinguish between working chart studies versus complex mathematical calculations and long-term analysis. Price movement is always going to rely on short-term factors pegged to supply and demand and economic news of the moment. Academic analysis tales solace in long-term averages and statistical likelihood of what will happen next, but realistically, price movement is always chaotic. A long-term statistical study may accurately indicate long-term *future* price movement, but cannot be relied upon to estimate price direction in the next five days. For that, you need to rely on the technical analysis that is involved directly with price trends.

Technical analysis is not simply the study of where price is and how strong or weak the trend's momentum is at the moment. On a more important level, this analysis helps you to quantify risk. In times of exceptional volatility, a stock's price might exhibit nothing except unpredictability. This by itself is a valuable indicator because it cautions you to stay away until more specific trends can be established and acted upon. When a trendline moves strongly in one direction but then falters, it could signal reversal; when confirmed by what the candlestick formations tell you, this process reduces risk by giving you the means for timely entry or exit before the reversal occurs.

The Significance of Gaps

Past chapters have often referred to gaps as confirming signals for a conclusion based on movement in candlesticks, support and resistance, and trendlines. Gaps are among the most important of technical indicators because they represent a departure from the orderly trading of shares of stock between trading sessions. Incidentally, this general observation applies to the most commonly used trading session period of a trading day, but it applies equally to sessions of any duration—including weekly, hourly, or even five-minute trading sessions. The advantage of observing specific patterns in trades (such as gaps) is that the meaning of those patterns can be applied to any trading duration.

Gaps have a number of different meanings. A gap may be simply a common occurrence within price change from one day to the next. It may be part of a breakout above resistance or below support. There are four specific types of gaps.

1. *Common gap.* This is a gap that is common and is easily found. It has no special significance until common gaps begin to appear one after another as part of a developing trend.

Common gap: A commonly occurring gap in price between one day's close and another day's open, which by itself has no special significance

---

2. *Breakaway gap.* A gap with significance, signaling a departure from the establishing trading range; price moves above resistance or below support with a gap in price.

Breakaway gap: A gap in price that takes the price range above established resistance or below established support.

---

3. *Runaway gap.* The third type is a gap or series of gaps occurring during a strong and rapid trend.

Runaway gap: A gap or series of gaps appearing as part of a strong and fast-moving trend.

---

4. *Exhaustion gap.* A gap appearing at or near the end of a trend, signaling that the price direction is overextended and is about to stop or reverse and fill.

Exhaustion gap: A gap showing up at or near the end of a trend, signaling an impending reversal to fill the overextended price run.

The chart in Figure 10.2 contains several examples of all four types of gaps. Common gaps are found on most charts with regularity. The breakaway gap occurs as price moves out of the established range. In the chart, this gap took place as price broke through support and began a downward movement. At the end of a fast run, an exhaustion gap signals the end of the trend and likely reversal. Between May and June, price rose quickly and did not stop until the peak identified by the exhaustion gap. One problem with this price pattern is that the gap is not specifically identifiable as exhaustion until after price has reversed and turned in the opposite direction. By that time, the exhaustion gap will be recognized as a confirming signal of reversal.

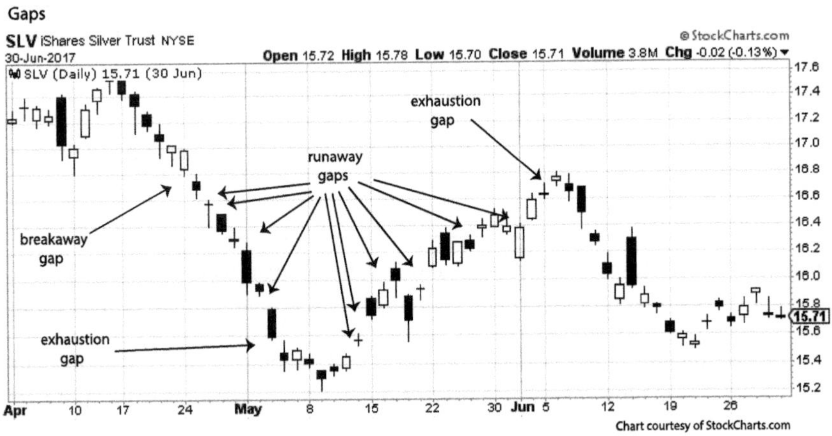

Figure 10.2: Gaps

The exhaustion indicator in this case did not precede a downward price movement, but it did signal the end of the run-up. As a confirming signal, you expect to see reversal. However, in some cases, the exhaustion gap only signals the end of a gapping pattern. What follows could be reversal or continuation.

An example of continuation following an exhaustion gap is seen in Figure 10.3. The exhaustion gap contained exceptionally long shadows, with the top shadow challenging resistance. Because this pattern occurred after three previous sessions of rapid price advance, it was unclear in the moment what would be likely to occur next. The question was answered quickly, however, with the appearance of the windows rising pattern, a bullish continuation. This was further confirmed with a second bullish continuation, the upside *tasuki* gap.

Continuation after exhaustion gap

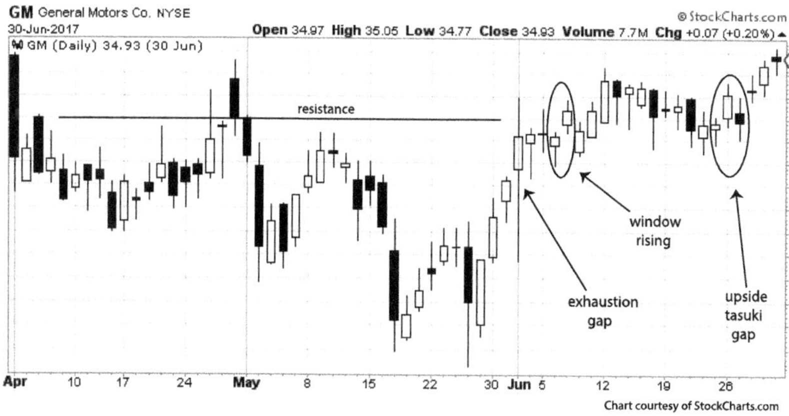

Figure 10.3: Continuation after exhaustion gap

This chart demonstrates how the exhaustion gap is properly interpreted. It is easy to assume that exhaustion always signals reversal; it may also signal consolidation, as it did in this case. In all cases of gaps, confirmation is essential. The discovery of bullish continuation signals strengthened what the original exhaustion gap predicted. Part of the likelihood for continuation versus reversal was the preceding bullish short-term trend. It moved rapidly and quickly went through resistance, adding to the possibility of continuation and reducing the chances for a bearish reversal.

A Framework for Interpretation: Support and Resistance

Gaps often signal changes in the existing trading range. This range, bordered on the top by resistance and on the bottom by support, is the foundation of technical analysis. It adds a sense of order to how price trends are read. You expect short-term trends to remain inside the borders for a period of time, even if that occurs only so that buyers and sellers can determine what should happen next. In any technical test of trading range limits, the need for confirmation is greater than ever because several possible outcomes may occur.

Only observing the trading range and how support and resistance are tested is not enough analysis to know how to proceed. Some tests of the range lead to breakouts, whereas other breakouts fail and retreat. How do you know which is taking place as breakout occurs? You cannot know just by virtue of the breakout. This is where candlestick patterns are helpful. The confirmation obtained by observing breakouts, gaps, tests of support or resistance, and candlestick formations all help in determining whether one of the two events is most likely to occur: failed breakout or successful breakout. These possible outcomes occur frequently, and both can be confirmed by candlestick formations.

1. *Attempts at breakout fail.* When well-known patterns like double or triple tops (or bottoms) or head and shoulders form, it often precedes strong price movement in the opposite direction. That may also mean a breakout in the direction opposite to the initial failed breakout attempt. Thus prices move upward after failing to break through support or move downward after failed breakout above resistance.

   An example of repeated trading range tests without successful breakouts is seen in Figure 10.4. The consolidation range between $156 and $160 per share held firmly throughout the period shown, even with breakout attempts.

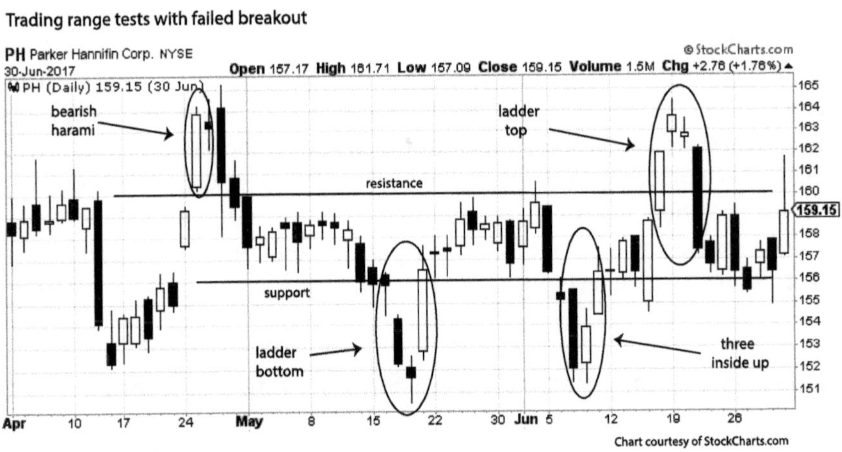

Figure 10.4: Trading range tests with failed breakout

The first breakout above resistance appeared to be exceptionally strong. It was preceded by strong price gaps moving to the upside. However, as soon as price moved above resistance, it formed a bearish *harami*, which led almost immediately to it retreating into range.

The second breakout attempt moved price below support. This also appeared strong due to repeated downward-moving gaps. However, the breakout was brief, and the ladder bottom was a strong bullish reversal indicator.

The third instance was another move below support. For a third time, the breakout was preceded by price gaps. Even so, an immediate bullish reversal appeared, the three inside up. The final attempt moved above resistance, also with gapping price action. But the ladder top led price back into range.

This was an example of a chronic consolidation trend with interim volatility. The gapping price action made the breakouts look like successful changes in the trading range, but throughout the period consolidation held.

2. *Tests become breakouts.* If prices move strongly away from the trading range, a breakout may occur in the opposite direction. While a breakout can occur unexpectedly due to indicators beyond price patterns, a predictable event includes the failed test of the opposite border. So a failed double bottom may precede an upside breakout, and vice versa.

   The chart in Figure 10.5 demonstrates how a failed breakout in one direction can lead to a successful breakout in the opposite direction. A fairly narrow trading range between $78 and $82 was first broken with a strong upward movement and gaps. However, it immediately formed a bearish reversal signal, the three inside down. This led to a rapid decline below support.

Trading range tests with successful breakout

Chart courtesy of StockCharts.com

Figure 10.5: Trading range tests with successful breakout

The value of traditional trading range testing patterns, specifically candlestick reversals or traditional Western reversals, such double tops and bottoms or the well-known head and shoulders formation, provide strong early warning signs. However, the appearance of these patterns does not always mean a breakout is going to occur in the opposite direction. It could mean simply that the price range will remain within existing borders and that the failed test merely strengthens support (at the bottom) or resistance (at the top)

On the other side of the breakout, you cannot always rely on its staying power. Some breakouts are going to set new trading ranges and hold, but many others fail and prices retreat. Candlestick confirmation of either event improves your ability to know which event is most likely to follow.

Overbought and Oversold Indicators

Virtually every chartist or technical trader recognizes the more popular price patterns, including those that test support or resistance, trendlines and their conclusions, and price gaps. These easily recognized price changes are strongly confirmed (or contradicted) by observations of candlestick signs, moves, and patterns. You can augment your analysis further by combining candlestick analysis with even more advanced indicators that calculate whether the current stock price is overbought or oversold.

These indicators are often mathematically intensive, and before the Internet, your ability to make use of them was limited. Today, however, automated chart generation provides you with instant availability of valuable advanced indicators. In past chapters, some of these were introduced and demonstrated as valuable for confirming trends. The on-balance volume, CMF, and moving average indicators are easily comprehended and work well with traditional technical price patterns and candlesticks. In addition, three technical indicators are worth following because they define whether stocks are overbought or oversold. Four are RSI, Stochastics, MACD, and Bollinger bands.

Relative Strength Index (RSI)

The RSI compares the strength of uptrend days to that of downtrend days. It often leads the price trend and is especially valuable when other technical indicators do not clearly define the direction of impending price changes.

The RSI is expressed on an index of 100 and is one of the most reliable of the *momentum oscillators*. This combined terminology refers to the trend direction (momentum) combined with the quantified value (index) of RSI.

Relative strength index (RSI): A momentum oscillator that compares the strength of uptrend and downtrend days and expresses the value on an index between 1 and 100.

Momentum oscillator: An indicator such as RSI, expressing a quantified dominance of the trend direction (momentum) on an index (oscillator).

RSI provides a single index value telling you whether a stock is currently *overbought* or *oversold*. The RSI standard, first introduced by J. Welles Wilder in his 1978 book *New Concepts in Technical Trading Systems*, identifies the RSI level of 70 as overbought and 30 as oversold. This single-digit valuation of the stock's condition makes the RSI an exceptionally easy to use technical indicator.

Overbought/oversold: The quantified status of a stock identified through the RSI value as overbought above 70 or as oversold below 30.

To calculate RSI, both upward and downward price changes over a number of sessions (normally fourteen) are added together and then averaged. Next the up-day average is divided by the down-day average. The result is multiplied by 100 to find the RSI value. However, you do not need to go through the tedium of making these calculations because many online sites provide free stock charts with RSI included.

An example of how RSI can be used is seen in Figure 10.6. Here, RSI gives an early warning that the stock is in overbought range. This anticipates a correction in price. However, the correction was delayed nearly a full month.

Even so, RSI should not be ignored. As the bullish trend rose, the overbought condition anticipated the reversal that occurred in mid-June. The three outside down is a strong bearish signal that confirmed what RSI forecast one month before.

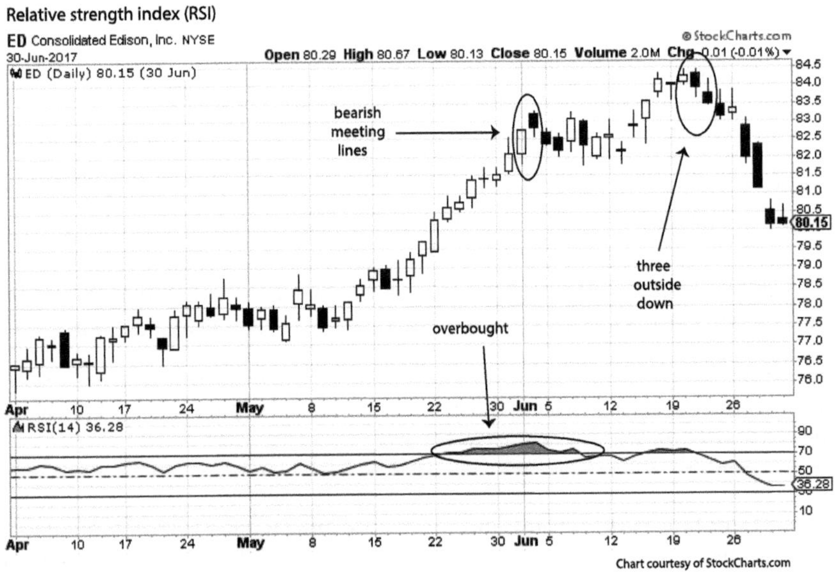

Figure 10.6: Relative strength index (RSI)

Stochastics

The next advanced technical indicator is called Stochastics. This is a *price oscillator*, which is a calculation of the differences between two moving averages. This price oscillator provides a percentage difference that shifts between positive and negative.

Figure 10.7 shows that Stochastic is similar to RSI in the sense that it identifies overbought and oversold conditions. In this indicator, those default levels are index values of 80 and 20. Like RSI, Stochastic may anticipate a coming reversal. It shows overbought from late May forward, even though price did not turn until late June. During June, three bearish engulfing patterns provided further warning of a downtrend to follow. In fact, in the period following this chart, the stock declined fifty points below the $361.61 level in the figure.

Stochastics

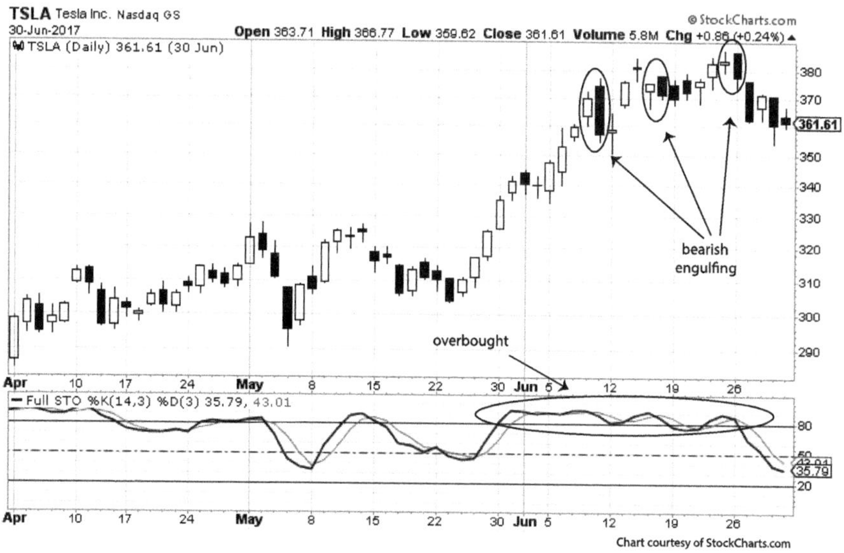

Figure 10.7: Stochastics

Stochastics: A momentum indicator identifying current price in relationship to the current trading range; the word means "random" and is a means for calculating the likely price movement in the near future.

Price oscillator: A technical indicator based on comparisons between two moving averages.

MACD

The final oscillator is moving average convergence divergence (MACD). This is the most complex of all because it involves three separate moving averages. As shown in Figure 10.8, the key indicators occur when the twelve-day and twenty-six-day signals reverse direction. In mid-May, MACD anticipated a downtrend when the averages peaked and then began moving downward. At the same time, two bearish engulfing signals appeared.

Moving average convergence divergence (MACD)

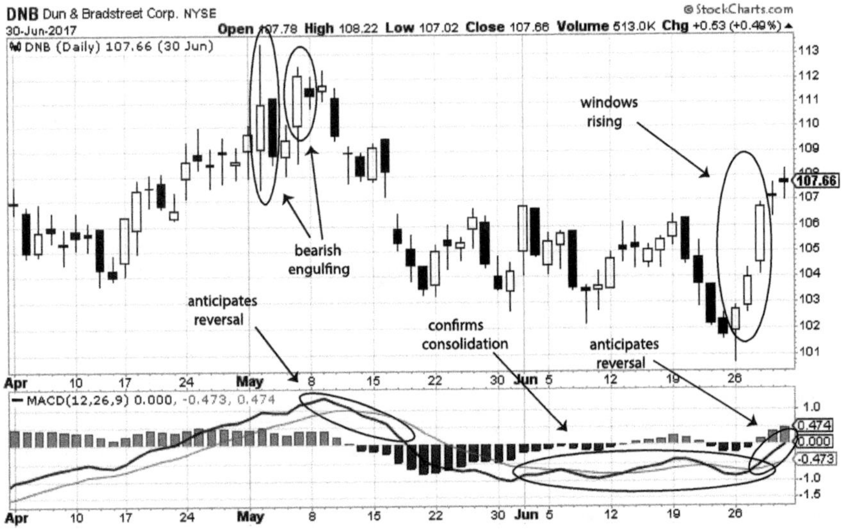

Figure 10.8: Moving average con vergence divergence (MACD)

After a decline, price moved into a consolidation trend, which was confirmed by lack of movement in the MACD averages. However, in the last week of June, that changed suddenly as the two lines moved rapidly toward the signal line. At the same time, a windows rising signal marked the beginning of a breakout from consolidation and the start of a bullish trend.

MACD: The moving average convergence/divergence, a technical calculation comparing the trend between two fixed moving averages.

Bollinger Bands

The final overbought/oversold indicator is called Bollinger bands, named after the technician John Bollinger, who introduced the concept in the 1980s. The method begins with a calculation of a moving average over a specified period of time (Bollinger recommended using twenty days). The next step applies the statistical calculation known as standard deviation to quantify the "highness" or "lowness" of price in relation to previous price levels. This produces bands running above and below the moving average at a distance of two standard deviations. The distance between the average and the bands measures volatility.

Bollinger bands: A technical indicator that tracks the relative distance of current price from a moving average, visually displaying price volatility levels.

Combined with RSI, Stochastics, and MACD, Bollinger bands prominently define overbought and oversold conditions with powerful accuracy. Volatility levels are easily viewed on Bollinger bands, with the upper and lower bands easily compared to current price levels.

All four of these indicators can be studied together to provide technical confirmation; when used in conjunction with traditional chart patterns and candlesticks, they round out your program of technical analysis. For example, the chart in Figure 10.9 shows price with Bollinger bands overlaid. The upper and lower bands are solid lines and the middle band (twenty-day simple moving average) is the broken line in the middle.

Bollinger bands

Chart courtesy of StockCharts.com

Figure 10.9: Bollinger bands

Several interesting and worthwhile signals are found on this chart, revealing the exceptional value of Bollinger bands as a signaling device. At several points, price violated the bandwidth, but immediately formed reveal signals and saw price move back into range. The first of these occurred where price moved below the lower and formed a three identical soldiers signal. The second was a move above the upper band, forming a bearish engulfing and correctly predicting a reversal down into range. The third was a ladder bottom, a bullish reversal located at the point where price once again moved below the lower band. The final signal was the bearish engulfing located at the end of the chart as price again moved above the upper band. In the two months following the period shown, price declined as predicted by this final signal.

There is more to be gained from analysis of this chart. Although reversal is easily spotted by the identification of a candlestick signal, a retracement is an opposite move signifying price adjustment but not a new trend. Using Bollinger bands, retracements are easy to spot. They are found in the many spots on this chart where price moved outside of the bands and then retraced back into bandwidth range. However, the lack of a reversal signal helped to identify these patterns as retracements. Bollinger bands clarify these events and make their appearance and subsequent price action highly predictable.

Bollinger bands offer another benefit, which is improved channel line tracking and identification of trend reversals. This occurs when Bollinger bands are accompanied by the indicator known as the t-line. This is an exponential moving average of price for the most recent eight sessions.

T-line: An indicator consisting of an eight-day exponential moving average of price, yielding buy or sell signals based on crossover between the line and price.

The t-line signals action based on crossover. When price crosses above the t-line and closes there for two or more consecutive days, it is a bullish signal. When price crosses below the t-line and closes there for two or more consecutive days, it is a bearish indicator.

T-line is a simple but useful confirming signal. However, when combined with Bollinger bands, it sets up a powerful and expanded version of the channel. When price is moving upward, the upper Bollinger band forms an advancing resistance level, and the t-line forms an advancing support level. An example is found in Figure 10.10.

Figure 10.10: Expanded upward channel

In this case, the channel is easily identified. The Bollinger upper band is a solid dark line and the t-line is a solid lighter line. Both advance together. With this combined signal, it is easy to spot continuation of the channel as well as the moment when that trend is ending. It would consist of price crossing below the t-line and remaining below with trading leveling out or declining.

The same benefit is found in declining trends as well. Figure 10.11 contains an example of a bearish trend forming a channel with a falling t-line as resistance and lower Bollinger band as declining support. At several points, price crossed the t-line but was not able to sustain trading at that level.

Figure 10.11: Expanded downward channel

When this combined Bollinger band and t-line overlay is used in conjunction with candlestick analysis, timing of trades is more readily confirmed and identified. However, the narrow channel forms only in trending price patterns; in these cases, seeking reversal in the form of candlesticks is the most effective system for timing entry of a new trade or exit of a current position.

The Potential of Candlestick Signals

No indicators or combination of indicators provides a guarantee that signals are always reliable. By the same argument, no candlestick formations can provide assurance that entry and exit timing will be flawless. All of these indicators, when used to confirm one another or to provide agreement on the continuation or reversal of a trend, will improve the instances of well-timed trading decisions.

The possibility of false signals is ever present. With this in mind, it is imperative that candlesticks be viewed as one of many technical tests worth performing. The candlestick signs, moves, and patterns presented in this book and shown in the context of reversal and continuation are probably more accurate as predictive indicators than most other forms of price analysis. However, as dozens of past examples have shown, *confirmation* is the necessary attribute to a sensible program of technical analysis. Different candlestick formations may confirm one another when they appear side by side, and indicators other than candlesticks, including moving averages, trendlines, volume, and advanced technical indices, all aid in the development of an accurate and reliable system.

Emphasis has been placed not only on confirmation, but also on the possibility that even the strongest indicator may be false—even when confirmed by any number of other indicators. No trader should expect to rely on a timing system to the extent that risks become higher than acceptable. The purpose of all of these indicator studies is not to completely eliminate risk, but to reduce it and facilitate risk management. In the process, improved and more reliable systems are designed to increase the success of trade timing. By combining a singular analytical system with a series of confirming signals, you may expect to realize a much higher degree of success.

The application of technical analysis based on candlestick patterns is not a fixed practice. It evolves. This is due to technological advances in information sciences as well as enlightened views of practical technical analysis as it moves away from academic theory and acknowledges the reality of how traders improve their abilities to time trades. This involves many advanced techniques:

> As computers have become more powerful and their use more widespread, analysts have begun to combine fundamental economic data with the more traditional price and volume data to produce new indicators. More recently, concepts like chaos theory, fuzzy logic, artificial neural network, genetic algorithms, and so on, have been applied to the financial markets. This could well be the next stage of the evolution of technical analysis.[viii]

However, even with the most advanced network of information and algorithms, the individual trader observing the patterns on a stock chart will remain the ultimate judge of how to best employ the full range of signals. Candlestick analysis involves dozens of potential formations, and each has its own degree of significance. Some are bullish, others bearish; some indicate coming reversal, others tell you continuation is more likely. A few are significant only to the degree of proximity within a trend (for example, appearing at the conclusion of an uptrend versus a downtrend). With this in mind, candlestick analysis cannot be oversimplified or expected to always provide an identical conclusion. That relies on the momentum of the trend, confirmation in many forms, and acceptance of the reality that even the strongest predictive indicator is going to be wrong sometimes.

The "right or wrong" of a decision is not determined by the degree of accuracy in how you read the signals. The percentage of well-timed decisions and the use of candlesticks for the purpose of increasing this percentage is where your advantage lies. In that sense, candlestick analysis is not an absolute science. However, it is effective at improving the quality of the estimate involved in your timing decisions. To a degree, all trading decisions involve part guesswork. Candlestick analysis is a method for improving the success of the guesses you need to make.

---

[i] Nikola Gradojevic, N., & Gençay, R. (February 2013). Fuzzy Logic, Trading Uncertainty and Technical Trading. *Journal of Banking and Finance*, 37, No. 2, 578–587.
[ii] Malkiel, B. (1996). *A Random Walk Down Wall Street*, 6th ed. New York: W. W. Norton, 139.
[iii] Marshall, B. R., Young, M. R., & Rose, C. R. (2006). Candlestick Technical Trading Strategies: Can They Create Value for Investors? *Journal of Banking & Finance*, 30, 2303–2323.
[iv] Caginalp, G., & Laurent, H. (1998). The Predictive Power of Price Patterns. *Applied Mathematical Finance*, 5, 181–205.
[v] Lee, C., & Swaminathan, B. (2000). Price Momentum and Trading Volume. *The Journal of Finance* LV, No. 5, 2017–2069.
[vi] Friesen, G. C., Weller, P. A., & Dunham. L. M. (June 2009). Price Trends and Patterns in Technical Analysis: A Theoretical and Empirical Examination. *Journal of Banking & Finance*, 33, No. 6, 1089–1100.
[vii] Sullivan, R., Timmermann, A., & White, H. (October 1999). Data-Snooping, Technical Trading Rule Performance, and the Bootstrap. *The Journal of Finance*, LIV, No. 5, 1647–1691.
[viii] Wong, W. K., Manzur, M., & Chew, B-K. (2010). How Rewarding Is Technical Analysis? Evidence from Singapore Stock Market. *Applied Financial Economics*, 13, No. 7, 543–551.

Glossary

Accumulation/distribution (A/D line): A technical indicator measuring proportionate degrees of buyer and seller volume, which acts as a momentum indicator.

Advance block: A set of three consecutive white candlesticks, each opening and closing higher than the one before.

After top gap down: A bearish reversal pattern consisting of upward movement, a downward gap, and a black session.

After bottom gap up: A bullish reversal pattern consisting of downward movement, an upward gap, and a white session.

Ascending triangle: A bullish triangle characterized by a level resistance and rising support level.

Bear abandoned baby: A complex formation consisting of a bear *doji* star (an upward day, upward gap, and *doji*) followed by a downward gap and then a downward day.

Bear squeeze alert: A three-session candle with the first one upward, the second with a narrower opening and closing range, and the third with yet narrower ranges. Although second- and third-session candles may be upward or downward, the strongest version of the squeeze alert contains three white candles.

Belt hold, bearish: A reversal signal consisting of multiple sessions: upward-trending white sessions, a higher-opening black session with little or no lower shadow, and finally a series of downward-moving sessions.

Belt hold, bullish: A reversal signal consisting of multiple sessions: downward-trending black sessions, a lower-opening white session with little or no lower shadow, and finally a series of upward-moving sessions.

Beta: A measure of how closely a security moves with the market. Beta of 1 indicates exact movement with the larger market; beta under 1 indicates low responsiveness. Beta above 1 is a sign of greater risk than overall markets.

DOI 10.1515/9781501507397-011

Bollinger bands: A technical indicator that tracks the relative distance of current price from a moving average, visually displaying price volatility levels.

Breakaway, bearish: A multi-session pattern of three or more white and advancing days, concluding with a downward black session identifying a reversal.

Breakaway, bullish: A multi-session pattern of three or more black and declining days, concluding with an upward white session identifying a reversal.

Breakaway gap: A gap in price that takes the price range above established resistance or below established support.

Bull abandoned baby: A complex pattern consisting of a bull *doji* star (a downward day, downward gap, and *doji*) followed by an upward gap and then an upward day.

Bull squeeze alert: A three-session candle with the first one downward, the second with a narrower opening and closing range, and the third with yet narrower ranges. Although second- and third-session candles may be upward or downward, the strongest version of the squeeze alert contains three black candles.

Candlestick chart: A visual summary of all the trading action in a single period, showing the opening and closing prices, breadth of trading, and upward or downward movement in price.

Channel line: A variation of the trendline in which resistance and support move together but without a change in the breadth of trading.

Coil: Alternate name for the symmetrical triangle.

Common gap: A commonly occurring gap in price between one day's close and another day's open, which by itself has no special significance.

Complex patterns: Candlestick formations consisting of three or more consecutive trading sessions and creating one of several specific reversal or directional indicators.

Concealing baby swallow: A bull reversal pattern consisting of four black candles; the first two are *marubozus*, followed by a downside gap, a third black candle, and then an engulfing black candle. This pattern sets a new support level for the trading range.

Confirmation: The use of an indicator to verify the meaning of a separate indicator occurring at the same time or earlier, consisting of movement in an index or individual stock price, changes in price trend direction, or initiation of an entry or exit signal.

Confirming indicators: Candlestick formations that anticipate the current trend is likely to continue in the same direction.

Consolidation: A period in which a narrow trading range is in effect and little if any movement occurs. This is likely to occur in between upward or downward trends and reflects uncertainty in the market about future price direction.

Contrarian investor: A trader or investor who recognizes that markets overreact to news, and who makes buy and sell decisions in a direction opposite to the prevailing trend.

Convergence/divergence: The tendency for two long-term moving averages of price to move toward one another (converge) or away from one another (diverge).

Dark cloud cover: Alternate name for the bear piercing lines move.

Deliberation, bearish: A set of four signals. The first two are white and trade in close range to one another. The third session is also white and occurs after an upward gap, and the fourth session is black, moving price lower.

Deliberation, bullish: A set of four signals. The first two are black and trade in close range to one another. The third session is also black and occurs after a downward gap, and the fourth session is white, moving price higher.

Descending triangle: A bearish continuation pattern consisting of steady support price and declining resistance.

Descent block: A set of three consecutive black candlesticks, each opening and closing lower than the one before.

***Doji*:** A candlestick sign developed when the day's opening and closing prices are identical or very close; the real body is a horizontal line rather than a box.

***Doji* sandwich, bearish:** A reversal with black sessions in the first and third positions and a *doji* in between.

***Doji* sandwich, bullish:** A reversal with white sessions in the first and third positions and a *doji* in between.

***Doji* star:** A variation of the inverted hammer in which the signal day forms as a *doji* instead of a hammer candle.

Downside gap filled: A bear complex pattern with a downward session, a downside gap, a second downside session, and then a third session moving to the upside. However, although the third session fills the gap, it does not move above the resistance level set by the first day's opening price.

Downside *tasuki* gap: A complex pattern creating a bear trend with a downward candle, a downside gap, a second downward candle, and then an upside candle that does not fill the gap. It is a bear formation because the gap holds up.

Downtrend: A short-term pattern of three or more periods, characterized by each period's lower low price levels and lower high price levels.

Dragonfly *doji*: A type of *doji* with a lower shadow; the longer the shadow, the greater the bullish indication.

Dumpling top: A series of narrow days setting up a resistance level after an uptrend, forecasting reversal and a new downtrend to follow.

Eight new price lines, bearish: A run of eight consecutive sessions, all white and rising. This predicts a turnaround and resulting bearish trend as reaction to the unusual pattern over eight days.

Eight new price lines, bullish: A run of eight consecutive sessions, all black and falling. This predicts a turnaround and resulting bullish trend as reaction to the unusual pattern over eight days.

Engulfing pattern: A double stick move in which the range of the set-up period's stick is surpassed by the range of the signal period and in which the setup stick's shadows are longer than those of the signal period.

Evening star: A bear three-stick pattern combining a bear inverted hammer with a subsequent third day moving downward, with spaces between the sessions.

Exhaustion gap: A gap showing up at or near the end of a trend, signaling an impending reversal to fill the overextended price run.

Falling three method (bearish mat hold): A complex bearish continuation pattern combining downward movement, a gap, three or more upward-moving days, and a resumption of the downtrend.

Falling wedge: A reversal pattern in which prices fall while the price range narrows, anticipating a coming price rise.

Frypan bottom: A bullish reversal signal consisting of several sessions setting up new support after a downtrend and predicting the end of the trend.

Gapping play, low price: A bearish continuation signal consisting of black sessions, a downside gap, another black session, and further movement in the same direction.

Gapping play, high price: A bullish continuation signal consisting of white sessions, an upside gap, another white session, and further movement in the same direction.

Gapping trend: Any trend involving price gaps, especially between trading sessions in which the gaps are not immediately visible.

Gravestone *doji*: A type of *doji* with an upper shadow; the longer the shadow, the greater the bearish indication.

Hammer: A pattern with a small ready body, no upper shadow, and a longer than usual lower shadow. It appears at the bottom of a downtrend and is a bullish day indicating an impending reversal, or it appears as confirmation during an uptrend.

Hanging man: A pattern with a small real body, no upper shadow, and a longer than usual lower shadow. It appears at the top of an uptrend and is a bearish day indicating an impending reversal, or it appears as confirmation during a downtrend.

***Harami*:** Meaning "pregnant," a double stick move in which the set-up day's range is longer than the signal's days, extending above the high and below the low, and when the set-up's shadows are longer than those of the stick in the signal period.

***Harami* cross:** A type of *harami* in which the signal day forms a *doji* and is subject to the same range requirements of other *harami* moves.

High waves: A signal of several sessions setting up new resistance and signaling likely bearish reversal.

Identical three crows: A bearish reversal of three black sessions. Each one's opening price is the same as or close to the previous session's closing price.

Identical white soldiers: A bullish reversal of three white sessions. Each one's opening price is the same as or close to the previous session's closing price.

In neck: A variation of the neck line move in which the two days' real bodies overlap somewhat in price levels.

Inside down: A three-stick formation with a bear *harami* in the first two sessions (a white first day and a smaller black second day in a narrower range) and then a third downward day.

Inside up: A three-stick formation with a bull *harami* in the first two sessions (a black first day and a smaller white second day in a narrower range) and then a third upward day.

Inverted hammer: A double stick move made up of a downward trending long candle, a low-side gap, and a hammer (a bull formation), or an upward moving long candle, a high-side gap, and a hammer (a bear formation).

Kicking, bearish: A two-session bullish reversal consisting of a white day, a downward gap, and a black day.

Kicking, bullish: A two-session bullish reversal consisting of a black day, an upward gap, and a white day.

Ladder bottom: A reversal pattern beginning with a series of black candles trending down, a gap moving up, and a final white candle.

Ladder top: A reversal pattern beginning with a series of white candles trending up, a gap moving down, and a final black candle.

Long-legged *doji*: A *doji* sign with exceptionally large upper and lower shadows, indicating a coming reversal in the current trend.

MACD: The moving average convergence/divergence, a technical calculation comparing the trend between two fixed moving averages.

Major yang: A bullish reversal of three sessions: two black sessions gapping downward and a third white session closing within the range of the first session.

Major yin: A bearish reversal of three sessions: two white sessions gapping upward and a third black session closing within the range of the first session.

***Marubozu*:** A long candlestick with varying lengths of upper and lower shadows. The word in Japanese means "with little hair."

Mat hold: A bull reversal pattern beginning with a long white candle, followed by an upside gap, downward black candles, and a final white candle closing higher than the first candle.

Matching high: A bearish reversal consisting of two white sessions with matching closing prices, which sets up a new bearish price move.

Matching low: A bullish reversal consisting of two black sessions with matching closing prices, which sets up a new bullish price move.

Meeting lines: A double stick move with the bottom of the set-up day's real body meeting the top of the real body in the signal day. In a bull move, the set-up day is downward moving and the signal day is upward, creating a downward gap between the closing price of the set-up and the opening price of the signal. A bear meeting lines move exhibits the opposite direction in both sessions and an upside gap in between.

Momentum oscillator: An indicator such as RSI, expressing a quantified dominance of the trend direction (momentum) on an index (oscillator).

Money flow index (MFI): A momentum indicator measuring positive and negative money flow in a stock's price over a twenty-one-day moving average, creating an oscillator ranging between 1 and 100; the indicator is also known as the Chaikin Money Flow (CMF).

Money flow: A technical test of volume trends employing the average of each day's high, low, and close to develop a cumulative trend direction in price.

Morning star: A bull three-stick pattern combining a bull inverted hammer with a subsequent third day moving upward, with spaces between the sessions.

Move: A double-stick formation that foreshadows either a reversal or continuation in the current price trend.

Near *doji*: A candlestick with an exceptionally thin space between opening and closing prices; while these are not identical, the range is so small that the candle is granted the same significance as a perfect *doji*.

Neck line: A double stick confirming move with long candlesticks. The set-up is upward and a higher signal is downward (bull pattern) or the set-up is downward and the signal is upward (bear pattern). In both cases, a gap is closed in the set-up day, confirming the current trend.

Northern *doji*: Any *doji* appearing above a previous uptrend, considered a strong bear signal.

OHLC chart: Abbreviation of "open, high, low, close." A type of stock chart showing a vertical stick for the day's trading range and two vertical, shorter protrusions showing opening and closing prices.

On neck: A variation of the neck line move in which the two days' real bodies intersect at approximately the same price level.

On-balance volume: A cumulative indicator measuring dominance of daily trading by either buyers or sellers, used to anticipate emerging trends.

Outside down: A complex pattern consisting of a bear engulfing (two sticks made up of a white day and then a larger black day with higher high and higher low) and a third day moving lower.

Outside up: A complex pattern consisting of a bull engulfing (two sticks made up of a black day and then a larger white day with higher high and higher low) and a third day moving higher.

Overbought/oversold: The quantified status of a stock identified through the RSI value as overbought above 70 or as oversold below 30.

Paper trading: A method for becoming familiar with strategies, in which a fictitious portfolio is traded using "virtual money." This enables you to see the outcomes of different timing strategies, but without losing real money.

Pattern: A candlestick formation of three or more trading periods that strongly indicates a reversal or continuation of the current trend.

Percentage swing system: A method of timing entry and exit based on the percentage by which price moves above or below the previously established trading range.

Piercing lines: A double stick move with two long candles. A bull formation has a downward movement in the set-up and a lower, upward movement in the signal, with trading ranges overlapping to form an invisible gap.

Price oscillator: A technical indicator based on comparisons between two moving averages.

Primary trend: The overall price direction in the market, either bull (upward) or bear (downward). Within each primary trend, offsetting secondary trends occur.

Reaction swing: A tendency for short-term prices to return to an established trading range following a price spike.

Real body: The rectangle in a candlestick, representing the area between the day's opening and closing price but excluding the total range above and below those levels (upper and lower shadows).

Relative strength index (RSI): A momentum oscillator that compares the strength of uptrend and downtrend days and expresses the value on an index between 1 and 100.

Rest after battle: A bullish continuation signal that follows strong upward movement. It consists of a white session followed by two smaller black sessions, likely to be followed by a continuation of the bullish trend.

Reversal formations: Candlestick developments signaling the end of the current trend and anticipating the likelihood that price will next move in the opposite direction.

Reversion to the mean: A tendency for prices to reverse course and move back toward their longer-term average.

Rising three method (bullish mat hold): A complex bullish continuation pattern combining upward movement, a gap, three downward-moving days, and a resumption of the uptrend.

Rising wedge: A reversal pattern in which prices rise while the price range narrows, anticipating a coming price decline.

Risk tolerance: The degree of risk you are willing and able to take in your portfolio based on many factors, including knowledge about the market, experience, capital, budget, portfolio size, and personal financial situation. The defined risk tolerance level identifies the kinds of investments anyone can afford to make.

Runaway gap: A gap or series of gaps appearing as part of a strong and fast-moving trend.

Separating lines: A confirming double stick move creating a gap equal to the real body of the set-up day. A bull formation is formed with a downward set-up and a higher upward signal. A bear move is formed with an upward set-up and a lower downward signal.

Set-up: The first trading period in a multi-stick formation, followed by the signal trading period.

Shadow: The portion of the candlestick above and below the real body. The upper shadow shows the distance between the trading range (open to close) and the highest price of the day, and the lower shadow shows the distance between the trading range and the lowest price of the day.

Side-by-side black lines bear: A formation of three black sessions. The first is followed by a downside gap and then two additional downward-moving sessions.

Side-by-side black lines bull: A formation of one white session, an upside gap, and two black sessions. Price support prevents the bears from moving price down to fill the gap and forms new support, making this a bullish indicator.

Side-by-side white lines bear: A pattern of one black session, an upside gap, and two white sessions. Price resistance prevents the bulls from moving price up to fill the gap, making this a bearish indicator.

Side-by-side white lines bull: A pattern of three white sessions. The first is followed by an upside gap and then two additional upward-moving sessions.

Sign: A single candlestick that provides initial indications about a reversal or continuation in the overall trend.

Signal: The last trading period in a multi-stick formation, which occurs after the set-up.

Southern *doji*: Any *doji* appearing below a previous downtrend, considered a strong bull signal.

Spike: A sudden price move above or below the trading range, which is followed by a return to that range within a few trading sessions.

Spinning top: A candlestick with a relatively small real body and upper and lower shadows. The real body is approximately midway in the day's range, and both shadows are at least the same size as the real body.

Stick sandwich, bearish: A reversal pattern of three consecutive sessions. The first and third are white, and the middle session is black. The middle session's real body should reside within the real bodies of the other two sessions.

Stick sandwich, bullish: A reversal pattern of three consecutive sessions. The first and third are black, and the middle session is white. The middle session's real body should reside within the real bodies of the other two sessions.

Stochastics: A momentum indicator identifying current price in relationship to the current trading range; the word means "random" and is a means for calculating the likely price movement in the near future.

Swing trade: A trade with a short time in a position, entered after price spikes or percentages above the norm of movement. The purpose is to time short-term profits by trading contrary to the market tendency.

Symmetrical triangle: A continuation pattern consisting of a trading range of the same breadth in both the beginning of the triangle and the continuation.

T-line: An indicator consisting of an eight-day exponential moving average of price, yielding buy or sell signals based on crossover between the line and price.

Tails: An alternate term for especially long upper and lower shadows, used as indicators of the degree of strength in bullish or bearish trends.

Ten new price lines, bearish: A run of ten consecutive sessions, all white and rising. This predicts a turnaround and resulting bearish trend as reaction to the unusual pattern over ten days.

Ten new price lines, bullish: A run of ten consecutive sessions, all black and falling. This predicts a turnaround and resulting bullish trend as reaction to the unusual pattern over ten days.

Thirteen new price lines, bearish: A run of thirteen consecutive sessions, all white and rising. This predicts a turnaround and resulting bearish trend as reaction to the unusual pattern over thirteen days.

Thirteen new price lines, bullish: A run of thirteen consecutive sessions, all black and falling. This predicts a turnaround and resulting bullish trend as reaction to the unusual pattern over thirteen days.

Three black crows: A complex candlestick formation consisting of three or more consecutive downward candles. Each has a lower opening and a lower closing than the previous candle.

Three Buddha bottom: A bullish reversal signal with three price valleys, the middle one lower than the first and third; a Sakata version of the Western inverse head and shoulders pattern.

Three Buddha top: A bearish reversal signal with three price peaks, the middle one higher than the first and third; a Sakata version of the Western head and shoulders pattern.

Three gap downside: A bullish reversal pattern involving repetitive gaps, but not necessarily accompanied by specific candlestick signals. The pattern reveals excessive momentum and likely reversal to follow.

Three gap upside: A bearish reversal pattern involving repetitive gaps, but not necessarily accompanied by specific candlestick signals. The pattern reveals excessive momentum and likely reversal to follow.

Three gaps down: A set of four candlesticks, three black and gapping downward, and one white reversing direction.

Three gaps up: A set of four candlesticks, three white and gapping upward, and one black reversing direction.

Three line strike, bearish: A pattern of three or more white sessions, concluding with a black session that forms a bearish engulfing signal.

Three line strike, bullish: A pattern of three or more black sessions, concluding with a white session that forms a bullish engulfing signal.

Three mountains: A pattern signal marking high price resistance and forecasting a bearish reversal.

Three rivers: A reversal formation consisting of a long black candle, a lower black and a short white candle closing lower (three rivers bottom, a bull formation), or a long white candle, a white higher candle, and a short black candle closing higher (three rivers top, a bear formation).

Three stars in the north: A bearish reversal signal with three white sessions. The second trades above the first, and the third is engulfed entirely within the range of the second session.

Three stars in the south: A bull reversal consisting of three black sessions. The second trades below the first, and the third is engulfed entirely within the range of the second session.

Three white soldiers: A complex candlestick formation consisting of three or more consecutive upward candles. Each has a higher opening and a higher closing than the previous candle.

Thrusting lines: A double stick confirming move consisting of two long candles. In a bull formation, set-up is upward and a higher signal day is downward. In a bear formation, set-up is downward and a lower signal day is upward moving.

Total capitalization: The sum of capital that funds a company's operations, consisting of equity (shareholders' capital) and debt (long-term loans and bonds).

Tower bottom: A bullish reversal clearly marking the final black session of the downtrend, two bottoming days, and introduction of an uptrend with a higher white session.

Tower top: A bearish reversal clearly marking the final white session of the uptrend, two topping days, and introduction of a downtrend with a lower black session.

Trading range: The price spread between highest and lowest points on a daily bar or over a period of time; the breadth of trading between those two points.

Trend: The direction of price movement over time, which continues in the same movement until it weakens and moves sideways or reverses.

Trendline: A series of straight lines bordering the highest and lowest point in a current price trend.

Triangles: Continuation patterns characterized by a narrowing trading range over time; these may be symmetrical, ascending, or descending.

Tri-star, bearish: A three-session bearish reversal consisting of three *doji* sessions, the middle one higher than the first two.

Tri-star, bullish: A three-session bullish reversal consisting of three *doji* sessions, the middle one lower than the first two.

True range: A stock's trading range within a trend rather than a single trading session. It includes the previous session's closing price and the current session's price movement.

Tweezer bottom: A bullish reversal with two or more low price sessions and lower shadows, forecasting reversal and a new uptrend.

Tweezer top: A bearish reversal with two or more high price sessions and upper shadows, forecasting reversal and a new downtrend.

Upside gap filled: A bull complex pattern with an upward session, an upside gap, a second upside session, and then a third session moving to the downside. However, although the third session fills the gap, it does not fall below the support level set by the first day's opening price.

Upside *tasuki* gap: A complex pattern creating a bull trend with an upward candle, an upside gap, a second upward candle, and then a downside candle that does not fill the gap. It is a bull formation because the gap holds up.

Uptrend: A short-term pattern of three or more periods characterized by each period's higher high price levels and higher low price levels.

Wedge: A reversal pattern in one of two shapes: a rising wedge is bearish and anticipates a reversal from the existing uptrend to a downtrend, and a falling wedge is bullish, anticipating a reversal from the existing downtrend to an uptrend.

Index

DOI 10.1515/9781501507397-012

S